Classroom Success for the LD and ADHD Child

Also by Suzanne Stevens

The LD Child and the ADHD Child:
Ways Parents and Professionals Can Help

Getting the Horse to Drink:
How to Motivate Unmotivated Students

Classroom Success for the LD and ADHD Child

BY SUZANNE H. STEVENS

John F. Blair, Publisher
Winston-Salem, North Carolina

Printed in the United States of America

The paper in this book meets the guidelines for permanence and durability of the Committee on Production Guidelines for Book Longevity of the Council on Library Resources.

Library of Congress Cataloging-in-Publication Data
Stevens, Suzanne H., 1938–
Classroom success for the LD and ADHD child / by Suzanne H. Stevens.
p. cm.
Rev. ed. of: Classroom success for the learning disabled. c1984.
Includes bibliographical references and index.
ISBN 0-89587-159-9 (alk. paper)
1. Learning disabled children—Education—United States—Case studies. 2. Attention-deficit-disordered children—Education—United States. 3. Slow learning children—United States—Case studies. 4. Educational change—United States. I. Stevens, Suzanne H., 1938– Classroom success for the learning disabled. II. Title.
LC4705.S74 1996
371.92'6—dc21 96-47283

Cover design by Debra Long Hampton and Liza Langrall
Layout design by Liza Langrall

Contents

PART IV

Introduction

THROUGHOUT THE 1970S AND 1980S, many states recognized learning disabilities as worthy of attention and services in public schools. Programs were established. Teachers were trained to go a step beyond remedial reading and instruct students who had information-processing problems that made it hard for them to master reading, writing, spelling, and/or math despite the fact that they were bright, healthy, and emotionally stable. Along with their difficulties in learning basic academic skills, almost all of these youngsters had a short attention span, problems with distractibility, and difficulty with concentration. Some were *hyperactive*; a few were *hypoactive*. A tiny minority couldn't control their focus of attention at all. Only a handful of these learning-disabled children were girls.

During those years, LD specialists were trained to teach by a variety of methods, almost all of them aimed at reading. A few of the remedial methods focused on the full spectrum of skills involved in dealing with written language. Those approaches usually used multisensory techniques to teach a sequentially organized phonics-based program. In addition to working to develop students' decoding skills, they addressed the needs of LD children in the areas of handwriting, spelling, and expressive writing. Amidst much controversy over instructional methods, many teachers used an "eclectic approach," with the intention that they would do "whatever was necessary." Regardless of their method or their background, very few of those certified to teach LD children had any training in remedial techniques for math.

Over the next twenty years, the trouble learning-disabled youngsters had with concentration and disorganization became more pronounced. When my first book (*The Learning-Disabled Child: Ways That Parents Can Help*) came out in 1980, very few children were on Ritalin, and of those who were, the majority were classified as LD, with hyperactivity and distractibility considered to be part of the attention problems associated with their learning disability.

Whether children were officially diagnosed and labeled or not, every classroom had one or two students who stood out because of their failure to learn to read, write, and spell. The school behavior of those who had trouble with concentration and organization made it obvious that their attention problems were not the primary cause of their academic difficulties.

A second group of children who had trouble with concentration and organization were termed *hyperkinetic*. These overactive youngsters were bouncing off the walls and hanging from the rafters. They were out of control, and their behavior was outrageous. Fortunately, there were very few of them. The regular classroom teacher would run into one of these hyperactive children every few years. When she did, she didn't have time to notice if the youngster had a learning problem; she was too busy keeping him from tearing down the building. For this handful of high-energy wildcats, Ritalin and other medications were a godsend. As these unruly little terrors settled down, parents, teachers, and classmates rejoiced. It was assumed that once they gained enough control to sit still and pay attention, they would learn just fine.

In 1980, the term *Attention Deficit Hyperactivity Disorder* was coined by the *Diagnostic and Statistical Manual of Mental Disorders*, third edition. At that time, ADD was considered rare. Over the next ten years, many LD children were diagnosed as having an attention deficit disorder in addition to their learning disability. During that period, ADD became increasingly common, and it grew obvious that most of the youngsters given the label had trouble with spelling, math, and expressive writing. Many of them, especially the girls, also had problems with reading comprehension. For some of these students, their academic difficulties were serious enough to warrant an extensive reevaluation and the secondary label of *learning disabled.* As youngsters identified as having an attention deficit disorder matured, it became increasingly common for further testing to recognize their learning problems as part of a previously unrecognized learning disability. By 1990, experts in the two fields began to realize that researchers who were studying learning disabilities and doctors who were investigating attention deficit disorder were exploring two sides of the same coin.

Thus, for the purposes of this book, the two groups of students will be dealt with together. Whether their primary problem is academic (LD) or behavioral (ADD), both groups need classroom accommodations to help them overcome difficulties with concentration and organization. And both groups need remedial training in spelling, handwriting, and expressive writing.

Both groups also tend to have the strengths and talents associated with the "global learners" described in the last chapter of this book. Recognition of the special areas of giftedness typically found among LD/ADD students leads quite naturally to speculation about educational alternatives that go far beyond the remediation, modification, and accommodation techniques suggested here.

A few words about terminology and usage are necessary.

There have been a number of variations on the term *Attention Deficit Hyperactivity Disorder* since it first appeared. The current "correct" label is *Attention-Deficit/Hyperactivity Disorder*, abbreviated *ADHD*. Contrary to "proper" usage, *learning disability* and *attention deficit disorder* will not be capitalized in this book, on the theory that the idea of "defectiveness" should not be given more emphasis than it deserves.

The term *learning disability* should not be abbreviated when it is used as a noun. No one has an LD. Instead, it is correct to say, "John has a learning disability." Also note that learning disabilities come one per person. A student may have many different learning problems, but taken together they comprise his own personal learning disability. No matter how many problems he has, John does not have *learning disabilities*. He has *a learning disability*. These phrases are correct: his learning disability, some learning disabilities, a learning disability, John's learning disability.

The abbreviation *LD* may be used as an adjective in describing those with a learning disability, their instructors, and their classes. These phrases are correct: the LD child, the LD teacher, the LD class.

Experts used to say that 70 percent of those with learning disabilities were male; though they are indeed in the minority, females make up a larger percentage than was previously suspected, as has been revealed by more sophisticated testing and a clearer understanding of how LD characteristics are manifested in girls. Similarly, current research suggests that 70 to 80 percent of those with an attention deficit disorder are male.

With these figures in mind, the pronoun *he* will generally be used in this book to refer to individual LD/ADD students. No gender bias is intended; this usage merely reflects reality and avoids the cumbersome *he/she*.

Likewise, *she* will be used to refer to individual teachers, psychologists, and learning-disabilities specialists. Though there are men who work with LD/ADD students in various capacities, most of the specialists are women, especially on the elementary-school level.

Finally, it should be noted that, for this revised edition, pertinent material has been incorporated from four of my other titles that are now out of print: *How to Rescue At-Risk Students; Shifters: How to Help Students Concentrate; Enabling Disorganized Students to Succeed*; and *Helping the LD Child with Homework*.

PART I

An Afternoon with Al

CHAPTER 1

WHILE ON A LECTURE TOUR, I FOUND MYSELF in a strange town with a whole afternoon free. It was a very hot, sultry day. I decided to find a shady spot down by the river and laze away the hours.

Before I'd even had a chance to pick my spot, a cruising policeman stopped to warn me, "This is no place for a lady."

Scanning the gravel parking lot and weed-choked field adjoining it, I saw no sign of human activity. The place was cut off from the rest of the downtown area but certainly didn't look dangerous.

"A lot of bums and winos hang out down there," the cop explained, gesturing over his shoulder toward a clump of large poplars at the river's edge.

A glance in that direction revealed nothing. A small knoll blocked the base of the trees from view. With a confident smile, I assured the patrolman that I was perfectly safe. "I've got my dog with me," I said, pointing to my Weimaraner, Max.

The officer didn't seem impressed with my seventy-pound protector and traveling companion. "You be careful," he cautioned, and drove off.

Never having been a person to take someone else's word for something, I gathered lawn chair, lunch, books, and dog and headed for the shade of the poplars. I'd gotten about halfway to the trees when I noticed the sound of voices coming from that direction. Moving more slowly, I proceeded forward until the weeds thinned enough to allow a glimpse of the area. Sure enough, some men were lounging on the rocks at the river's edge. It irked me that they had the best shady spot, right down by the water.

I beat a hasty retreat to the only other shady area available. Max and I set ourselves up in a patch of grass in the shadow of a cement wall about a hundred yards back from the river. It was too hot for him to be interested in exploring or for me to pursue thoughts of irritation about the bums. With a pleasant breeze and a magnificent view, he and I dozed contentedly.

After about an hour, one of the winos came staggering up from the water's edge. He was gaunt beneath a shock of unkempt gray hair. Our eyes never met as he passed. He returned shortly, the neck of a bottle sticking out of the brown bag he was carrying. Following his lurching gait as he returned to the shade of the poplars, I was relieved that he hadn't stopped to bother me or ask for a handout.

Max and I drifted through another peaceful hour. Then, again, one of the winos approached from the river. This time, it was a young man. He had blond hair sticking out around a cloth cap, a T-shirt covering his husky torso, and blue jeans. He looked straight at me. Max barked furiously. I drew him in on his chain so that he stood close by my side, and hoped the youth would just pass on by.

Max acted as though he'd rip the boy's arms and legs right off if given half a chance.

"Will he bite?" the youth asked casually.

"Only if you do something to make him feel threatened," I

replied curtly. The policeman's warning echoed in my mind and made me suspicious of the young man's easy manner and unknown intentions. From the way he walked, it was apparent he'd been drinking. From his eyes, I could tell he'd been smoking marijuana. Whatever the reason for his friendliness, I tried to discourage him with a cool, aloof attitude.

He asked a lot of questions about Max. I stuck to one-word answers in the hope that he'd see my lack of enthusiasm and go away.

Instead, he moved into the shadow of my wall, hunkered down in the grass, and told me about his own dog.

It took a long time, but gradually I realized that the boy meant no harm. He was just lonely and wanted to talk. Max and I became comfortable with the stranger as he told us about his home on the other side of the river, places he'd been, things he'd seen. More and more, he revealed himself to be a perceptive, intelligent, sensitive, resourceful person.

As my interest grew, I began asking questions and taking a more active part in the conversation. He talked freely about dropping out of school when he was in the eighth grade. Except for his winning a third-grade poetry contest and having one good history teacher in junior high, school had been nothing but a source of pain. He said he was a poor reader, a dismal speller, and never could learn math at all. He said he often got "mixed up" and couldn't keep letters and numbers in the right order. At fourteen, he had joined a rock band. For the next two years, he had spent his nights playing in bars and his days skipping school and doing drugs. As soon as he turned sixteen, he had dropped out of school and hit the road. He'd been hitchhiking all over the country and living by his wits ever since.

By this time, our conversation was flowing along as smoothly and easily as the river before us.

"What are you doing here in town?" he asked me. "I can tell from your accent you ain't from around here."

My crusade to help the learning disabled interested him tremendously. He knew firsthand about the pain of failure. When I explained that LD and ADD children are badly hurt by adults who accuse them of being stupid and lazy, my companion nodded his head sadly. "Oh, yeah. Tell me about it. That was the story of my life until I dropped out of school. Really, I guess that was the *reason* I dropped out—the kids always thinking I was stupid and the grownups telling me I was lazy." He paused, staring at me earnestly. "But you know, they were wrong. I ain't lazy. If I'm broke and I need money, I'll work to earn it. I don't mind working. I built a redwood deck for a lady this summer. She paid me over four hundred dollars. And it didn't take but a few days. If I need money, I can earn money."

"How could you build a deck if you can't use numbers?" I asked. "How'd you do the measuring?"

"Shoot, don't need to use 'rithmetic for that. You just give me a piece of string, a T square, and a level, and I can build you anything you want. And not just carpentry work either. Ain't nothing I can't build."

The topic of how he made money when he needed it was all but inexhaustible. He'd done every imaginable kind of construction job and had even worked with an animal trainer for a while. It became increasingly apparent, and reassuringly so, that panhandling and larceny were not part of his approach to living by his wits. Except for drugs and vagrancy, he lived within the law.

When the subject worked its way back to success and failure, his philosophy amazed me. He understood that real achievement motivates by offering more than the hollow rewards of money and approval. He knew why life was worth living.

"What's the biggest success you've ever had in your life?" he asked.

For that one, I didn't even have to think. "The publication of my first book."

"Oh, wow, what a high!" His eyes widened with understanding. We shared the thrill of my success for a while, then he asked, "Do you want to know my biggest success, the thing that makes me *know* I'm not stupid or lazy?"

I nodded.

"I was a junkie—and I kicked the habit all by myself."

"A heroin addict?"

"Yeah, smack. It was going to kill me and I knew it."

"And you got off it without any help?"

Nodding slowly, he smiled with deep pride. "All by myself."

"I thought that couldn't be done."

"It can. I did it." He shared the delight of that success, then added, "I was a speed freak for a while, too."

By this time, my companion seemed clear-headed and sober, and the afternoon sun was rapidly eating into our small area of shade. We'd been talking for well over an hour but had no desire to quit. He had no commitments. I still had nearly four hours until my seven o'clock speaking engagement.

"Hey, there's a little pond over on the other side of the river, my most favorite place in the whole world. Let me take you there." He paused to see what my reaction would be, then continued enthusiastically. "It's so beautiful. I'd really like you to see it. We could even go swimming."

In the face of the afternoon heat, the idea of an old schoolmarm and an eighteen-year-old bum traipsing off to a swimming hole together didn't seem at all ridiculous. We quickly gathered up my belongings and started toward the car.

As the youth opened the door, he said, "By the way, my name is Alvin," and stuck out his hand. "My friends call me Al."

"Okay, Al it is," I said as I started the car. I gave him my name and we shook warmly. "Don't forget you're going to have to navigate. I don't know a thing about this town," I reminded him as we pulled out of the parking lot.

"No problem," he replied. "I know this place like the back of my hand." Pointing ahead, he instructed, "Go down to that first light and take a left. We want to go up over the bridge."

The huge steel girders rose in plain sight on our right. When we reached the traffic signal, it was red. As we waited, I gestured in the direction of the bridge. "That way?" I asked, to get verification of the right turn I was about to make.

He nodded. "Yup."

Up over the bridge, down into a small area of heavy traffic, past a few stores and a row of houses—in less than five minutes, we were on a winding country road. Al pointed out the interesting sights. He seemed to know who lived in every house we passed and had a story to tell about each. In an easy, free-flowing style, he told of living by himself in the woods for months, of fishing, camping, and living off the land.

The pond that was our destination was even lovelier than I'd imagined. Its clear green water was rimmed by cattails, lush, tall grass, and woods. The scene had the perfection of a picture postcard. Al helped me out onto the rickety old dock. Removing our shoes, we sat on the weathered gray boards and dangled our feet in the cool water.

Al broke our comfortable silence by asking, "If I get my jeans wet, you got something I could sit on so I won't ruin your seats?"

"Yes, I've got an old towel in the trunk."

"Good, then I'm going in for a swim." With that, he stripped off his shirt, removed his leather belt, and slid from the dock into the water.

For a while, time and appointments just didn't exist. Al floated lazily on his back, tried to touch bottom, gathered a handful of moss from a leg of the dock and studied it carefully. I splashed my feet in the water, relaxing and talking and enjoying.

A powerful thirst, an uncomfortable awareness of a No Trespassing sign, and five o'clock all hit me at about the same time. Al picked a couple of the cattails I wanted and helped me off the wobbly dock, and we headed back to town.

He wanted to go by his house on the way so he could change into some dry jeans. But first, we stopped at a tiny gas station/grocery store to pick up cold drinks.

Al and I stood side by side surveying the contents of the store's drink cooler. Noticing what I wanted way down at the end near him, I requested, "Fish me out a Coke, will you?"

He reached in with his left hand, snapped the top off in the opener attached to the cooler, and handed me the bottle.

"I didn't know you were left-handed," I commented casually.

"I'm not," he replied, removing a drink for himself with his right hand by way of demonstration. "Most of the things I can do with my right hand, I can do just about as good with my left." With a grin, he added, "Comes in handy when you're working in tight places trying to tack up molding and stuff."

The little old lady behind the counter exchanged greetings with Al but obviously didn't approve of him. She asked me a lot of questions in an effort to find out just what I was doing with such riffraff. Al was oddly silent. We finished our drinks and left.

Al's house was on a small side road just a mile or two from the country store. As we pulled up the steep gravel driveway, I gasped, "Your house is an authentic log cabin?"

"Yup." Al grinned. "The real thing."

We parked by the side door. While Al went in to change, Max and I prowled around the backyard. A couple of junked cars and a varied assortment of old, rusty parts rimmed one side of the area. A small house trailer, the cinder-block foundation of a building, and two old wooden sheds circled the other side.

Al returned, bringing his young Doberman with him. After proudly telling me how he'd trained his loving, obedient pet, he asked, "You want to see the pigs before we go?"

I nodded with interest and followed the youth over to the cinder-block foundation walls. There, penned inside, three mammoth hogs snuffled and snorted at us in greeting.

"Did you know pigs are smart?" Al asked. Without waiting for my reply, he picked up a long, stout stick. "And they love to have their backs scratched." As soon as they saw the stick, the huge beasts pushed and shoved to get closer, grunting with anticipation. Al leaned contentedly against the wall, rubbing the stick up and down the broad, bristly backs and explaining to me about raising pigs.

The subject was fascinating. But the stench and the heat were overwhelming. As gracefully as possible, I proposed that we leave. "I want to be at the university by six, and it's quarter of now. I think it's time we headed back toward town."

After the pigpen, the country air on the ride back to town

seemed especially cool and sweet. As we crossed the bridge, I asked Al where he wanted me to drop him off.

"There's one more thing I'd like to show you," he replied.

I checked my watch. "It's five to six."

"From the top of this one building downtown, you can see the whole city," he said.

"Will it take long?"

He pointed off to the left. "It's just right there."

"If we run short of time, I'll have to leave you downtown," I half-apologized.

"That's okay. Ain't nowhere I need to get to that I can't get there by thumbing."

We agreed to take in this one last sight before parting.

Al directed me to the entrance of a large parking deck. We took a ticket and drove to the top. Happy to be released from the car, Max loped joyfully around the vast expanse of concrete. Al moved slowly from one vantage point to another, pointing out special features in the panoramic view of city, river, and hills beyond. As we looked away from the river and back toward the downtown area, even the rooftops across the back alley were interesting. We were particularly captivated by a tiny vegetable garden planted in tin cans and clay pots on a roof below. Languidly leaning against the railing, Al speculated about the size and quality of the small crop about to be harvested by some city farmer.

Increasingly anxious about my tight schedule, I tried to hurry my companion along. He didn't seem to notice my concern. He was digging through the pocket of his jeans, looking for something. As I was about to mention my schedule once more, Al produced a nickel, held it up for me to see, and grinned. Without a word of explanation, he reached far out over the edge, dropped the coin, then watched and listened closely as it fell the five floors to the pavement.

A quick glance at my watch startled me into realizing that time was becoming a serious problem. It was ten after six. Mentally, I computed how long it would take to drop Al off, drive to the university, change clothes, eat dinner, and get to the meeting. Quickly deciding I could forgo dinner if necessary, I announced, "Al, we have *got* to go. It's nearly quarter after six."

In our fascination with the view, we'd forgotten all about Max. Now, he was nowhere in sight. I called him. Al whistled.

Some rather frustrated barking came from one of the corner stairwells. I hurried over and looked down. My poor dog, confused by one level that looked the same as the next, was moving farther down the stairs in his attempt to get back to where we were.

"Come on, Max!" I shouted. "Up. We're up here."

Al sauntered over, sized up the situation, and said, "I'll go get him." Talking to the dog in calm, soothing tones, the youth padded casually down the stairs. "You just stay there, Max. I'll come get you. See, I'm up here. No, don't go down—you need to go the other way. Attaboy, now you got it."

From above, I could hear slowly moving sneakers and clicking canine toenails on concrete. Max bounded out at the top; Al followed shortly with a grin. "Ol' Max don't know up from down," he chuckled, and gave the dog a fond pat.

I was so far behind schedule that Al and I had to part without much fanfare. Clasping hands warmly, we said our good-byes.

Several times during the afternoon, the youth had said he often wondered if dropping out of school was a mistake. As I pulled away, I wanted to shout out to him in farewell, "It was no mistake. You're learning disabled. They had ten years to recognize you. What makes you think it might be different now? The first nine years, they damaged you. The next four might have destroyed you." But I didn't say anything. With tears in my eyes, silently, I waved good-bye.

Recognizing the LD/ADD Child

Chapter 2

How did I *know* that Al was learning disabled? What did I observe in such an informal encounter?

To those who know what they're looking for, Al revealed a tremendous amount of information strongly suggesting a severe learning disability combined with an attention deficit disorder with hypoactivity. From his own words and the circumstances of his life, there was ample evidence that the youth had failed to learn successfully in school. Anyone who's only in the eighth grade when he drops out at age sixteen can be safely categorized as an academic failure.

But Al's poor scholastic performance was merely one of many pieces of evidence suggesting that the youth had problems associated with learning disabilities and attention deficit disorder. His strengths and successes pointed just as surely to the same conclusion. Al's entire pattern was typical of LD and ADD individuals. A definitive diagnosis would include careful probing for physical, intellectual, and psychological assets and deficiencies. Yet even without benefit of such formal procedures, clues were readily available to any observant person.

Causes of Failure

The LD/ADD child's failure to succeed in school is not caused by a physical handicap. If it is to be suggested that Al had a learning disability, and probably an attention deficit disorder as well, then it must be shown that his learning failure was not the result of some physical condition.

In vision, hearing, and general state of health, Al showed no signs of any physical problem. It takes good visual acuity plus tracking ability to follow a nickel as it drops from a parking deck to the pavement five floors below. And it takes good ears to hear it when it hits the ground. No hearing problem was observed or mentioned. Al showed that he was well coordinated. Playing a musical instrument in a rock band, doing carpentry, and engaging in heavy construction work all demand at least adequate agility. Long-distance hitchhiking and living off the land are not for the weak, sickly, or faint-hearted. All of the evidence strongly suggests that Al was alert, quick, responsive, and strong and had a great deal of stamina. From the things Al *could* do, it would not be logical to assume that his learning problems were caused by a physical condition.

Also by definition, the LD/ADD child's academic failure is *not* caused by lack of mental ability. The problem is not mental retardation. To be classified as having a learning disability, a youngster must have average or better intelligence.

There is much evidence to indicate that Al had adequate mental ability. At fourteen, he could play a musical instrument well enough to make money in a rock group. From sixteen to eighteen, he managed to support himself as a carpenter and construction worker. By the age of eighteen, he had come to realize that his parents, friends, teachers, and classmates were wrong in believing that he was stupid. He knew about raising pigs, training dogs, and fishing. Al hitchhiked all over the country without getting lost or arrested. Despite his poor grammar and slang expressions, he had a rich vocabulary and communicated effectively. He asked intelligent questions, had an abundance of curiosity, and was highly observant of his surroundings. Al was definitely not retarded or "slow."

In addition to the type of mental ability that is measured by an IQ test, Al seemed to have a great deal of common sense. Anyone who could figure out a way to build a redwood deck with a piece of string, a T square, and a level would have to possess considerable ingenuity. Living off the land and living by his wits demanded alertness and quickness of mind. There *are* LD/ADD children who don't have sense enough to come in out of the rain—but they are not in the majority.

The legal definitions exclude psychological problems as the cause of the LD child's lack of success in school. This distinction does not always apply to those who are labeled ADD. Problems with concentration, distractibility, impulse control, and activity level are commonly found among those who have a behavior disorder or are emotionally disturbed. In such cases, the ADD is part of the larger, more pervasive problem. Theoretically, those whose ADD is part of some larger problem should be identified with *both* labels, but it doesn't always work that way. Many doctors use the ADD classification when a more specific diagnosis cannot be determined. It is also commonly applied by psychologists and physicians who are reluctant to place a child in a category that carries a heavy social stigma. Parents who would never accept some more precise diagnostic label are often able to acknowledge the fact that their child's behavior does fit with the symptoms of an attention deficit disorder.

This is a tricky area. Any child who is the dum-dum of the class develops strange behavior patterns out of frustration, shame, and anger. By the time he gets to junior high, the unrecognized LD/ADD student is usually unmotivated and either hostile or withdrawn. In the classroom, he is a behavior problem. Outside class, he has social problems. Al's truancy and drug use at age fourteen are typical examples. Obviously, he was not a model student.

By the age of eighteen, Al could demonstrate his emotional stability and flexibility. Despite the drugs and alcohol, he lived in and talked about reality. He was respectful of a dog that might bite him but was neither recklessly bold nor unreasonably afraid. Asking about wet pants damaging my car seat before deciding to go for a swim shows that Al considered the consequences of his behavior *before* acting.

Although school had been a miserable experience for the youth, he expressed no anger or hatred toward former teachers, schools, or society in general. His thoughts on the past were not full of guilt or despair. His thoughts about the future were not full of impossible dreams. By being honest about both his weakness in math and his capability at building, he showed that he had a realistic attitude about himself. Al said he gave up heroin because he didn't want to die. That action demonstrated that he not only valued life but considered the quality of life important as well. The will power to overcome heroin addiction can be found only in a person with a very strong desire to have control over his life.

Al's attitude toward me provided further evidence of emotional stability. While being friendly and unusually assertive, he was always respectful and considerate. He was careful not to hurt my car seats, kindly rescued my dog, and even seemed to watch his language to avoid four-letter words that might have been offensive.

Al never did anything odd or peculiar. He was "oddly silent" in the grocery store, but that was an understandable and logical way for him to deal with the situation. We were in a tiny rural community. He was a "local." The old lady at the cash register not only knew him but openly showed her disapproval. She asked me a lot of nosy questions in her attempt to find out what I was doing with a person she considered a good-for-nothing bum. Under the circumstances, Al's polite silence was extremely reasonable behavior.

There are those who would say, "A healthy, intelligent eighteen-year-old who spends his days drinking and smoking dope with the winos—there's got to be something wrong with his head." The young man definitely was a misfit. It would take a psychological examination to evaluate his state of mental health precisely, but from everything that happened during that afternoon, there was no reason to consider him emotionally disturbed.

Mixed Dominance and Directional Confusion

Human beings have a natural tendency to develop a strong preference for using one half of their body over the other. In strength, agility, coordination, and acquisition of skills, the body becomes increasingly one-sided. When an activity allows a choice of feet, hands, eyes, or ears, one side will be consistently favored. For most people, the dominant half is the right.

The learning disabled and those with an attention deficit disorder aren't necessarily built that way. They often have mixed dominance. Their bodies aren't strongly one-sided. Al was partially ambidextrous. Although he did most things with his right hand, he sometimes found it more convenient to use his left. In getting our soft drinks, Al used his left hand for both removing the bottle from the cooler and applying the top to the opener. Very few right-handed people would attempt such a maneuver. For most people, the nonfavored hand is just hanging there for ballast, and occasionally for holding things while the other hand works on them. Al was proud of the fact that this was not the case for him. He commented that his ability to switch back and forth came in handy when doing things like tacking up molding.

There is nothing wrong with having mixed dominance. Sometimes, it's an advantage, as with Al's carpentry and those who become switch hitters in baseball. Sometimes, it's a disadvantage, as with a youngster who tries to learn to shoot a gun right-handed while sighting with the left eye. When dealing with concrete objects and body movement, right-sided, left-sided, and mixed all work out about the same.

The inability to tell left from right is one of the most common symptoms of a learning disability and is frequently found among those labeled ADD. Al demonstrated his problem in this area when he gave me the instruction to turn left at the bridge, though he and I could plainly see the big steel structure looming over us on the right. From any person over the age of seven or eight, such a mistake should not be considered a meaningless slip of the tongue. And noticing and correcting the error does not change the fact that it was made. Those who are LD/ADD do *not* have trouble with the labels *left* and *right* every time they use them. But most people never have trouble with them at all.

Poor Concept of Time

Al never once talked about what time it was. Even when my schedule was tight and we were discussing the possibility of seeing the view from the parking deck, he responded without ever referring to time. I announced the hour; he said there was a great view of the city from the top of a building downtown. I asked how long it would take; he pointed, replying that the building was right over there. I explained that my schedule might force me to leave him abruptly; he responded that he could get anywhere he needed to go by hitchhiking. Throughout the entire exchange, Al and I were operating on different wavelengths. I was very conscious of the minutes moving past. He was totally oblivious of them.

All through their lives, LD and ADD individuals tend to live in the here and now. As youngsters in school, this shows up in many ways.

LD/ADD children often have extreme difficulty learning to use a clock. But it is very unusual for a teacher to notice or even suspect that one of her students can't tell time. It just never comes up. Everyone assumes that once a child passes the second or third grade, the skills involved have been mastered. Teachers often say, "I told you to have that paper finished by one o'clock. It's now quarter after, and you still haven't handed it in." Teachers never ask, "What time is it?" If, by some fluke, an LD/ADD child gets trapped into a showdown, he can be counted on to use his wits to bail himself out. In such an emergency, a wide assortment of non-answers can allow the student to avoid revealing his problem. The humorous response of immediate innocent cooperation usually works well. "What time is it? Oops, it's time for me to give you my paper." All smiles, he dashes forward, scribbles his name at the top of the page, gives the paper a pat, and nods as he leaves it on the teacher's desk. If the inquiry is made by a classmate, a flippant "You got eyes, look for yourself" will usually suffice. As for the LD/ADD child's revealing his weakness by asking someone else to tell him the time, it never happens. He doesn't *care* what time it is! Like Al, those with a learning disability and/or an attention deficit disorder just flow along in the present. They're not big on plans and schedules.

Once we were on top of the building, Al and I clearly demonstrated the difference in our approaches to time. I was in a hurry. I scurried around trying to get as much as possible out of the few moments available. But not Al. He sauntered casually from one vantage point to another, pointing out the sights. Despite the fact that I emphasized the need to hurry, he oozed along at his usual slow speed. He leaned against the wall in easy comfort while offering his observations on a roof garden below. Fishing the nickel out of his pocket and dropping it over the edge was done at a relaxed pace. The unhurried movements with which he savored life were typical of the hypoactive and would have driven most people crazy! While hyperactivity is much more common, both forms of marching to a different drummer are typical of the nonvariable pace so commonly found among those labeled LD/ADD.

Clocks, time limits, and schedules do not motivate LD/ADD children. Those who move, think, and work slowly can seldom be forced to speed up. Those who run around in high gear tend to stay on fast no matter how strongly they're urged to slow down. Very few of those with a learning disability or an attention deficit disorder ever recognize the fact that their inflexible pace is an irritation and inconvenience to others. Instead, they think parents, teachers, and the world in general have made a moral virtue out of punctuality.

Because they live almost exclusively in the present—teachers often say these youngsters exist in a time warp!—LD/ADD individuals rarely consider the appropriate time for a particular action. If they think of something they want to do, they do it immediately. Psychologists label such behavior *impulsive*. Al showed some of this behavior in proposing that I join him in a trip to his favorite swimming hole. It was terribly hot. The idea of the cool water was very appealing. But he knew that middle-aged ladies don't usually join young vagrants in such adventures. His urge to act was expressed the minute it crossed his mind. When observed in the LD/ADD student, the quick decision to action is likely related to a sense of timing that allows only for *now*.

In addition to demonstrating a poor concept of time, Al described his inability to keep numbers, letters, and words in the right order. Although there was no opportunity to see it first-hand, it can be safely assumed that Al had all the difficulties with sequencing that are typical of a student with a learning disability and/or an attention deficit disorder.

Sequencing is a technique that orders objects or events in time. First comes this, then comes that, followed by something else. Since LD and ADD youngsters have such a poor concept of time, they have no feel for sequencing either.

This one problem has a devastating effect on almost all areas of schoolwork. From kindergarten, when they can't learn the alphabet, to high-school physics, when they can't keep the steps in an experiment straight, the inability to sequence makes routine tasks impossible for many of those with a learning disability and/or an attention deficit disorder. Their difficulty is particularly obvious in their poor spelling and their confusion and frustration when trying to follow sequential directions.

The majority of the activities in a traditional school program are based on doing things in a specific order.

1. Schedules.

Throughout the school day, segments of time are allocated for various subjects. As long as the periods stay in a fixed order, the LD/ADD student develops a feel for the rhythm of the day. But he'll never remember that art replaces science every other Tuesday. And he'll frequently forget that there's a vocabulary test every Wednesday. It's pointless to hope that he'll fulfill some obligation that comes up once a month, unless it's an activity in which he is passionately interested. To keep an LD/ADD child moving smoothly on schedule, teachers have to supply a lot of advance warnings and gentle reminders. They also have to systematically teach these youngsters to rely on a "memory jogger" type of calendar from a very early age.

2. Instructions.

Explanations of assignments almost always include directions that must be followed in a particular order. Details such as breaking words into syllables and then marking the vowels are likely to be overlooked by LD/ADD youngsters. Unless there's some necessary reason for one step to come after another, the progression is often forgotten or ignored. Multiple assignments are especially likely to cause frustration. If the child can remember the directions for a single page of math problems, that's enough for one sitting. Adding some corrections from yesterday's work and a page in the workbook plus two story problems on the board will throw most LD/ADD youngsters into hopeless confusion. Sometimes, it helps to have students jot down all the instructions for a series of class activities in an assignment book or on a file card. Such a technique is especially valuable to those at the junior-high level and beyond.

3. Alphabetizing.

Dictionaries, encyclopedias, library shelves, glossaries, bibliographies, outlines, indexes, etc., are based on alphabetical order. Because of the difficulty LD/ADD children have with sequencing, all forms of alphabetizing are likely to be troublesome for them. This means they are often unable to use materials necessary in completing an assignment. Yes, they can find a word in the dictionary. But it takes them three to four times as long as other students—provided they don't get furious and quit, get desperate and cheat, or lose interest in the assigned task and start reading about some fascinating topic they run across by chance.

4. Teaching techniques.

The human brain uses gimmicks to aid memory. For most people, it would be impossible to name the months of the year without saying them in order. Sequencing is a trick that enables us to recall all twelve easily. In teaching anything to anybody, the method of instruction is likely to use sequencing as the tool that makes learning possible. First-graders are told, "To make an *m*, first you make a stick, then you make a hump, then you add another hump." For most of them, this makes the process as easy as one, two, three. But not for those with a learning disability or an attention deficit disorder. No amount of repetition teaches them to put two humps on an *m* if their memory must rely on sequencing.

"What comes next?" "What do I do now?" LD/ADD students ask these questions constantly. Every time they express such confusion, they're announcing the fact that they're having trouble with sequencing.

Unusual Powers of Observation

From the way Al studied the moss on the dock, told me about raising pigs, dropped the nickel from the building and watched it fall, it was clear that he was observant and perceptive. He had a huge amount of curiosity and was interested in what went on around him. He noticed everything.

Those with a learning disability, and especially those with an attention deficit disorder, seem to look at the world through a wide-angle lens. Nothing escapes their attention. They do not focus narrowly on one task and tune out everything else—unless they go into the "hyperfocus" they apply when involved in their favorite activities. In a classroom, it seems to be impossible for them to ignore anything that's going on around them. They are the ones who comment on the teacher's new hairdo and the fact that her slip is showing. While they are supposed to be concentrating on an English test, their attention is drawn to footsteps in the hall, the glint of sunlight off the pencil sharpener, the cool breeze blowing across the room, shuffling feet, turning papers, tapping pencils, the feel of initials carved in the top of the desk, the breathing of other students, the great-looking skier on the calendar behind the teacher's desk, the rumbly emptiness of a hungry stomach. The LD/ADD student would make a splendid Sherlock Holmes. But in a traditional classroom, such powers of observation are a handicap. By not zeroing in on the work at hand, he fails to pay attention in a way acceptable to teachers. When a pupil is seated at a desk in school, the wide-angle-lens approach means he is distractible and has a short attention span.

Section 504 of the 1990 Individuals with Disabilities in Education Act (IDEA) makes generous allowances for adapting the environment so that LD/ADD youngsters' problem with distractibility does not deprive them of an opportunity to achieve academic success. Even those with mild attention problems must have a private, quiet area provided for testing and special projects upon request. This accommodation is commonly seen in medical schools as well as high schools and colleges. Within the public schools, it is one of the modifications frequently specified in the Individual Educational Plan (IEP).

For those LD/ADD youngsters who are super-observant, the tendency to notice everything does not apply merely to what can be seen, heard, and felt. Often, it also applies to people. The set of a shoulder, the tilt of a head, the raising of an eyebrow, the tone of a voice, body language, pauses—the unspoken messages in the realm of feelings are noticed by these very sensitive children. They are often unusually adept at reading people.

Al gave a good demonstration of this type of special sensitivity to people. While I was determined not to get involved with any of the bums and winos, he made light conversation until my defensive attitude evaporated. My haughty air of disinterest didn't fool him a bit. Somehow, Al sensed that my dog and I were both friendly. All afternoon, Al's consideration for me continually reflected his keen awareness of my feelings.

In recent years, more and more LD/ADD youngsters have been demonstrating a lack of these types of people skills. They can't read social signals; they say all the wrong things; they misinterpret what they're told; they have no friends. Their ability to notice everything in the concrete world around them is of no value in observing people, and they show absolutely no talent for interacting with their peers in ways that are socially desirable. This difficulty with social interaction has become so common that many programs designed for LD/ADD students now include social skills as a routine part of their curriculum, even at the college level.

Unusual Creativity

LD/ADD students are usually much more creative than their classmates. They approach problems in an exploratory manner and express themselves and their ideas in a more open-ended way. From poems to mechanical inventions to business ventures, they tend to keep tinkering with their design long after others consider the creative process complete. The products of their inventive thinking are often so simple, yet so totally original, that others gape in wonder, saying, "What an ingenious idea."

From an early age, Al showed unusual creativity. In the third grade, he won a poetry contest; at fourteen, he was in a rock band; at eighteen, he could figure out how to build a redwood deck without even measuring. Very few young people are creative enough to succeed in even one of these areas, let alone three.

Al's greatest strength was in building three-dimensional objects. "And not just carpentry work either." The LD/ADD child is the one who can build a go-cart out of an old lawn mower and a pile of scrap lumber. He tends to build things in unconventional ways, however. Part of this is due to his unusual creative ability, part to the fact that he's not likely to be using written directions or doing a lot of measuring or planning. With hammer and saw, screwdriver and pliers, LD/ADD children can do some amazing things.

Research has shown that most of the learning disabled are "spatially gifted." They tend to have a talent for understanding and creating objects that are three-dimensional. The boys are often good at drawing, fixing things, and working with lumber, pipe, or clay. This means they make good sculptors, mechanics, automotive designers, architects, plumbers, and engineers. The girls often have an unusual talent for working with fabrics and yarns. They have a good eye for color and a great flair for design and style. Their skills equip them to be fashion designers, interior decorators, and graphic artists. Even from a very young age, LD/ADD females take great pleasure in arts and crafts.

The mechanical wizardry so often found in LD/ADD students is pretty much common knowledge. The other areas of their exceptional creativity are not so often recognized. The walls of my classroom were always covered with outstanding artwork done by my students. They won many blue ribbons and awards at fairs, exhibits, and children's art contests. Some of them showed unusual skill in drawing, painting, and design. Almost all of them demonstrated a wonderful talent for coming up with original ideas. This special skill in producing novel ideas often carries over into creative writing and interpretation of literature, as well as dance and drama. Despite poor spelling and halting reading, the LD/ADD child often uses language with real flair. If appreciated for the imaginative person he is, an LD/ADD student can add sparkle, mirth, and new depths of insight to an entire class.

Misfits and Loners

To his classmates, the LD/ADD child almost always looks stupid or weird. Since the youngsters around his neighborhood know about his lack of success in school, they often consider him a loser. Teased, picked on, and rejected, the LD/ADD child is often forced into the role of outcast.

Generally, children with a learning disability and/or an attention deficit disorder do not find acceptance from the adults in their lives either. Teachers believe they're lazy. Parents accuse them of being stubborn. Relatives usually think they're spoiled. Neighbors consider them troublemakers. Socially, on all fronts, LD/ADD youngsters tend to be rejected.

Through no choice of his own, the LD/ADD child is forced to be a loner. The only companionship and acceptance available to him is from strangers or other losers.

Skipping school, doing drugs, dropping out, hitting the road—like Al, LD/ADD teenagers seek escape. They are frustrated and miserable in school. And their social life and home life are rarely much better. Life is *not* pleasant.

For such young people, escape-type activities hold great appeal. Among young children, doodling, drawing, and daydreaming are typical. For teenagers, it's escape through drugs, alcohol, sex, and travel. Traveling and bumming around become attractive because they offer opportunities for quick, easy acceptance among strangers.

Al's behavior was typical of this pattern. For the most part, he was a loner, escaping through drugs and alcohol. With me, a stranger, he was relaxed, friendly, and comfortably outgoing. With the old woman in the country store, who knew all about him, he was quiet and withdrawn. And faraway places held a special attraction for him. Outside the school and neighborhood where he was known, he could be accepted as totally normal and okay.

It's unfortunate that psychiatry probably would not have helped Al. Teaching children to live joyously with failure has been tried many times. It doesn't work. The LD/ADD youngster doesn't need counseling. He needs to learn to read. He needs to learn to do his math. He needs acceptance. He needs confidence. He needs success.

Poor Organization

If there's any group that has *no* natural inclination toward organization, it's those with a learning disability and/or an attention deficit disorder. They are the original absent-minded professors. They can't find their glasses, lost their pencil, don't know what day it is, forgot where they put their jacket, left their book home on the dining-room table. Their work is messy, their environment a shambles. They're forgetful, preoccupied, frequently off in the clouds. Mothers, teachers, wives, roommates, and colleagues are driven crazy by their total lack of order.

Al was a beautiful example of the lack of organization so typical of LD/ADD people. By the age of eighteen, he'd completely abandoned attempts to live within any kind of structure. No plans, no regular job, no commitments, no schedules—he just went along with the flow. Al created a lifestyle in which it didn't matter if he knew what day it was. He turned lack of organization into an asset.

LD/ADD individuals are unable to live comfortably on deadlines. As children, they're chronically tardy. As adults, they're famous for being late for most of their appointments. This is not simply part of their lack of a concept of time. It is also a result of their lack of organization.

The little square on the LD/ADD student's report card for "Uses time wisely" is likely to be checked "Needs improvement." When faced with a task, he has a standard ineffective pattern. First, he gets ready to get started. This usually includes a trip to the wastebasket or drinking fountain, a joke with a classmate, and some fun with a toy stashed in his pocket. Teachers often put an abrupt end to this stage with admonitions like "John, get down to business." Second, he takes a long time to get out his materials. The jumbled mess in his desk makes the search for pencils, paper, and books a slow process. And he also tends to dawdle. When the child finally picks up his pencil to begin work, his classmates are already way ahead of him. (That is, of course, assuming he can find a pencil at all!) Third, the LD/ADD youngster struggles to figure out the directions. He never seems to remember what the teacher said to do. His tendency toward impulsiveness often prompts him to wade in, figuring it out as best he can. Sometimes, he pesters his neighbors for guidance. Often, he comes running up to the teacher's desk for help. His confusion and uncertainty are usually obvious. Fourth, he makes his big attempt. He fills in a few answers. When that proves difficult or boring, he shifts to some part of the assignment that looks easier or more interesting. As he proves equally unsuccessful at that, he resorts to pure guessing. Frustrated, he pauses to sharpen a pencil, take a breather, or gaze out the window. And fifth, his mind drifts off to something else as the rest of the class period slips by.

This pattern isn't just the result of poor reading skills or distractibility. It's also caused by an inability to get organized.

Failure in the Basic Skills

LD/ADD students fail to succeed in learning the basic skills. As a third-grader, Al understood poetry well enough to create a contest-winning poem. As a junior-high student, he succeeded in learning history. This is typical of LD/ADD students. They can learn the material in subject-matter courses, but they have trouble mastering reading, writing, spelling, and/or math. When they fail subject-matter courses, it's usually because they can't read the book, can't (or won't) write the answers for assignments and tests, don't pay attention in class, or don't study. Academically, students with a learning disability and/or an attention deficit disorder have a problem acquiring the basic skills.

From the teacher's side of the desk, it is rarely obvious that the LD/ADD student's newest failure is caused by lack of success in learning the basic skills. It almost always looks as if his problem is laziness, lack of motivation, poor attitude, or absences. The academic failure usually appears to be the *result*, rather than the *cause*, of his behavior problems.

When faced with real LD/ADD children in real classrooms, teachers fail to recognize what they're seeing.

They say, "If there's anybody who can't afford to sleep through math class, it's you. The least you could do is *try*!"

Why should he try to do multiplication? He can't even write the numbers so they face in the proper direction! After three or four or five years of trying, the multiplication tables are still not stored in his memory. Trying has never paid off before.

Teachers snarl, "Young man, I'll take that yo-yo you've been playing with, and you can get to work right now. You can get all four of those English worksheets done before lunch if you put your mind to it."

Why should he put his mind to writing sentences? He can't read the questions or the story they're based on. If he did know the answers, he could neither spell the words correctly nor copy them out of the book accurately. And if by some miracle he could manage all of the above tasks, his illegible penmanship would draw ridicule and demands that the paper be copied over.

With a stern tone of voice, classroom authorities demand, "You take this note home to your mother. And when you walk in that door Monday morning, I want to see that book you say you're reading for your book report."

Why should he bring that book to school with him? He can read only about half the words in it. If he skips over the hard parts and ignores all the boring parts, he still can't follow the action. He can't spell, can't express his ideas in writing. He's never written a decent sentence in his life. Even if he could read the book, he couldn't possibly write an acceptable book report. So why should he bring that book to school on Monday? It would be just another hassle.

To LD/ADD students, effort is pointless. Failure is inevitable.

To teachers, the child doesn't look as if he *can't* do the work. He looks as if he *won't* do it.

For many students who are diagnosed as having an attention deficit disorder, with no recognition of LD tendencies, inability to get motivated causes more problems than lack of skills. Even very bright ADD students with only minor academic difficulties grow to hate the subjects that cause them confusion and frustration. These youngsters rarely recognize the fact that they find math or spelling or foreign languages or handwriting or report writing to be difficult. Instead, they think of it as a matter of preferences, of likes and dislikes. Despite the fact that it is possible to produce work of acceptable quality, they grow to hate the subject so thoroughly that they avoid completing assignments even when their grades suffer dramatically for the lack of effort. To find out which academic areas a student finds difficult, ask, "Which subjects do you hate most?"

Even if a teacher is fully aware of an LD/ADD child's lack of skill in reading, spelling, and math, there is a strong tendency to find excuses to justify his poor performance—"He doesn't pay attention" or "He's too busy fooling around" or "He just doesn't really care." Adults are almost always convinced that if the youngster would really try, he could succeed. Al's teachers probably blamed socioeconomic factors with questions such as "What can you expect from a kid who lives in a shack?" Because he came from the wrong side of the tracks, Al wouldn't have been expected to succeed.

When a student with a learning disability and/or an attention deficit disorder has a pencil in his hand, it is obvious that the real cause of his difficulties is not lack of motivation. I didn't get to see Al do any writing. If I had, he'd probably have made many of the writing errors that are typical of LD/ADD students.

1. LD/ADD children often have strange methods of gripping a pencil. They hold it at an odd angle, wrap their thumb around to some weird, useless position, use four fingers instead of three, entwine their fingers around the instrument much in the manner of a claw. The traditional three-finger triangle formed by thumb, index finger, and middle finger is rarely the grip they prefer. And they are very resistant toward changing their style of holding a pencil, no matter how much the teacher insists.

2. Their papers are messy. Although they can control their hands well enough to make great spit wads and paper airplanes, they are seldom able to do a nice, neat job of handwriting, even when they try.

3. When they are motivated to do their best, their papers show that they've made many errors which were corrected. LD/ADD students erase a lot.

4. Older LD/ADD pupils usually prefer to print. They continue to use manuscript writing even when pressured to do cursive. By the seventh or eighth grade, they may improve their skill in printing but often refuse to shift to cursive.

5. They tend to use only their first name on papers. LD/ADD youngsters often have trouble learning to spell and write their first name. Last names are usually more difficult, and the young child doesn't get much practice writing his surname. Many teenage LD/ADD youngsters *cannot* write their last name correctly.

6. Most of the errors look as if they're caused by carelessness. Some of the common mistakes are undotted *i*'s, uncrossed *t*'s, *m*'s with missing humps; letters facing the wrong way, put in the wrong place, or missing altogether; letters that are the wrong size or shape, or not placed properly on the line; strange mixtures of manuscript and cursive writing.

7. Much to their teacher's dismay, LD/ADD students can't even write well when all they have to do is copy. In their attempt to reproduce what they see written before them, they leave out words and letters and make all their usual reversals and handwriting errors.

All of the writing difficulties described here are much more commonly seen in boys than girls. Many LD/ADD females have lovely penmanship. Some of them have no trouble with spelling. When a girl has a problem with writing, it usually revolves around an inability to organize her thoughts logically and express her ideas clearly.

For children who are learning disabled, the same kinds of problems seen in writing also appear in reading.

1. Letters are read upside down or backwards, so that *bad* becomes *dad* or *mash* becomes *wash.*

2. Letters are reversed or scrambled out of their proper order, so that *slot* becomes *lots* or *salt* becomes *slat.*

3. Entire syllables, words, or phrases are rearranged or omitted altogether. Suffixes frequently get left off, and little words get changed at random. *For* becomes *from, who* becomes *which, he* becomes *she, mother* becomes *mom.*

For students who are labeled as having an attention deficit disorder with no mention of a learning disability, these same reversals, inversions, omissions, and transformations are often seen in attempts to write numbers. Youngsters who are diagnosed as purely ADD rarely have major problems with reading. Their academic difficulties more typically fall in the areas of handwriting, spelling, expressive writing, and math.

Although it is traditionally assumed that most LD/ADD children have adequate or good reading comprehension, that is more and more frequently found *not* to be the case. Many female students develop excellent decoding skills but have a terrible time understanding and/or remembering what they read. And in both genders, it is becoming increasingly common to find students who have extreme difficulty expressing their ideas in any form of language—written or spoken. They may read accurately and seem to take in information adequately, yet when asked to demonstrate their grasp of the content by writing a summary, answering questions, or creating a project, they are totally unable to do so. For such youngsters, the problem is not so much reading or writing or even reading comprehension. It's a more pervasive inability to process or think with language.

Spelling is the most sensitive indicator of a learning disability and is a good indicator of an attention deficit disorder. By combining the demands of sequencing with those of writing, it hits LD/ADD children in two of their weakest spots. In trying to spell even the simplest words, they make reversals, omissions, and strange alterations. The relationships between sounds and symbols rarely make sense to them, so without special instruction they seldom even spell phonetically. Even with a high IQ and the finest therapy, very few LD/ADD individuals ever become better than barely adequate spellers. Most never do that well.

Although poor handwriting and spelling mean that LD/ADD children cannot express themselves well in writing, they usually have no difficulty expressing themselves orally. Al was typical of the learning disabled in that he loved to talk and was a good conversationalist. One of the most commonly recognized characteristics of an attention deficit disorder is a tendency to be overly talkative. The typical ADD child never seems to know when to shut up! He talks constantly.

On what little work they do, LD/ADD students tend to confine themselves to writing very brief answers. A worksheet that requires complete sentences will get answers of one or two words. An assignment that asks for paragraphs will get a few sentence fragments. When allowed to respond orally, LD/ADD pupils can almost always think of several intelligent sentences in answer to a question. Yet when the ideas have to be put into writing, they condense it all down to one word. As a general rule, the more writing an assignment requires, the less likely it is that an LD/ADD student will complete it successfully.

Al's main area of disability was math. From what could be observed directly, it is easy to surmise the types of difficulties he had. Mixed dominance and directional confusion would have given Al a strong tendency to turn numbers around or scramble them so they were out of order. Twenty-seven would become 72; 465 would become 564 or 645 or 456 or 654 or 546. This means that he would have made errors even copying the problems out of the book.

Al said he couldn't learn math at all. As is often the case with LD/ADD youngsters, no amount of practice would have helped get the multiplication facts planted in his memory. And even if he had mastered the facts, it can be assumed that he would have had a lot of trouble manipulating numbers. In the process of working a problem, Al's directional confusion would have made him get lost in the maze of up, down, right, left. Carrying would have caused problems because he would have had trouble remembering which number to write down and which to carry. In subtraction, Al would have been perfectly comfortable taking the top number from the bottom one. And of course, borrowing would have been impossible for him. Multiplication, division, fractions, decimals—all advanced arithmetic depends on the student's having a sure sense of direction. By his own admission, Al never did learn to work math problems. His total lack of ability in this basic skill no doubt had far-reaching effects on many other areas of schoolwork.

Like most LD/ADD children, Al failed because he couldn't successfully use the tools that—in our educational system—make all learning possible. All of his unsatisfactory grades were really Fs in reading, writing, spelling, and math. Because he lacked the basic skills, he was locked out of a chance for success in all academic areas. Effort was totally pointless.

Learning disabilities and attention deficit disorder cut across all racial, economic, and cultural lines. Many children have unusual family situations that can be mistaken for the cause of learning failure. The very poor and the very rich, the baby of the family, the spoiled child, the child from a broken home, the youngster who has moved a lot, foster children, adopted children, abused children, runaways, youthful offenders; children whose parents are alcoholic, physically handicapped, chronically sick, mentally ill, hospitalized, institutionalized, in jail—many youngsters live in horrible home situations. Their family problems can make it hard for them to concentrate or take a serious interest in school. But to the unwary teacher, a child's home situation can mask a learning disability or an attention deficit disorder. Worse still, teachers often respond to students with troubled backgrounds by lowering their expectations. Instead of seeing youngsters as doomed to failure, we need to lead them to think of school as a safe haven—the one place where they have an opportunity to experience the delights of total success.

It can be devilishly difficult to recognize LD/ADD youngsters. To be successful, the process of investigation must be a child-centered activity. That's why this book focuses on the child: the child's schoolwork, the child's attitude, the child's behavior, the child's strengths and weaknesses, the child's failures and successes. Always, the emphasis will be on direct observation narrowly focused on a specific child. What is he doing in class? What do his papers look like? What are the things he can't do no matter how hard he tries? Always, the aim will be to explore beneath the surface, to probe with an open, investigative, problem-solving attitude, to find and understand what's really there.

These children *can* be found and helped. Classroom teachers *are* capable of recognizing symptoms of a learning disability and/or an attention deficit disorder, recommending youngsters for testing, understanding the special needs of LD/ADD students, and making the classroom adjustments that enable many of them to succeed.

Beautiful young people like Al do not have to be crushed by the system. The vicious cycle of failure and frustration that damages LD/ADD children needlessly can be stopped by caring, well-informed classroom teachers. No matter what is or is not going on to help these students outside the classroom, every teacher has the opportunity to create an academic atmosphere that will breed success for youngsters who exhibit the behavior patterns commonly seen among those with a learning disability and/or an attention deficit disorder.

For the LD/ADD Child, First Grade Isn't Much Fun

Chapter 3

Let's pretend that Al, the young wino I met on the river in chapter 1, could take us back to relive his experiences in school. In our imagination, we can return to the first grade with him and let him show us what his days were like. In our mind's eye, we will then let Al guide us through one of his days in the fifth grade. Through fiction, we can later witness his classroom struggles as an unrecognized, undiagnosed LD/ADD teenager.

The journey back into the classroom with Al offers an opportunity to witness three vital aspects of the LD/ADD child's failure in school.

1. Al clearly demonstrates almost all of the characteristics that are typical of the LD/ADD youngster. Although it is much more common for such a child to be hyperactive, Al's attention deficit disorder is readily observable in his hypoactivity, a nonvariable slow pace that is particularly difficult to deal with.

2. Al's teachers demonstrate that standard classroom procedures are generally ineffective, if not downright destructive, for LD/ADD pupils.

3. Over the ten-year period of the three observations, Al's attitude toward himself and the world gradually deteriorates. He steadily draws in on himself and becomes removed from any but the most superficial contact with his peers. Until he gets free of the schools and has a chance to watch himself attain a few impressive successes, he suffers under the weight of his acceptance of the system's condemnation of him as lazy and stupid. He feels guilty for giving up. He is ashamed of himself for not being tough enough to stand up to the system and win. Many of those who have suffered such academic failure have *LOSER* tattooed on their knuckles. Al's emotional scars weren't quite that visible but are likely to be just as indelible.

Most of the children were already in their seats when the bell rang to start the day. The teacher took her place behind her desk and waited for Al to finish hanging up his jacket on the coatrack at the back of the room. The boy stooped, peeped into a grocery sack he'd brought with him, folded the top of the bag, and carried it with him toward his seat.

The traditional greeting began the day. "Good morning, class."

"Good morning, Miss Dowell," thirty-four small voices chorused back.

Al was nearly to his seat at the front of the room next to the teacher's desk, so roll call began. After the fifth name, Miss Dowell glanced up from her record book. She was not at all surprised to find that Al had gotten sidetracked on his way to his seat. The youngster was leaning over the cage of hamsters kept by the window.

"Al," the teacher called gently.

The boy was so engrossed in tapping on the glass and talking to the furry creatures that he didn't seem to hear.

In a louder voice, Miss Dowell called, "Al."

Startled, the child looked over his shoulder. "Huh?" he grunted.

"Will you please take your seat? It's time for class to get started."

The youngster started toward his desk, returned for the paper sack he'd left by the hamsters, stuck his face near the cage to whisper a parting word, and moved slowly toward his place.

Convinced that Al would actually reach his destination this time, Miss Dowell went back to taking the roll. She glanced up to see the boy nearing his chair. Encouraged by his progress, she resumed her morning routine.

But the child didn't stop at his seat. Al walked right by it and up to the teacher's desk.

"For lunch today, we have beef stew with—"

"I found this great big lizard down by the creek last night," a little voice said right beside Miss Dowell's shoulder.

The teacher jumped with surprise, then turned to look at the child who had interrupted her. She wanted to pick him up by his scrawny little shoulders and carry him to his seat.

Al was bending over to remove something from his brown bag. "I ain't never seen a lizard as big as this one. And he's a weird color, too—got all red around his head and back there where his tail is broke off. He must of lost that tail piece in a fight, but it'll grow back." Rising with his prize displayed in a jar gently cradled in his hands, the child looked straight at his teacher. "Did you know lizards can grow new tails?" he asked.

He was stunned into silence by the glowering look in Miss Dowell's eyes.

"Al," she snarled in a dangerous low voice. "This is *not* the time for that. Put the lizard away and get into your seat."

The child started to say, "I just wanted—"

But the teacher cut him off. "Get into your seat, Al—*now*!"

The little boy's eyes watered, and he swallowed hard. The whole room was deathly quiet as he carefully put the jar back into the bag, folded the brown paper securely over the top, and slunk to his chair.

His teacher waited in outraged silence, thinking how unfortunate it was that most of Al's days started off this way.

Once the announcements were finished, the morning's writing lesson began. As a warmup exercise, each child printed the alphabet across the top of his paper. Miss Dowell moved around the class checking the work. One by one, the children got their star for the alphabet and began copying the day's penmanship assignment that the teacher had neatly lettered on the board. Al was always the last to finish the alphabet. In fact, the teacher usually had to stand at his side and help him if there was to be any hope that he'd complete it at all. It was part of the daily routine.

Miss Dowell took her customary position next to the struggling youngster. "Al, you're doing well today. You're already up to *o*, and you haven't got any letters in the wrong place."

The child was concentrating so hard that he didn't even look up. His brows were furrowed and his lips were set in a thin, straight, determined line. He clutched the thick first-grader's pencil in a vicelike grip.

"Want me to help you?" the teacher asked softly.

The tousled head nodded.

"Are you stuck?"

"Yeah. I can't figure out what comes next."

"Well, before we start, how about holding the pencil the way I showed you?"

The boy's dirty fingers strained to find the correct position.

Taking the child's right hand, the teacher gently moved his thumb so that it no longer curled over the top of the lower knuckles. "The way you hold it, it's a wonder you can write at all," she chuckled. She knew Al hated to hold the pencil properly. He'd often told her it didn't feel right. Today, he didn't complain.

A glance around the room assured Miss Dowell that the rest of the class was hard at work, so she pointed to the *o* on Al's paper and whispered, "Now, let's have a look. You need to figure out what comes after *o*. Let's try the little song. That usually helps." Singing the ABCs in a low voice next to her student's ear, she got him started again.

Al's eyes lit up. "*P*!" he shouted with delight, in a voice way too loud.

There were a few snickers from the other students. Miss Dowell stood up tall, surveyed the room sternly, and warned, "Class, you have work to do. And it doesn't require *any* noise." The quiet resumed.

Returning her attention to Al, the teacher found three letters had been added to his alphabet: *p*, *q*, and *u*. "Oh, Al, you're not stuck anymore. That's good."

The boy grinned.

"But one of those letters doesn't belong there. Let's do the little song again and you can figure out which one."

They tried the song twice. It didn't help.

Children were starting to move about the room as they finished their handwriting and looked for other activities. Miss Dowell glanced at the clock. It was time to start reading.

Anxious that Al at least finish his alphabet, she told him, "The *u* doesn't go there. It's *p, q, r, s, t, u*." She helped Al struggle through *v* while trying to keep an eye on the increasingly restless class.

By this time, Al was feeling a great deal of pressure to finish. Quickly, he slapped down the *w, x, y, z*, then looked up with relief.

Miss Dowell scanned his messy paper, then took out her red pencil. As she began marking the errors, she explained, "You make the corrections on these letters, and we'll let the rest of the assignment wait until recess."

The child sighed and slumped in his chair. He hated it when he missed recess because he hadn't finished his work.

"Al, you're not listening."

The little boy looked up at his teacher. She'd been telling him something, but he hadn't heard. His mind had drifted off to thoughts of recess. And Miss Dowell knew it.

"Al, I'm trying to help you," she said in an impatient voice. "If you would just pay attention."

The boy returned his gaze to the paper in front of him. It now had bright red circles around four of the letters.

"You need to make these corrections, Al. Your *d*—it's backwards. See?" The red pencil pointed. "Your circle is on the wrong side. It looks like a *b*. Look over here next to your *a*. This is your *b*. Which side is the circle on?"

The youngster thought a minute, then ventured, "The left?"

"Write a *b* for me here at the bottom," Miss Dowell instructed.

Al drew the vertical line, paused, glanced at the letter next to *a* in his alphabet above, then put the circle in its proper place.

"Now, which side did you put the circle on in order to make that lovely *b*?" the teacher asked.

"The right?"

"Yes, the right." The teacher looked at her pupil. "Show me your right hand."

The child looked at his hands, then held out the correct one.

"Yes." Miss Dowell nodded with approval. "Your right hand is the one you write with, isn't it?"

Al nodded in agreement.

The teacher's desire to finish with Al and get the reading lesson started put a quick, no-nonsense clip in her voice. She was straining to maintain her patience as she tried to divide her attention between this one struggling child and her increasingly restless class.

The teacher continued, "To make a *d*, you put the ball on which side of the stick?"

Al glanced at his hands, then replied, "The right."

"No, that would be a *b*." In frustration, the teacher checked her watch. "Look, Al, I'll write out the first four letters of the alphabet for you and you copy them exactly, okay?"

As soon as the four letters were there before him, the child nodded, reached for his pencil, and tried to do as requested. But Miss Dowell's hand was still on his paper.

"Not yet, Al," she said crossly. "Wait until after I tell you about *all* the corrections."

He withdrew his hand.

The teacher hurriedly continued, "The *m* needs another hump. The way it is, you have an *n*. The *j* is backwards. It needs to face the other way. And down here at the end, the *w* is upside down." Miss Dowell stood up, adding, "Now, you work real fast, and make those letters right. It's time for reading."

As the teacher moved away, Al followed her with his eyes. Students clustered around her to turn in their papers. He wondered if they ever noticed how pretty Miss Dowell was when she smiled, and especially how pretty she was when she wore her hair all bunched up in the back like today.

The sound of footsteps at his side didn't register fast enough to spare Al a surprise thump on his head, delivered with an accompanying snicker. "Hey, dummy. Ain't you done yet?"

Al took a quick swing at Bobby, the boy who had stopped by to taunt him.

"What's so hard that's taking you so long?" the tormentor asked, then grabbed the paper from Al's desk to have a look. "You ain't even got started on the stuff to copy off the board." The child stabbed a finger at the incomplete paper in accusation. "All you got here is the alphabet—and it ain't even right!"

As the color rose in Al's face, another boy joined the fun. "You mean he took all that long just to write that little dab?" Tom asked with a laugh. "Golly, I didn't know *anybody* was that stupid."

Jumping from his seat, Al grabbed for his paper.

"What's going on over there?" Miss Dowell challenged.

The paper was quickly placed back on Al's desk. The three boys faced each other in hostile silence.

The teacher surveyed the scene. "Bobby and Tom, get back to your seats and get ready for reading. You've got no business over there." Miss Dowell motioned for the two to move along. "Al, have you finished your handwriting?"

"No," he mumbled.

"Young man," the teacher said in that special warning voice, "you've got one minute to finish your corrections and get your paper turned in."

Since he'd forgotten what Miss Dowell had told him to do with the letters circled in red, he copied them down below—more neatly, but facing in the same direction—and handed in his paper.

"The Eagles, the Robins, and the Cardinals, get out your pencils and your reading workbooks," the teacher instructed from the front of the room. "And the Bluebirds, bring your books and come up into the reading circle." Al was a Bluebird. Everybody knew it would have been more appropriate to call them the Buzzards. They were the low group.

As Al bent over to get his book out of his desk, his attention was caught by the grocery bag on the floor next to his chair. He pulled back the paper and peeped inside just to be sure the lizard was all right. Thinking maybe the animal wasn't getting enough air, he removed the lid of the jar and fanned his hand across the top several times. The lizard scurried to make an escape, but Al clapped the top back on and twisted it down tight. He was glad to know his little friend was fine.

"Al." Miss Dowell's voice sounded threatening. "You're supposed to be getting out your reading book, not playing with your lizard."

He eased the jar back into the bag.

"We're all up here waiting for you, Al." The teacher lapsed into a meaningful pause, hoping to hurry him along.

Reading class started. Al shuffled up to join the Bluebirds. They were not very good readers. The rest of the class had already finished three or four reading books. The other children were into nice, thick books with interesting stories and hard words. The Bluebirds were still trying to get through the baby books with the big print and big pictures.

The half-hour in the reading circle with the Bluebirds was one of the most trying periods of Miss Dowell's day. The students in the group found reading difficult. They constantly lost their place and stumbled over easy words. Most of them had an unusually short attention span. This meant the teacher always had to contend with a lot of wiggling and looking out the window. In all these things, Al was just like the other Bluebirds. He found it difficult to sit still and pay attention. He hated reading. And his oral reading sounded absolutely awful.

Many of the youngsters in the group had trouble understanding the simple stories. When asked the comprehension questions, they couldn't remember the details and often weren't able to explain the main ideas either. However, Al had no such difficulties with comprehension. Once he knew what a passage said, he always understood what it meant.

The reading circle was torture for Al. It was his least favorite part of the school day. He dreaded sitting there knowing his turn was coming. It was hard to pay attention when he knew that in just a few minutes he was going to have to go through the agony of trying to read out loud. All too quickly, his turn came.

"Al," Miss Dowell asked, "do you know where we are?"

He shook his head.

"Carol, will you show Al the place, please?"

The boy tried to cooperate as the little girl next to him fumbled to turn several pages of his book and point out where he should start.

Al pressed his finger hard against the page to keep the place, then began.

Al: "Mother was—"

Teacher: Not *was*, Al. *Saw*.

Al: "Mother saw . . . Bill . . . on top of the . . . house. He—"

Teacher: Not *he*, Al. The word starts with *s h*, as in *shhh*.

Al: "She saw—"

Teacher: *Was.*

Al: "She was not . . ."

The child paused, then looked up at the teacher.

Teacher: You know that word. Joe, tell us what that word is.

Joe: *Happy*.

Teacher: Right, *happy*.

Al: ". . . happy to see . . . him up . . . here—"

Teacher: Not *here*, Al. *There*.

Al: ". . . there. 'Come down, Bill,' Mother called."

Teacher: *Called Mother*.

Al: ". . . called Mother. 'Come down off—'"

Teacher: *From*.

Al: "'Come down from there this minute—'"

Teacher: No, Al. It doesn't say *this minute*. Take another look. What are those last two words?

The reading circle finally ended. Miss Dowell gave her low group three worksheets, carefully explained the directions for each, sent the Bluebirds back to their seats, and called for the Robins to come up to the front.

Al made a circuit of the room on his way back to his desk. He stopped for a drink at the fountain, paused in front of the Indian mural to admire the part he was working on, sharpened his pencil, noticed the sharpener was nearly full of shavings, and started to empty it.

Miss Dowell called from her seat in the reading circle with the Robins, "Al, that doesn't need to be done now."

"But it's full," the child protested as he wrestled the little basket away from the cutting rotors.

"This is not the time for that," Miss Dowell repeated in a firm tone that made it clear she meant business.

Al carefully put the pencil sharpener back together and wandered toward his desk. Since the teacher's eyes followed him every step of the way, he went there slowly but directly.

A few other members of the Bluebirds were still just getting started. Most of the students were already hunched over their desks busily working. During the remaining hour of reading, Al stayed quietly in his seat. Ten minutes were devoted to getting out his crayons and ruler. Five minutes went to playing with a large rubber band he discovered in his desk. For ten minutes, he attempted to do the work assigned. For the first worksheet, he'd forgotten the directions, so he quickly and easily finished it but did it all wrong. The second page was a familiar type, but he kept getting stuck on the hard words. He knew better than to interrupt Miss Dowell while she was reading with another group. He figured out the words as best he could. Getting more and more frustrated, he began guessing at answers. By the end of the page, he was circling words he didn't know to answer questions he hadn't even tried to read. Before starting the third worksheet, Al colored the pictures on all three, took a peek at the lizard to be sure it was doing all right, drew several pictures of the lizard and the creek that was its home, watched a fly buzzing against the glass at the very top of the window, drew a picture of the lizard enjoying the fly for a meal, colored the large rubber band, used the now-striped rubber band to draw circles and ovals, tried doing some block printing by stamping the crayon-colored rubber band against his paper and pressing down hard. Before he knew it, reading class was over and it was time for recess.

Unfortunately, Al had to miss part of recess so he could finish his handwriting. The reading worksheets he had failed to finish would probably deprive him of *all* his recess tomorrow.

The children gathered their sweaters and jackets. The captains for the week got the kickball out of the closet. Chattering and laughing, the class lined up at the door, waited for the teacher's signal, and filed out to the playground.

Al was standing at the window trying to catch the fly when Miss Dowell came over to him with the penmanship paper. "I don't like you to miss your play period," she began. "You need a break like everybody else."

The boy left the window and returned to his seat. "I want to catch that fly and feed him to my lizard," he explained.

"That would be a good idea. I'll bet Granddaddy Lizard would like that. Maybe after we have our lunch, we could take a minute to catch him some lunch, too."

Al's eyes sparkled enthusiastically. "We could put the fly in the jar while it's still alive and watch to see how the lizard catches it. I'll bet he's got a long, sticky tongue like a frog and he'll shoot that tongue out—" The child's hands and mouth were acting out the process with dramatic flair.

"Hold it. Hold it." Miss Dowell stopped the excited youngster in mid-demonstration. "Let's get the handwriting done now. We'll see about the lizard's lunch later."

With one last longing glance at the fly, Al dutifully picked up his pencil.

"Since I think it's important for you to get at least part of your recess, I'm going to have you write just the first sentence of the story that's on the board." Miss Dowell patted the child's head to encourage him. She really could not afford to stay in with this one student while the rest of her class was outside playing. After all, it was her responsibility to supervise all her rambunctious pupils as they ran off their excess energy at recess. Hoping this one exceedingly slow worker would hurry up and get finished, she added, "You concentrate on doing a good job with just that one sentence. When you're done and I've corrected it, you and I are both going to go outside."

It took ten agonizing minutes and a lot of erasing, but Al put his heart and soul into that one sentence. His paper wasn't exactly neat, but for him it looked good. With a proud smile, he took his work up to his teacher for approval.

Miss Dowell looked at the words her student had copied from the board. Instead of reaching for her box of stars, she picked up her red pencil.

Al's heart sank.

"Al, I can understand that you have trouble writing your letters when you have nothing to go by. But I do not understand why you make so many mistakes when all you have to do is copy something off the board." The teacher's disappointment was easily seen in the way she frowned and shook her head. "First of all, you left out a whole word. Look at the third word on the board. It says *kite.* Look at your third word."

Al gulped. Sure enough. He didn't know what his third word said, but he knew it wasn't *kite* like it was supposed to be.

The teacher put a red *X* where the missing word should have been. Then she pointed to the fifth word and asked, "What's this word supposed to say?"

The boy studied what he had written. "*It*," he replied.

"How do you spell *it*?" Miss Dowell asked. Then she added, "You should be able to spell *it* without even looking at the board."

Nevertheless, Al checked to see the correct spelling on the blackboard. "Oh," he said, "I got the letters mixed up."

"Yes, you did. It's supposed to be *i t*, not *t i*." The red pencil put a big, ugly circle around the word that had been written backwards. "There are two other tiny mistakes." Miss Dowell paused to let the child attempt to figure out what they were. When he didn't respond, she said, "This *i* needs a dot." The red pencil supplied the small mark. "And this *t* is missing something."

Al reached over to his paper and crossed the *t* himself.

Finally, recess had arrived.

Al burst from the door and dashed across the playground to join his classmates. To get into the kickball game, which was already in progress, he took a position in the outfield. Enthusiastically, he danced around hoping to get some action.

When the captain noticed Al, he shouted, "You're not on *my* team! Go on in with the other side."

The opposing team's captain hollered back, "I didn't pick Al! He ain't on *my* team."

Al meandered up to the pitcher's mound to ask the captain, "Can I pitch?"

"You ain't even on my team, stupid," came the snarled reply.

The third baseman shouted, "Had to stay inside because he can't even write his alphabet! Get out of the way, baby. You're holding up the game."

Al started walking toward home plate.

Betsy, who was captain of the team at bat, confronted him with her hands on her hips. "I told you, you ain't on my team, retard. Go drop all the fly balls for those guys."

Miss Dowell arrived just in time to settle the issue. She forced Betsy to accept Al on her team, then hovered behind the backstop to observe. Al was at the end of the line. With luck, he'd get one chance to kick before recess ended.

Fate gave the team's new addition a turn at bat. With two outs and two men on, Al stepped up to the plate.

"Oh, boy," groaned the captain. "Here comes our last out."

Nervously, Al waited. As the ball bounced along the ground toward him, he ran up and gave it a walloping kick with his left foot. The ball sailed out of bounds by third base. On the second pitch, he tried again. This time, he missed the ball entirely and, worst of all, his shoe flew off and sailed into the middle of the infield. Blushing crimson, Al hopped out to retrieve it and returned to his position behind the plate as his teammates jeered, "Can't you do anything right?"

The next pitch dribbled toward him. Somehow, Al's left foot managed to catch the ball way underneath and squarely in the middle. It was a high infield fly. Four different children moved into position for the catch. Each one called, "I got it! I got it!" It looked like an easy out.

Al's legs churned up a cloud of dust as he raced toward first base. To his delight, the ball plopped to the ground amid the four scrambling infielders. He was safe.

The next child at bat made the third out, and recess was over.

Al bounded inside to get a drink, then had to start on the long hour of math that separated him from lunch. Arithmetic presented all the difficulties of reading and writing put together. The child had trouble getting organized, paying attention, and following directions. He read some numbers backwards and often wrote them facing the wrong way. Although he understood what math was all about, he couldn't deal with it effectively when it had to be put on paper. As usual, the class was over before Al's messy, error-filled paper was finished.

Lunch was a cinch as long as Al was careful to avoid Bobby and Tom and some of their friends. Then came the afternoon. That was the good part of the day.

Story hour was a great time for Al. While the teacher read aloud to the class, the children were free to move about the room doing anything they liked, as long as they were quiet. Al was good at that. He loved to build with Legos, watch the hamsters, draw, look at the pictures in books, play with the collection of toys he kept in his desk. He could wander all over doing whatever he liked and still never miss a word of the story.

After the story, it was time for show and tell. Al expected this to be the best part of the day, next to getting safely to first base. Miss Dowell let the children come up and sit on the floor in a circle. When it was Al's turn, the jar with Granddaddy Lizard was passed carefully from hand to hand. The lizard's proud owner told all about how he'd caught the wonderful creature. The children asked questions, and Al demonstrated an amazingly comprehensive knowledge of the habits of his captured prize.

"Will he bite?" one of the girls wanted to know.

"No, he ain't got no teeth," Al replied. "They're fast and try to run away, but they won't bite."

"Well, if he ain't got teeth, how does he eat?"

"He just grabs a bug whole and swallows it down." Al demonstrated with his hands. "To see them little bitty bugs, I think a lizard must have pretty good eyes," he added.

The last hour of the day was social studies. The children were studying about Indians. Miss Dowell had read them stories and taken them to a local museum. Today, she showed a filmstrip and then let the children work on the mural that covered the whole length of the wall at the back of the room. Al loved it. He knew a lot about Indians. One of his uncles had taken him into the fields and taught him how to find arrowheads. He had quite an impressive collection. He'd been eagerly awaiting his chance to work on the huge panorama the class was creating.

Before the children cleaned up and put their paints away, the teacher had each one stand by what he or she had done that day and explain it to the class. Some had painted a tepee, a horse, or a warrior. Most had worked on sky, grass, trees, and other background. Al had done a bush. He proudly showed the bright green leafy mass to his classmates. "I even put in some of the branches and twigs," he explained. "And a bird's next," he added, pointing to a grayish circle off to one side.

"What are those two red things sticking out of the top?" Miss Dowell asked.

"Them's feathers." Al grinned playfully. "There's a Indian hiding behind my bush. He don't know it, but his feathers are sticking out, so *I* know he's there."

"That's stupid," Tommy chortled.

Miss Dowell ignored the unkind remark and beamed. "What a clever idea."

Anita flounced her curls with a huff. "I think it looks silly."

"Two ugly red blobs sticking out of a bush," another girl added. "That's dumb. Those don't look like feathers."

The teacher stepped quickly to Al's side. "That's enough of that," she snapped at the two girls. "Nobody criticized *your* work like that."

"But we didn't do anything that looks that stupid," Anita protested.

"He's ruined our mural," chorused several of the children.

"Al hasn't ruined anything. And there won't be another word about it," the teacher concluded in a very firm warning voice.

Half the class worked on cleaning brushes, picking up the newspapers spread on the floor, and other jobs related to the messy painting project. The rest of the children were involved with routine end-of-the-day chores.

It was Al's week to wash the blackboards. He was a cooperative but unreliable worker. It took him a long time to get the sponge and water because he spent a few minutes playing with the faucet. Then he stopped to admire the mural on his way by. And once he did get started, he worked very slowly. The bell rang before Al finished, despite repeated warnings that he needed to hurry. "You can go, Al," the teacher offered.

"I'm almost done," the child explained, without speeding up his slow pace.

Miss Dowell went to the door to see the other children off. They said their good-byes, broke into small groups, and left.

By the time Al finished, his classmates were long gone. But he always walked home alone anyway. At least he had his lizard to keep him company this day—and it had been an especially good day, too.

As a six-year-old, Al was eager to learn. His amazing powers of observation and his inquisitive nature made him interested in everything. He was hungry for information and had a wonderful memory for overall concepts as well as minute details about a huge assortment of plants, animals, and machines. The fact that he just couldn't seem to get the hang of reading, writing, and math didn't appear to bother him. With his exploratory approach to life, he had a real flair for figuring things out for himself. He felt that, with time, he'd catch on to this school stuff, too. His super-slow, nonvariable pace looked more like a personality trait than the hypoactivity sometimes associated with ADD. His undeveloped social skills made him so quick to forgive that he remained optimistic and trusting of his peers despite their repeated rejection and ridicule. Although constantly criticized for his behavior, Al was innocently oblivious of the ways in which his actions irritated others.

Fifth Grade and Still Failing

CHAPTER 4

"AL, YOU'RE TEN MINUTES LATE." Mrs. Carswell looked up over her bifocals as the student casually approached her desk.

"I had to stop at the office," the boy replied, fishing around in the hip pocket of his jeans. "I got an excuse."

"Speaking of excuses, do you have the note you promised me? Remember? You were absent Monday and Tuesday. You were supposed to get your mother to write an excuse."

"My mom didn't get off work until late last night," Al answered, rummaging through the other back pocket.

Mrs. Carswell set her spelling book aside. "Al, you and I need to have a talk," she said, motioning for the boy to follow her to the hall. As she led the youngster toward the door, Mrs. Carswell announced to the class, "The spelling test will begin at ten minutes to nine. Please get your papers ready." Al followed his teacher out of the room. She closed the door behind them.

Mrs. Carswell set a hand on her pupil's shoulder and tried to look into his face. "Al, it's the middle of April and you have F's in almost every subject. If things don't improve, you're going to have to repeat the fifth grade." She sought the boy's eyes, but he was staring at the floor. The youth had been held back once. He was already a misfit—bigger and older than his classmates. "Al, I don't *want* you to fail." The teacher's tone was almost pleading.

Al shifted his weight, then stuffed his hands in his back pockets so they no longer dangled limply. He made no remark.

Mrs. Carswell opened her record book and held it down where her student could see it. He stared at the page with unfocused eyes.

"You have missed . . ." The teacher paused, counting under her breath. "You've missed eighteen days of school this semester. Of course, two whole weeks of that were the ear infection you had in February. But you've gotten so far behind in your work."

Al said nothing.

The teacher flipped the pages in her book. "In language arts, we've had four book reports." She pointed to the four zeros representing Al's grades. "You were absent for the first one and never got around to making it up. For the second one, you picked a book that was too hard and didn't finish it. On the third one, I helped you select a book; you got halfway through and decided you didn't like it."

"I lost the book," the boy muttered.

"Yes. Then you lost the book. The fourth report was due Monday. But you were absent Monday." Assuming a no-nonsense attitude, the teacher sternly asked, "Have you read a book for this report?"

"I ain't done with it yet," the youth muttered.

"What book are you reading?"

"It's one I got at home."

"You know I'm supposed to approve the books that are used for the reports."

"This is a good book. It's all about a pioneer family living out on the prairie." Al gave a brief summary of the plot. As he warmed to his subject, he began describing an especially exciting scene.

"There's one part where the Indians are about to attack the cabin. The father knows he can't stand them off by himself. So he leaves his wife and the children locked inside the house, and he slips off out the back and sneaks up into the woods behind the Indians. They're all up there sitting around a campfire waiting for the moon to come up before they attack."

Swept along by her student's enthusiasm, the teacher's eyes lit up with recognition. "Oh, I know that story. That's a very famous Western." Mrs. Carswell pondered, then added, "Al, that's an adult Western. It'll take you forever to wade through that great big thick book."

"But it's a good story."

"I think you're making a mistake to try to read such a difficult book, Al. That's way too hard for you."

"I'm doing okay," he reassured her.

Mrs. Carswell was delighted that Al had finally found a book that interested him. Smiling, she offered encouragement. "Well, if you can read it, more power to you. Did you know they made a movie out of it?"

"Yeah."

"In fact, it was on TV not long ago."

"Yeah, I seen it. That's how come I got interested in the book."

"Al," Mrs. Carswell sighed. "You already know the story. If you saw the whole thing on television, there's no point in reading the book."

"But it's a interesting story. I like the part where the chief's two sons have the contest to see who gets to keep the pony."

"Have you gotten to that part in the book?"

"No, not yet."

It was time to start the spelling test. The teacher decided to settle two issues immediately and drop the others until later. "On Monday, you are to bring two things to school with you. One, I want to *see* this book you say you're reading." For emphasis, she tapped the first line of the note she was writing to the boy's mother. "Monday, you bring the book." She paused for Al to nod that he understood, then moved on to her second point.

"With the two days you were out this week, you now have five days of unexcused absences. I've written the dates down here." Again, she tapped the note for emphasis. "You give this message to your mother. And when you walk in that door Monday morning, you'd better have that book in one hand and a note to excuse your absences in the other—*or else*!"

Al stared at the bright red letters of the message to his mother. Slowly, he took the paper, folded it, and stuffed it into his pocket.

The noises made by thirty-two restless students drifted into the corridor. It was past nine o'clock. Mrs. Carswell could not ignore her class any longer.

Opening the door, she announced in a loud, threatening voice, "The spelling test will begin in thirty seconds." She paused, returning her attention to the boy still standing beside her in the hall. "Al, for Monday," she insisted gently. "The absence excuses and the book. Okay?"

Al's only response was a small nod. Head lowered, eyes on the floor, he slipped quietly by her and moved toward his seat in the back row.

The teacher knew there was only a slim chance she would ever see either the book or the note. In fact, it was possible that the issue might never come up again. Al had a habit of being absent on Mondays.

As Al got to his seat, Charles, the boy in the desk next to his, teased, "Hey, Al, you in trouble with the teacher again, boy?"

Al grinned, then climbed into his seat by throwing a leg over the back as though mounting a horse. "I'm *always* in trouble with the teacher," he chuckled. He lightly punched the heavyset boy seated diagonally in front of him. "Right, Larry?"

"That sure is right, Al." Larry nodded as he pivoted in his chair to look directly at his pal. Grinning and bobbing his head in agreement, he stated, "You're in trouble just about more than anybody else in the class."

A whoop of laughter burst from the youth in the desk directly behind Larry. "You said that right," Todd chortled. He gave Al a cuff on the shoulder, then teased in a falsetto voice that was a good imitation of the teacher, "Always in trouble—you just never do behave."

Al shrugged his shoulders. "What do you expect from us guys here in the back?" Charles and Todd snickered under their breath. Larry snorted.

"The boys in the back—ain't no way we can keep out of trouble." Charles snapped his fingers and rolled his black body to an imaginary beat. "The boys in the back—we back here because we *bad*." He rolled the last word on his breath. To cover their laughter, Al, Todd, and Larry bent over and pretended to be getting out some books.

At that moment, the teacher called, "Al, would you come up here for a minute, please?"

Todd's eyebrows shot up in feigned alarm. "Uh-oh. You're in trouble now."

Al slowly got out of his chair.

Charles prodded him in the behind. "Now you gonna get it, boy. Get on up there and take your licks."

Al bent over as though to pick up something he'd dropped. While out of the teacher's line of vision, he quickly untied Todd's sneaker, shoved a wad of paper under Charles's shirt, and smiled in triumph. With Mrs. Carswell watching, there was no way his friends could get even.

From the front of the room came a repeat of the teacher's request. "Alvin, I need to see you *now*."

Impatiently, the teacher waited.

One of the students near the front complained in a loud voice, "Aw, come on, Al. We want to get started."

It was 9:14. Thirty-two children had just spent nearly thirty minutes waiting for their spelling test. That one disgusted voice expressed the way most of the class felt toward Al.

Rather than scold about wise remarks, the teacher carefully enunciated the first spelling word and gave a sentence to go with it. The room fell silent immediately. She pronounced the second word, then the third. By then, Al was standing awkwardly at her side. As she continued with the spelling list, her conversation with

Al was squeezed into the pauses between words. "You got here so late this morning that I'd already sent down the lunch count and attendance," Mrs. Carswell explained. She said a spelling word for the class, told Al the two selections on the lunch menu, gave the class another word, wrote down Al's decision, pronounced a spelling word, filled out an adjusted attendance slip. When Mrs. Carswell removed a hall pass from her drawer, Al reached his hand for the messages he assumed he would be taking to the office.

The teacher scanned the room, then fastened her gaze on a bubbly little blue-eyed blond in the front row. "Sally," she requested sweetly, "would you come up here for a minute, dear?"

While Sally set her pencil aside and turned her letter-perfect paper face down on her desk, Mrs. Carswell explained tartly to Al, "It's too bad I can't trust you to go on errands. Every time I let you out of the room, you're gone for at least half an hour. You've wasted enough of our time this morning already." With a firm nod, she sent Al to his seat and Sally to the office.

At 9:20, on spelling word number eleven, Al's school day finally began.

Throughout the rest of the test, Al struggled to get out of the mess he was in. "Hey, Charles," he whispered. "Call out them first ten words for me." His friend tried, but it didn't work out very well. Even with his paper right in front of him, Charles didn't know for sure what most of the words were supposed to say.

Al tried the same approach on Barb, the girl sitting in front of him. Mumbling behind her hand, she tried to help him. That didn't work either. The teacher overheard them and issued a loud order. "I don't want to hear any whispering back there. Al, you leave Barb alone."

At the end of the test, Mrs. Carswell instructed the students to pass their papers forward.

Al left his seat and started toward the front. He had to find out what to do about those words he'd missed.

The boy had gotten only a few feet from his desk when the teacher stopped him cold in his tracks. "Alvin, there is no need for you to be up walking around. *Pass* your paper in like everybody else."

"But I need to ask you a question," Al protested. He paused, then proceeded toward his teacher.

"Go back to your seat, Al," Mrs. Carswell ordered. "If you have a question, raise your hand and ask it from there. That is the accepted procedure."

Cheeks flushed, fists clenched, Al returned to his chair. An uncomfortable silence fell over the room. Even Todd and Charles found no humor in the situation and made no comment.

Angrily, Al folded his spelling test and shoved it into his desk.

From the front of the room, the teacher commanded, "Get that paper out of your desk, Alvin, and pass it up to the front."

"It ain't finished," the infuriated youth snorted.

Mrs. Carswell stalked over to Al's desk and glared down at him. "You're the one who's just about finished, young man."

The boy's cheek muscles twitched over his clenched jaw and stiffly set lips. A thin film of tears washed over the anger and hatred in his eyes.

The teacher fought to keep control. She had seen Al explode before. At all costs, she wanted to avoid a really ugly scene. Forcing calmness into her voice, she requested with icy quiet, "May I *see* your paper?"

Halfheartedly, Al rummaged among his books. When he found the spelling test, he unfolded it, pressed it out flat, printed his name at the top, then shoved it at his teacher.

"I see that numbers one through ten are missing," Mrs. Carswell observed without emotion. "Is that what you wanted to talk to me about?"

"Yeah," the boy replied sharply. "I wanted you to call them out so I could finish."

The teacher wanted to sneer, "Why would I waste my time?" Instead, she explained in cool, smooth tones, "Because of you, the class was over twenty minutes late getting started. I don't think it would be fair to make thirty-two others wait for you *again*." She was tempted to add, "Besides, you haven't passed a single spelling test this year. Why pretend you might spell even one of those words right?" But from the way the youngster slouched in his seat, she saw it wasn't necessary. For the sake of fairness, she concluded, "I'll dictate the rest of the list for you at our ten-thirty break." Briskly, she placed Al's paper on the top of the stack, snapped a paper clip on to hold it in place, and strode back to the front of the room. "Get out your materials for reading," she instructed the class. "I'll work with Group 2 first today."

Al, Charles, Larry, Barb, and three others comprised Group 4, the low group. Theirs was a big, thick third-grade reading book—everybody knew it was a third-grade book from the pattern of dots on the back cover. For most of Group 4, even this easy book was too difficult.

Mrs. Carswell moved methodically from one reading group to another, handing out worksheets, making assignments, and explaining directions. Once all the children knew what they were supposed to be doing, she sat down to work with Group 2.

As usual, Al had trouble getting down to business. His pencil point was worn down, but he didn't want to risk a trip to the sharpener, so he spent several minutes gnawing the wood with his front teeth.

Disturbed by the sounds coming from his neighbor, Charles poked him in the ribs with an elbow. "Hey, boy, knock it off with all that noise. You sound like a rat."

Al curled his lips back to bare his front teeth and made smacking sounds with his tongue. "Nah, I ain't a rat. You don't know nothing. I'm gnawing on wood—see?" He smacked again on the pencil for effect. "I'm a beaver."

From his seat on Al's left, Todd interjected, "You sound more like Bugs Bunny."

Pretending the pencil was a carrot, Al shifted his voice to a high squeak. "Annhh, what's up, Doc?"

At this, Barb turned around in her seat to make a loud shushing noise.

Without even looking around, Mrs. Carswell called, "Al, Charles, Todd. Get to work!"

In imitation of Porky Pig, Charles stammered, "Th-th-that's all, folks!"

The three boys giggled for a minute, then turned to their work.

During the half-hour that Group 4 worked independently, the teacher had to speak to Al four times: once for making noise, once for getting out of his seat, again for making noise by punching holes in his paper with the pointed end of a compass, then for getting huffy when she took his compass away, at which time he slammed his book shut and refused to go back to work.

Promptly at ten o'clock, the students in Group 2 returned to their seats, and Mrs. Carswell called Group 4 up to the big table. The students were scheduled to work with the teacher for fifteen minutes.

"Be sure you have all four worksheets, your book, your pencil, and a checking pencil," the teacher warned the students who were gathering at the table around her. Al flopped into a seat.

"You have only two pages there, Al," Mrs. Carswell observed.

"I ain't done with the others," the boy replied, slouching further in his chair.

"Please go get the other two sheets," the teacher requested politely. "We're going to check all four of them. I want you at least to be able to follow along."

The youth made no move toward obeying. Instead, he shrugged casually and said, "I got nothing to correct."

In a voice that she forced to sound sweetly calm, the teacher replied, "I understand that. But I would like you to have your papers here with you so you can participate in the discussion."

As though the argument were too silly for serious consideration, Al sauntered over to his desk to get the two worksheets he'd never even touched.

Of the allotted fifteen minutes, five were gone before Mrs. Carswell managed to get Group 4 started.

As the students went around the circle reading the first page of comprehension questions, Al gave correct answers both times it was his turn. However, his responses in no way reflected what was written on his paper. He usually came up with good answers through the understanding he developed in the oral discussion, then insisted that his illegible scrawl was indeed the recorded version of what he had just voiced.

When the teacher got to the ninth question, it stumped everybody. Mrs. Carswell reread it: "Why did the horse run back into the fire after Bob had led it to safety?"

The children stared at their papers in silence. Nobody wanted to be the one called on. Carl got chosen first. "I got that he ran back in to try to get his friends out." Carl looked up and shook his head. "But you said that was wrong."

"Larry, what do you think?"

Words rolling slowly from his lips, Larry replied, "That was a real smart horse. I think he went back in to put out the fire. He could have stomped it out."

"Oh, the fire was too big for that," Mrs. Carswell explained gently. "The picture shows flames coming up clear through the roof."

The teacher searched the faces of her seven poor readers, then said, "Surely, some of you know about horses and animals."

Most of the children shook their heads. Carl, Larry, and Al just sat there.

"Al, what do you think?"

"He panicked," Al muttered.

"Who panicked?" Mrs. Carswell asked.

"The horse," Al said flatly.

With lively new interest, the teacher requested, "Could you explain what you mean?"

Al spoke as though he were bored by having to tell the group something everybody already knew. "Frightened animals don't always act logical. They get so scared they act crazy."

This piece of information supplied the spark needed to make the other students understand.

Racing against the clock, Mrs. Carswell got Group 4 through the rest of the first sheet and began entering the children's scores in her grade book. Out of fifteen questions, most of the students got ten or eleven right. When she called Al's name, he said, "Fourteen."

"Fourteen?" The teacher's eyebrows shot up in surprise. "You missed only one, Al?" Her amazement quickly turned to suspicion. "You'd better count that up again."

The boy nodded, stabbed a finger at each check mark as he added them aloud, then said, "Yup, I got fourteen."

"Let *me* have a look." The teacher took Al's paper and ran her eyes over it quickly. The youngster had filled all the blanks with single words and short phrases instead of the sentences the directions required. His handwriting was such a jumble that it was impossible to tell what any of the words said. "You don't get fourteen, young man. You get a zero. You didn't even follow the directions." She set the paper down with a disgusted snap.

"Them answers is all right," Al protested heatedly, then added, "Well, all but one. . . ." He paused to await a reconsideration of the verdict.

"Everybody else followed the directions and wrote sentences. It wouldn't be fair to them if I let you get away with one-word answers."

"That ain't fair," Al argued. "I got more right than anybody."

Returning her attention to the grade book, Mrs. Carswell asked, "How many did you get right, Barb?"

Al looked across the table at Charles. "I got more right than anybody else! Don't that count for nothing?"

Silently, Charles shrugged his shoulders.

The teacher wanted to stop Al's whining complaints with a starchy comment like "They spent *their* time working. You spent *yours* playing. And besides, you cheated. That mess you've got there doesn't even come close to saying all those great answers you claim." She wanted to shout right in his face, "You deserve exactly what you got!" But she refrained.

After Mrs. Carswell recorded all the scores for the first page, she gave Group 4 its new assignment. To Al, she added, "If you make those answers into sentences, I'll be happy to take the zero out of the grade book and put a fourteen in its place." Without responding, Al turned away and walked to his desk.

Al had the small, spring-powered motor from a windup toy in

his pocket. Careful that its whirring noise didn't attract the teacher's attention, he spent the remaining twenty minutes of reading class playing with it.

Morning break finally arrived. "Rows one and two may go to the lavatory and get a drink," Mrs. Carswell announced. "Al, bring your pencil and come up here."

Al took a seat beside the teacher's desk. She called out the words for him as she graded the rest of the spelling papers and supervised the class's free time. When Al's messy paper was complete, she took it from him and said, "While you're right here to watch, I'll go ahead and mark your test."

Al sank back into the chair and pretended not to care.

The red pencil flashed down the column of words. The boy couldn't do the arithmetic involved in figuring up his score, but he could see that he'd failed again.

Instead of letting the youth take his break, Mrs. Carswell leaned toward Al, explaining, "I want to take just a minute to direct your attention to some of the things that are wrong with this paper." Using her red pencil as a pointer, she said, "In the first place, the weekly spelling test is supposed to be done in cursive. You'll notice that you printed." Then she pointed to the heading across the top of the page. "You are supposed to have your full name—first *and* last—here on the right. You have just your first name."

Al watched Charles dance toward the door to go for a drink. Silently, he turned back to his teacher as she began a careful analysis of the types of spelling errors he'd made.

"I see you left out a number again," she observed crisply, then added, "You might not be able to spell, Al. But surely you can number a paper from one to twenty."

The boy made no comment.

"Two of these words would be right if you hadn't switched the letters around to the wrong places." The teacher fixed the youngster with an accusing gaze. "Careless errors, Al. Most of your mistakes are just carelessness." The fact that many of the words in the spelling list were so hard that he couldn't even read them never came up. The boy and his teacher both pretended that *if* he had taken the time to do the practice exercises and paid close attention to details, he'd have passed the test.

Todd sauntered into the room. From behind the teacher's back, he caught Al's eye, made a face, pointed at Mrs. Carswell, tossed off an obscene gesture, and grinned. He then ambled to the back of the room.

Mrs. Carswell was vigorously circling Al's mistakes. "This *f* is backwards. . . . You left out a whole syllable. . . . You wrote *b* instead of *d* twice in one word. . . ." She counted up the check marks, slapped a grade of 35 at the top, and told Al, "Go on and take your break." She then gathered up her sweater and purse and hurried toward the teachers' lounge.

Al strode to the door without drawing any interest from the other students. He was bigger and tougher than most of them. Trouble seemed to follow him. As much as possible, his classmates stayed clear.

But Charles had been waiting for his pal. Grabbing Al from behind in a surprise attack, the tall black youth playfully wrestled him to the ground. As they struggled to pin each other, Charles asked, "Hey, man, what'd you do with that little windup motor? Me and Larry want to look at it."

Larry moved closer to the two flailing bodies and bobbed his head. "Yeah, Al. Can I look at the little motor? I promise not to hurt it."

"Tell this hunk of junk to get off me so I can get it out of my pocket," Al grunted from under Charles.

Reaching into the squirming pile of arms and legs, Larry grabbed Charles's collar. "Get off of him. He's got it in his pocket."

A tearing noise came from the tautly stretched fabric around Charles's neck. "Hey, man, let go! You're ripping my new shirt," Charles barked up at Larry while trying to maintain his hold on his opponent.

The collar remained in Larry's strong grip.

"Let go, let go," Charles insisted, straining to pull his shirt free.

Several children came over to watch what they thought was a real fight. The teacher was still out of the room.

The tearing sound was heard again.

One of the onlookers charged over to Larry and shouted into his face, "Hey, retard, ain't you even smart enough to let go? Your hand can't be as dumb as your brains are!" Then he grabbed Larry by the wrist.

Charles and Al scrambled up from the floor. Todd raced toward the scene from the back of the room.

"You take that back," Al demanded.

"But he was ripping Charles's shirt," the youth protested.

"I don't care what he was doing. Don't you *never* call Larry names like that!" Al shouted.

Charles put an arm around Al's shoulder to draw him away. "Save your breath, man. They don't know nothin'." With a jerk of his head, he motioned Larry and Todd to follow. "Come on. Let's us four go get a drink. The air ain't so good in here." Charles herded his friends into the hall.

Al blustered under his breath. By the time he and his three buddies got to the fountain, he'd cooled down enough to sigh heavily and conclude, "We could beat the stew out of every one of them, Charles. But ain't no way they'd ever understand."

When Mrs. Carswell returned from the teachers' lounge, the classroom was unusually peaceful. Children were talking, reading, playing games. Even Al, Charles, and Larry were quietly amusing themselves with some toy.

Humming lightly to herself, the teacher moved about the room handing back math papers. To call the class to order, she announced, "You'll find yesterday's tests on your desks. Group 1 and Group 2, stay in your seats and make your corrections. Group 3, bring your tests and your pencils and come up to the table. I'm going to help you with your papers."

Groups 1 and 2 were doing fifth-grade arithmetic. Group 3 used the fourth-grade book and did a lot of worksheets. Al, Larry, Charles, Mary Lou, and Pam were the only students in the low group. The five joined their teacher at the table.

As soon as they were settled, Mrs. Carswell began. "Let's start with the addition problems at the top of the first page. Did anybody get all of the first row right?"

Pam's hand shot up.

"Okay, Pam, you go to the board." She handed the girl some chalk, then said, "Charles, did you miss the first problem?"

"Nah, I didn't miss nothing until the last one in the row," he replied.

Larry waved his hand. "I missed that one."

"Okay, Larry, tell Pam what to put on the board."

Slowly, the boy called out the numbers and told her what to do. Together, they arrived at an answer of ninety-three.

"Anybody who doesn't have ninety-three for the answer needs to figure out what went wrong," Mrs. Carswell said.

"I know what I did wrong," Larry spoke up. "I said three plus six equals eight. It should have been nine."

"Very good, Larry." The teacher scanned the papers for other errors on that problem. "Al, what did you do wrong?" she asked.

"I didn't do nothing wrong," the boy snapped.

"But it's got an *X* on it," Mrs. Carswell noted.

"I figured out the right answer," Al said. "You put a *X* on it because I messed up when I wrote it down."

"What does your answer say?"

Al studied his paper in silence, then said, "I got ninety-three."

"No, Al. That's what the answer is *supposed* to be."

"Oh, then I got thirty-nine."

"Right," Mrs. Carswell nodded.

Mumbling to himself about "stupid, dumb mistakes," Al changed the reversed numbers.

When they got to the harder addition that involved carrying, almost every problem on Al's paper was marked wrong.

"Charles, you go to the board," the teacher directed. "Al, you call out the first one to him."

Al began, "Twenty-six goes on the top."

Charles wrote the number.

"Put eighty-six underneath it."

Charles did as directed.

Al snorted in disgust. "That ain't eighty-six, Charles. Come on, be serious."

"Yeah, it is, man." The youngster at the board appealed to the teacher. "Ain't that eighty-six, Mrs. Carswell?"

She nodded. "It sure is."

With that, Al had reached his limit of frustration. Grabbing his pencil, he smashed it down on his paper. "I hate math. I hate math," he snarled.

"Yeah, man, I know that," Charles responded, not at all intimidated by his best friend's rage. "But what you want me to do with these here numbers?"

"You really want to know what you can do with them numbers, nigger?" Al challenged.

Mrs. Carswell gasped.

Still unruffled, Charles chuckled and gave his buddy a wide grin. "Nah," he drawled. "I mean other than that."

Al jumped out of his seat, snatched up his paper, and stuck it under Charles's nose. Stabbing at it frantically, he said, "Copy this . . . this number here."

"Oh, that. That's sixty-eight," Charles said casually.

"I don't care what it is! Just copy it down."

Charles did as he was told. Looking at Al, he asked, "Now what?"

"Now you just stay there and keep your big mouth shut. I'm going to tell you how to work it." Al yanked his chair out and flopped back into it.

Mrs. Carswell relaxed with a sigh of relief. Al had flared up and cooled off so quickly that there was no need for her to interfere. Charles had not been offended by his pal's ethnic slur, so she decided to let it go.

Al took a deep breath and cleared his throat. "Okay," he said in a calm, low voice. "Six plus eight is . . ." He counted on his fingers. "Fourteen."

Charles stood quietly, chalk poised.

"Put down the one and carry the four."

The numbers went on the board as ordered.

"Four plus six is . . ." Again, Al paused to count on his fingers. "Ten plus two is . . . twelve. Put down the twelve."

Larry leaned across the table and pointed to the problem on the board. "You did your carrying wrong, Al. You shouldn't have wrote down the one; that ought to have been the four."

Al couldn't follow what Larry was saying. Pam and Mary Lou chimed in. Charles wrote. Mrs. Carswell explained. Al tried. Finally, Larry went to the board. Al followed the boy's slow explanation carefully. And the light dawned. "I see what you mean, Larry. I see what you mean. The number is fourteen. I should have put the four down in the answer and carried the one!" Larry was so delighted that he patted Al on the shoulder. Al slapped Larry affectionately on the back. Exchanging a high-five, he said, "Thanks, man."

In congratulating Al on his success, Mrs. Carswell said, "Now that you know how to carry, you won't have any difficulty making your corrections."

Al looked down at the twenty problems he'd missed. The idea of reworking every one of them took the edge off his excitement.

To speed things up, the teacher sent all five pupils to the blackboard. That way, they could do a whole row at once. Al had a terrible time getting his problems copied correctly onto the board, but he had no further trouble working them.

Back at the table, the five started on the subtraction problems they'd missed on the test. Al's paper was covered with row after row of *X*'s. For every single set of numbers, he'd added instead of subtracted. Thoroughly disgusted, Al shoved his paper aside. "Ain't no way I can get all them done." Shaking his head, he silently sulked in defeat.

The other four took turns at the board reworking the subtraction problems. Al moped over his paper until Mrs. Carswell drew him aside and worked with him privately. Everything was fine until Al and the teacher got to subtraction problems that required borrowing. By reading the numbers in the wrong order, the boy made a mistake every time. On 46 –18, he said, "Eight take away six is two, four take away one is three."

The teacher carefully pointed out his error.

The next example was 73–45. Again, Al subtracted the smaller number from the larger one. "Three from five is two," he said.

Mrs. Carswell drew pictures of apples. She gave him beans from a jar. Al understood her illustrations. Yet on paper, he continued to work in the wrong direction.

Group 3 accomplished a lot in its thirty-minute session with the teacher. As the students were dismissed, they were rewarded. "You go back to your desks, finish your corrections, and then have a good time with this dot-to-dot puzzle." Most of them were delighted.

Al dragged himself back to his seat, tossed down his test and his puzzle, and sank slowly into his chair.

"What's the matter with you, boy?" Charles asked playfully.

"Oh, man, I got a headache," Al moaned. Folding his arms for a cushion, he put his head down on his desk.

It was lunchtime before the teacher noticed Al. As the other students prepared to leave for the cafeteria, she walked to the back row and asked Al, "Why do you have your head down?"

When the snoozing boy didn't respond, Todd gave him a gentle nudge.

Raising his drowsy head, Al looked up to see his teacher's angry face staring down at him.

"If there's anybody in this room who can't afford to sleep through math class, Al, it's you!"

"I had a headache," Al mumbled.

"Headache—humph!" The teacher blustered. "You get ready for lunch, young man. We'll talk about this later."

Flanked by Charles and Todd, Al left for the noon meal.

The twenty-minute period between lunch and physical education was story time. Mrs. Carswell read to the children as they remained in their seats drawing or quietly playing. The book for the week was a true story about the construction of the Golden Gate Bridge. Al found it fascinating. He got a box of Legos and a ball of string out of the cupboard. Once he'd spread all the pieces on his desk before him, he carefully removed the little windup motor from his pocket. He was going to make a building crane that really worked.

Al's hands deftly fit pieces together as he listened to every word Mrs. Carswell read. Running a string through the hole in a plastic ruler, he experimented with the boom until he hit on a design that worked.

Several times, Charles requested, "Hey, man, let me help."

Twice, Todd asked, "What are you making?"

The only response from Al was a brief "Shhh."

The last thing to go into place was the windup engine. Al used rubber bands to strap the motor to a platform at the back of his contraption. He even bent a paper clip so the derrick could hook onto the things it lifted. On the first trial, Al flipped the switch, the gears turned, and the string got all tangled up. After a few adjustments, he tested it again. This time, the weight of the object being lifted threw the whole thing out of balance. It toppled over and fell apart. With calm patience, Al snapped the pieces back together. Then he added an extra set of pieces as counterweights at the back. Two more tests and the machine was operational. A pack of chewing gum, a tiny model car, a roll of caps, a hunk of modeling clay, a golf ball—the machine hoisted each one with ease. Al, Todd, and Charles spent the rest of story time watching the crane lift an assortment of objects they dug from the depths of their desks.

During the forty-five-minute softball game in physical education, Al didn't get to play much. He was chosen last and put at the end of the batting order. When he dropped an easy fly ball, one of the boys on his team shouted, "Butterfingers! Can't you even catch a ball right?" Al lit into the youngster with fists and foul language. The other boy had to sit out for the rest of the inning. Al was sidelined for the rest of the game.

The last part of the day was devoted to working on projects for health class. Armed with pencils, paper, and dire warnings about good behavior, the class followed its teacher down the hall to the library. Once there, the children were split into two groups. The librarian supervised the research activities of twenty students.

Mrs. Carswell worked with a group of twelve. She made it a point to stay close to Al.

Charles, Larry, Al, and Todd scrambled into adjoining seats at the large, round library table. Chuckling and rolling his eyes, Charles whispered, "We got all the bad guys from the back row right here."

Todd nodded. "Mrs. Carswell is keeping us all to herself. I guess she doesn't trust us!"

The teacher gave her group a long explanation on how to use the card catalog. Then she sent the students two by two to look up their topic in the catalog drawers. When it was Al's turn, his partner was Mary Lou. Her topic was bones. His was teeth.

"Al, you go over and stand on the right side of the cabinet," Mrs. Carswell directed.

On his best behavior, Al took his pencil and paper and walked directly to the left side of the large set of drawers.

The teacher corrected him. "That's not the right side, Al."

The boy looked surprised. "It's not?" he muttered under his breath, then quickly moved to the other side.

"Yes." The teacher nodded her approval. "Now, Mary Lou, you go over to the left side."

With both pupils in the proper place, Mrs. Carswell said, "Mary Lou, where are you going to look to find *Bones*?"

"Under *B*," the girl replied.

"Then find the *B* drawer and pull it out." Looking at Al, the teacher asked, "Where are you going to find *Teeth*?"

"Under *T*," he replied with certainty.

"Good. Find the *T* drawer and pull it out."

Mary Lou already had the *B* drawer open and ready. Slowly, Al surveyed the drawers in front of him. When he couldn't locate the *T* right away, he ran his finger under the letters as he read each label. He started at *J*. In the back of his mind, he had a moment of panic as he wondered if his teacher had tricked him by sending him to the wrong side of the cabinet.

"Al," Mrs. Carswell called to him from the table. "You're looking at the middle of the alphabet there."

All the boy could figure out to do was speed up and read the labels faster. He wasn't at all sure he would be able to find the *T* drawer.

"No, Al," the teacher called. "Don't waste your time there. *T* is near the end of the alphabet. Move over to the drawers farther to your right."

Not wanting to make a second blunder on the right-and-left decision, Al hesitated for a second to think, then moved in the desired direction and began searching in earnest.

Mrs. Carswell left her chair and went up to help him. "Do you know where *t* comes in the alphabet?" she asked softly.

"Yeah. Near the end."

"Do you know what letters come before it or after it?"

Al looked at her blankly.

"Say the alphabet for me, Al. We'll figure out where the *t* is."

Quickly, he rattled off his version of the alphabet. He had a sticky place around *g, h, i, j,* but got to *o* safely. From there, it went *p, q, u, r, s, t, p, u, v* . . .

Apparently, his speed compensated for his lack of accuracy. The teacher did not complain about his errors. "What came just before the *t*?" she asked.

Under his breath, Al said the entire alphabet to himself. Unfortunately, he raced past the section he needed and had to repeat the process. Finally, he said, "*S*, then *t*."

"Good." Mrs. Carswell smiled. "And what came before *s*?"

Again, Al dashed through the alphabet before answering, "*R*."

The teacher patted him on the shoulder. "Very good—*r, s, t.* Now, you're ready to find the *T* drawer in the card catalog. It comes after the *R* and the *S* drawers."

It took a lot of help, but Al finally succeeded in finding three books on teeth. Back in the classroom, he used the research period to pore over them intently.

The teacher was delighted. It was the first time she had ever seen Al get really interested in a school assignment.

Al looked through all three of his library books. He studied the pictures and charts, copied some of the illustrations. He began drawing teeth—a human incisor, a whole set of human teeth, gorilla teeth, dog teeth, horse teeth, shark teeth, bat teeth, vampire teeth, Dracula's fangs, blood dripping off Dracula's fangs, a dead victim of Dracula, a werewolf howling over a corpse, Frankenstein. And before he knew it, the day was over.

As the students departed for home, Mrs. Carswell gave Al an unusually cheery good-bye. She felt very much encouraged by the interest he'd shown in the health project. It even seemed remotely possible that this time the boy might actually complete an assignment.

Al felt good about things, too. Between his success with the crane and the fun with the teeth, a typical day had turned out to be just a little bit special—and he hadn't been sent to the office once!

In six-plus years of school, Al had lost a lot of ground. His quick mind and good reasoning ability were still there but were no longer so readily apparent. His free-flowing interest in everything around him had all but disappeared. Very little remained of the enthusiasm that had formerly made the youngster eager to talk and share and express his ideas. He no longer trusted his classmates and was even suspicious of the teacher. Any motivation that might have been there was gone. His self-confidence had been pretty well destroyed. Socially, he'd become an outcast.

Fifteen and in the Eighth Grade

Chapter 5

Al paused in the doorway of the math lab and serenely contemplated the scene before him. The beak of his baseball cap arched up over his eyebrows to frame his watery, pink, translucent eyes. Affixed to the battered cap was an embroidered emblem advertising rolling papers. Next to the sweat-stained patch, a small tin button displayed a bright green marijuana leaf.

All the other students were at their seats working intently. No two were engaged in the same activity. Al's eyes took in the curve of open books, the reflections from plastic coatings on brightly colored work kits, and the exquisite geometry of the various cubicles, cubbyholes, and cupboards. Visually, the math lab was a feast for the eyes, and Al savored it thoroughly.

Miss Wintle looked up from her desk, surprised that any student would dare to enter her classroom a full forty minutes late.

Although she saw Al so infrequently that she couldn't remember his name, she was certain that he was on her roll as a member of this first-period remedial section.

Al couldn't remember Miss Wintle's name either. But that didn't worry him at all. In an emergency, he could call the wide-eyed first-year teacher "ma'am." The grin that radiated her idealistic optimism made him intensely uncomfortable. Math classes and math teachers always made Al uneasy.

Without fanfare, Al and Miss Wintle went through the ceremony of greetings, tardy slips, and checks in the roll book. Since lunch was cafeteria-style, no paperwork had to be taken to the office.

Noting that this student attended class on an average of once every two weeks, the young teacher thought to herself, "It's a good thing this program is individualized." She escorted her new arrival to the files and helped him get out his work folder.

"Ah, yes," Miss Wintle said, removing a page of problems from the manilla cover with Al's name on it. "You were half-finished with this subtraction sheet."

"I have to go get a pencil," Al muttered. He started toward the door, presumably on the way to his locker.

His exit was intercepted when Miss Wintle calmly pointed to a supply table in the front corner of the room. "No problem. Get one out of the pink coffee can." Then, stopping Al before he could start in the indicated direction, she patted her ears and said, "Oh, wait, better yet, take this one." With a chuckle, the young teacher pulled a long, new, freshly sharpened bright green pencil from behind her ear. "It even has a good eraser," she observed as she handed it to her student.

Al took a seat at one of the empty tables in the back. Miss Wintle pulled a chair beside him. The heavyset young woman was bouncy with enthusiasm.

Al stared at the worksheet in front of him and awaited instructions.

"Since you almost finished the first two rows before, I think you could just put today's date here at the beginning of the third row and pick up where you left off."

Al took up the pencil, put his hand in the proper position, began to write something, then looked up and asked, "What's the date?"

"November fourth," the teacher replied.

With flashy speed, Al dashed off 10/4/93.

"November's not the tenth month," Miss Wintle corrected.

Her pupil looked startled by his error.

Quickly, the teacher explained, "November is the *eleventh* month. That date should read 11/4."

Al made a dark one over the zero.

Miss Wintle paused as though debating something. Then she pointed to the four-digit subtraction problems he had previously completed. "What kind of problems are these?" she asked. When Al didn't respond immediately, she tapped the minus sign to give him a clue. "What does this sign tell you to do?"

"Oh, take away," Al said. "Yeah, those are take-away problems."

"Right," Miss Wintle agreed. "I'm going to sit here and watch to be sure you haven't forgotten how to do them. I want you to take the first problem in row three and work it out loud."

Al looked at the figures in question. "Let's see." His eyes narrowed as he thought. "Three take away three is zero." He wrote down the number with a nod of satisfaction and thought to himself, "So far, so good." "Four take away two . . ." His fingers tapped out the figures on the desk. "Two. Seven take away one . . ."

The teacher interrupted, "That's not seven take away one."

Pausing in confusion, Al stared at the problem, then corrected his mistake by saying, "Seven from one is . . ." Again, his fingers worked against the desk as he ticked through the calculation. He gave his answer, "Six," and wrote the number down.

Miss Wintle stopped him once more. "No, that won't work. You've got to do it in the other direction." With her finger, she pointed to the figures that illustrated what she was saying. "You have to start with the top number and take away the bottom number."

"Oh, yeah." Al nodded his head slowly. "I forgot."

"You have to say, 'One take away seven,'" the teacher coached.

"Right, right. One take away seven . . ." This time, his fingers flew through the computation. "One take away seven is six."

"No, that's still not quite it." Miss Wintle shook her head and pointed to the numbers. "You're *saying* it right, but you're still working it upside down."

"I am?" Al asked in total amazement.

The bell rang before Miss Wintle had drawn enough apples to get her pupil to understand borrowing. As the students put their folders away, she offered Al a parting word of encouragement. "We'll work on that borrowing one more time, and I think you'll have it."

He didn't reply. Instead, he handed her the pencil she'd loaned him, said, "Thanks," and ambled out of the room.

When Al sauntered into his second-period history class, no one seemed to notice his presence at all. The other teenagers were chattering and jostling. The teacher was writing on the blackboard. Without considering whether or not there were assigned seats, Al took a desk in the back row and slouched into a comfortable position. No one talked to him. He didn't say a word. Within his shell of isolated silence, he looked relaxed and content.

The bell rang. A few late arrivals hurried to their seats. The teacher, Mrs. Edmonds, took attendance and class began.

From her position front and center, Mrs. Edmonds cleared her throat and waited for quiet. "You should have before you your partially labeled world map. Monday, we did the continent of North America. Tuesday, we worked on Central and South America. Wednesday, it was Europe." Instead of looking at the class over her half-glasses, she took them off and used them as a pointer. "You'll find all the instructions you need right here on the board. This continent is to be labeled . . ." She touched the word *Asia*. "These major cities are to be located." Her finger swept across a long list of names. "Population figures are to be ascertained and appropriately noted." She looked sternly at her students and admonished, "After working on this project for three whole days, we can trust that you know how to do that." No one protested, so she went on. "You will, of course, locate and label these major geographical features." Her finger tapped the slate to indicate a long column of names of rivers, seas, and mountain ranges.

To the left of the teacher and just over her head, a large globe was suspended from the ceiling. In the glare of the morning sunlight, the orb's tiny, contoured mountains made a pattern of highlights and shadows across the surface of the garishly colored relief map. Al found the suspended ball intriguing. Staring at it, he could feel himself an astronaut coming back from outer space and trying to land on that little speck of a planet. He had progressed deep into his fantasy when an authoritative female voice said, "Alvin."

Al looked up to see the teacher moving toward his desk with a quizzical look knitting her brow. "Alvin—that *is* your name, isn't it?"

Al nodded. "Yeah."

Mrs. Edmonds flapped the back of her hand against Al's shoulder. "Sit up straight in your chair. Take off that hat."

Al quickly complied.

Fluttery motions accompanied the teacher's crisp, clipped words. She handed her pupil an atlas and a blank map of the world. "Since you missed the first three days of this assignment, it's pointless for you to try to catch up. Just start with the new work I put on the board this morning."

Al stuffed his cap into the hip pocket of his tattered jeans and bobbed his head in agreement.

Mrs. Edmonds started to walk away, then turned back to Al and added, "I'd suggest that you begin with the geographical features. After I get the rest of the class started, I'll come back and explain the proper procedure for putting in the cities and other political markings." Without waiting for a comment from her pupil, the teacher turned on her heel and walked away.

Al carefully spread out the large, blank world map he'd been given. He was intrigued by the strong black lines meandering around on it to form intricate designs. He noticed the oddly shaped enclosed areas and the patterns outlined within them by a network of lighter black lines. Al stared at the outlines through narrowed eyes. Just as children see shapes in the clouds, Al watched illusions emerge from the patterns of his map. The Baltic Sea became a rampaging elephant with its head thrown back. It seemed alive as he watched it charging across the area of the map representing northern Europe.

Al's interest in the fantasy shapes waned. His attention returned to the globe. While he was recreating the astronaut-searching-for-home experience, the oranges and browns seemed to pulsate against the blues that dominated the color scheme of the orb. With a jolt, Al realized, "That orange is supposed to be land!" This startling new perception made him see the globe in a whole new way and led him to wonder if he could tell the difference between the earth and the sea on the flat black-and-white map in front of him.

Al picked a spot, then stared at the globe in an attempt to find it. It took several tries. Finally, at the southern tip of Africa, he could see the relationship between his map and the globe. And he could see the difference between the land and the water. The continent stood out so clearly for him that he ran his finger around the black line that separated it from the surrounding oceans. Sometimes, an optical illusion would play tricks on his eyes. The Mediterranean Sea would stand out as the dominant landmass on his colorless map, and Africa would be seen as a large body of water. Every time such a visual reversal occurred, Al put his finger back on the southern tip of Africa and started over. He was in the midst of this process when Mrs. Edmonds returned to his side to give him the instructions she had offered earlier.

The teacher seemed startled by the fact that Al's map was still blank. She drew herself up tall, set her jaw and shoulders, and asked, "Young man, why are you not working?"

Al shrugged. "I ain't got no pencil."

To correct her pupil's grammar, Mrs. Edmonds said with precise emphasis, "You *don't* have colored pencils?" She paused, then continued, "Colored pencils are on the supply list for this course."

Al said nothing.

Disgust put a sharp edge on Mrs. Edmonds's clipped diction. "Do you have *any* pencil?"

Al shook his head. "No."

"Humph." The teacher glared at him over her glasses, shot a quick look at the clock, then snapped, "I suggest that you go to your locker and get one."

There *was* no pencil in Al's locker. He knew that before he left the history room. But he also knew that if one wandered the halls of a large school, a stray pencil could almost always be found on the floor somewhere.

A display of trophies in the hall caught the young man's attention. He paused to stare into the glass case to see if any were from the current year.

Farther down the hall, he wandered into the bathroom to have a cigarette. While there, he noticed that the paper towel dispenser was broken. It took him only a few minutes to remove the cover and determine the cause of the problem. Using the broken end of a ruler and the cardboard tube from a toilet paper roll as tools, he took the mechanism apart and fixed it.

Unfortunately, the bell rang before he got the cover back on. With young males streaming in to use the facilities, Al was forced to abandon his project and move on to his third-period class.

He strolled into the auditorium through a door near the stage. Fifty-five chattering teenagers were taking their places in the front section in preparation for health class. As the students clustered in groups with their friends, the huge theater echoed with the sounds of cushioned seats thudding down into place.

Al never even glanced at the crowd to check for familiar faces. He strode up the aisle, climbing the steps two at a time. With the casual certainty of one taking his favorite spot, the solitary youth eased into a seat in the center of the last row. Stretching his feet out on the chair in front of him, he leaned comfortably back until his head rested on the wall of the projection booth behind him. His blank, unfocused eyes stared calmly from beneath the visor of the baseball cap.

Noises from the projection booth indicated that the teacher was setting up a movie. Al closed his eyes and listened carefully to the sounds of celluloid being handled. He could hear sprockets moving, a tiny spring pulling into position, the rasp and whir of an empty reel. In his mind's eye, he pictured the activity of hands, film, and machine. In his imagination, he could see every step of the threading process in 3-D wide-screen Technicolor.

Mr. Armsley, the school's baseball coach, bounded out of the projection booth and down the steps toward the front of his class. His strong, enthusiastic voice perfectly complemented his vigorous, sure movements. "Okay, troops. Let's get it together here." With his straight white teeth, close-cropped hair, starched plaid shirt, and conservative tie, Coach Armsley was so vibrantly wholesome that he looked as if he'd just stepped out of an ad for physical fitness equipment. "Got a film on diet," he announced. "It's a long one, so we'll see it today and have a discussion and a quiz on it tomorrow." All bustle and efficiency, he grabbed his roll book off his desk and looked out at the sea of faces. "Adams."

"Here," a male voice called.

"Andrews."

"Present."

"Arrington."

Al listened until the roll call got to his name and gave a sharp, snappy "Yo."

As soon as the lights were dimmed, Al leaned farther back in his seat, pulled the brim of his cap over his eyes, and settled down for a nap. As far as he was concerned, green, leafy vegetables were boring.

Al awoke when the lights came back on. He flexed his shoulders and stretched his neck to get the kinks out. Craving a cigarette, he eagerly awaited the sound of the bell. When it finally came, he flowed down the aisle, eased past the swarm of departing classmates, skirted around the edge of the throng in the halls, and headed for the back door.

Outside, Al dug his lighter out of his pocket. A cigarette was in his lips before he got halfway across the lawn. At the curb, he paused, checked for traffic, flicked his lighter, stepped into the street, and applied the flame to the tobacco. All tension drained out of him with the first cloud of smoke. Al stopped on the road's centerline, took a second pull on his cigarette, and sighed with content. From his vantage point, he scanned the faces of the young males who had already attained the safety of the territory just across the street. Most had long hair and wore blue jeans. Many had the sparsely whiskered goatees of adolescence. A few had full beards or sweeping mustaches. Many wore hats. The ones in leather, chains, and assorted motorcycle paraphernalia looked muscular and violent. Those in denim, bandannas, and T-shirts emblazoned with slogans appeared gentle and idealistic.

Al crossed the street and joined the crowd on the curb.

A tall, thin young man with a huge, drooping mustache clapped him on the shoulder. "Hey, man, good to see you." The two joined closed hands to form one bonded fist in the ritualistic handshake of hippies.

"You still makin' music?" Al asked.

"Yeah. Yeah." The full length of Joel's slender body undulated as an extension of the movement of his nodding head. He stared into Al's face with open affection. A broad grin stretched across his mouth as he said, "Yeah, I'm still makin' music."

The two fell silent. Al lit a second cigarette from the butt of the first. His mind drifted momentarily.

"Got a light?"

Al didn't bother to come out of his reverie. Automatically, he fished out his lighter and offered it.

The smell of burning marijuana caught his attention. With casual, slow-moving eyes, Al turned his gaze back to Joel.

The tall, lean youth allowed a large cloud of smoke to burst from his lungs, then took a series of noisy little puffs, inhaled powerfully, and, while holding his breath, offered the joint to Al.

With an easy movement like that of an athlete, Al took the joint and pivoted on one foot so his back was to the school. Sucking in one steady draw, Al filled his lungs to capacity.

The crowd started to thin. Joel cocked his head to one side and looked at his companion with hooded, dreamy eyes. "Want one more toke?" he asked.

Al stayed for another round.

The bell rang as he and a host of others crossed the street back to school. Al had a couple of candy bars stashed in his locker. At that moment, he wanted one so badly that his tongue tingled. It didn't occur to him that he was already late for his fourth-period biology class. It didn't strike him as odd that he walked right by the biology room on the way to his locker. With a confident swagger, humming a rock tune under his breath and beating out the rhythm on an imaginary guitar, he strode through the empty halls intent on his mission.

As he walked into his fourth-period class, Al was licking chocolate off his fingers and lips. The room was totally silent. The students were huddled over their desks writing answers on machine-scored answer sheets.

The teacher, Mrs. Tuttle, rose from her desk and motioned for Al to join her in the hall. Her glorious smile and short Afro made the tiny black woman look almost playful as she led her student to a spot just outside the door. "The rest of the students are taking a unit test," she whispered. "Since you've missed so many classes, you couldn't possibly make a passing grade on this test." She cocked her head and looked at Al knowingly. "I think we'd better put you back in the workroom with a filmstrip so you can catch up on the work that you've missed."

Al looked confused.

"Does that seem fair to you?" the teacher asked, then explained without waiting for a response. "You can get ready to take a makeup test sometime next week."

Al nodded his head slowly.

"Get some paper and colored pencils off the corner of my desk and meet me in the little back room."

Again, Al nodded.

Mrs. Tuttle thrust her head forward to look her pupil in the eye. "Is this okay with you?" she asked.

"Yeah, sure." Al actually grinned.

Mrs. Tuttle and her tardy student tiptoed through the quiet classroom. Very few students looked up. Al gathered his materials while the teacher took a small, shiny red box out of her file cabinet. They softly padded into the workroom and closed the door.

As though unveiling a treasure, the biology teacher slid open the red box and revealed its contents to Al. "With these four filmstrips, we're going to introduce you to the anatomy of a frog," she explained.

Al stared at the small film canisters and cassette tapes nestled in their neat rows. With respect bordering on reverence, he stretched out his hands and accepted the offered gift.

"Do you know how to work these filmstrip machines?" Mrs. Tuttle queried.

Al was so enthralled with the red box that he didn't respond.

"Here," the teacher called gently. "Come over here and let me show you how to work the projector."

The youth took the chair indicated, then watched closely as the procedures were demonstrated. He was eager to don the headset and begin his private showing.

The teacher gave Al his final instructions. "Don't forget, you won't have time to see all four today, so take as long as you want to look at them in any order that suits you."

Al nodded.

Mrs. Tuttle smiled and left the room.

The filmstrips featured the giant American bullfrog. The frogs were the biggest Al had ever seen. He was fascinated. He viewed the first tape and was on his second time through the third tape when the teacher had to roust him out of her back room and force him to go to lunch.

"You ever seen any of them big frogs?" he asked.

"We've got some of the tadpoles," she replied.

Al's eyes widened. "Where?"

"In that first aquarium by my desk."

"Can I see 'em?"

The teacher was glad she'd just finished locking the door. Al was so enthusiastic about the tadpoles that he seemed eager to forgo his meal to see them right then. "We have to go to lunch now," she answered. "But next time you're in class, go over and take a look."

Al strolled along beside his biology teacher. His slow, languid gait easily kept up with her quick, tiny steps. "Did you hatch 'em from eggs?"

"No, we don't have the proper equipment for that."

"That sure would be interesting."

Mrs. Tuttle's fast-moving high heels clicked down the wide marble stairs, then paused for a second at the entrance to the faculty dining room. She laid a hand lightly on Al's shoulder. In farewell, she reminded him, "The aquarium is right next to my desk. They really are wonderful. Come by tomorrow and see."

The school cafeteria held no appeal for Al. No one he knew would be there. He wasn't interested in nutritious institutional food anyway. He headed across the street, where vending machines offered the soft drinks and snack foods he liked. He could eat outside with the gang at the curb.

Al started off with a packet of peanut butter crackers and a bottle of cola. He was thinking of heading back to the machine for something sweet when he heard talk of amphetamines. Try as he might, he couldn't figure out who had the uppers, so he wove his way through the crowd making inquiries. Several youths told him to see J. C.

The small-time dealer grinned as Al approached. J. C.'s frizzy hair stuck out around the edges of the greasy red bandanna he used as a headband. Except for his massive size, there was no reason to suspect that he had once been the star of the football team.

Al and J. C. had known each other since grade school. They clasped hands in warm greeting. After exchanging a few pleasantries, Al asked, "You really got some good speed?"

"White cross," the former athlete responded. Lowering his eyelids and sighing blissfully, the dealer added, "Pharmaceutical quality for the connoisseur."

"Real white cross, huh?"

J. C. reassured him. "Same stuff they use in the hospital."

Al pondered a moment, then nodded. "How much?"

"Fifty cents a hit."

"All I got on me is a buck," Al protested.

"This is good stuff, man. Two hits of this and you'll be right until past midnight."

A crumpled dollar bill emerged from the customer's hip pocket, and the transaction was completed.

Al washed both pills down with the remaining swallow of his soft drink. Since speed didn't mix well with school, he headed for the highway. Al didn't have a particular destination in mind. He just felt like hitching a ride.

At the age of fifteen, on the eve of abandoning his attempt at formal education, Al displayed few of the true causes of his academic difficulties. His apathetic attitude masked the intense shame he felt about his repeated lack of success in school. Since he produced almost no work, he rarely demonstrated his terribly inadequate basic skills. He seemed to be a loner by choice. Nearly every aspect of Al's scholastic failure was obscured by absences, drugs, and lack of motivation.

Yet behind it all, there still remained a spark of curiosity and delight in the world around him.

PART 2

A New Approach to an Old Problem

CHAPTER 6

STUDENTS WITH A LEARNING DISABILITY and/or an attention deficit disorder have always been in regular classrooms. They were the wiggly and disorganized ones. They socialized and horsed around a lot. They rarely paid attention to what was going on in class. Their work was messy, incomplete, and full of errors. They were in the bottom reading group. Or they were in one of the higher groups but never got their work finished. Bribes, punishments, and special attention didn't help. No matter what was done on their behalf, these youngsters continued to fail.

We teachers consoled ourselves by saying, "This year, I helped thirty-three out of thirty-four children. I didn't do a bit of good for Al. But you can't win them all. Maybe next year, he'll . . ."

Years ago, these unsuccessful students were passed on through the grades, and their lack of academic achievement was accepted. Nothing much was expected of them. They were those sweet but rambunctious boys destined to fill the low group. Since they weren't retarded, hard of hearing, blind, or physically handicapped, there were no special programs for them. They were simply a part of every class—the unmotivated nonachievers in the back row.

In the 1990s, we can no longer take comfort in figures that keep the Als of the world in a tiny minority. Of a teacher's twenty-six to twenty-eight youngsters, as many as a third—and with alarming frequency, up to a half!—have a learning disability and/or an attention deficit disorder severe enough to warrant the use of stimulant medication. Inability to concentrate, extreme difficulty with organization, unwillingness to develop even the most basic time-management skills, and a general ignorance of study skills and learning strategies have become significant problems with a huge portion of today's youngsters. Pediatric neurologists report that over half of their patients are brought to them because of an inability to pay attention in school. And rarely is the attention problem separate from some serious learning deficit in spelling, handwriting, expressive writing, math, or reading. Today's children are different. The learning problems are the same, but the number of those who can legitimately be labeled LD and/or ADD has vastly increased. The group we used to ignore can't be disregarded anymore. There are just too many of them!

Our present-day approach to education emphasizes development of strengths that are the direct opposite of those possessed by LD and ADD youngsters. Anything that enables these children to succeed in today's schools is at best a compromise.

Teachers want LD/ADD students to succeed with the regular program. For the vast majority of them, this is not possible. When faced with regular classwork, LD/ADD pupils fail to succeed. They become discouraged and lose interest, motivation, and self-confidence. When they are assigned appropriately adjusted schoolwork, their chances of success are vastly improved.

The choice of whether or not to adjust an LD/ADD student's schoolwork is basically a question of whether the focal point of education should be the system or the individual child. We often get so caught up in the ethical ramifications of this issue that youngsters with learning disabilities and/or attention deficit disorder end up going unhelped.

Every special modification designed to accommodate a student's unique difficulties can be condemned as unfair to those who are forced to abide by "normal procedure." As long as we hold to the "one size fits all" approach to education, there will be no way to adjust a student's assignments in a way that is totally fair to his classmates, future teachers, college admissions officers, and prospective employers.

This discussion is aimed at helping LD/ADD children succeed. As much as possible, the established structure of education and business will be taken into account. But when there is a conflict, the best interests of the individual student will take precedence over all else. Others will have to solve the ethical questions. The goal here is to solve the academic difficulties of students who have a learning disability and/or an attention deficit disorder.

The Teacher's Role

As long as there are laws preventing schools from singling out LD/ADD students for special instruction in small groups separate from their classmates, regular classroom teachers will be forced to figure out ways to meet the demands of a few without sacrificing the needs of the many. There are alternate teaching techniques that can enable teachers to create a learning environment where all but a tiny minority of LD/ADD students can thrive, techniques that simultaneously enhance the academic atmosphere for the rest of the class. But most teachers have no training or experience in these radically different approaches. And with the budget cuts so typical of current fiscal policy, it is highly unlikely that staff-development funds will provide the training required for such a major transformation. Some schools have strong support services to help teachers make the modifications that can give LD/ADD pupils a genuine opportunity to achieve academic success in the regular program. Most do not. Once again, teachers will have to make do with ideas gleaned from books and gathered through workshops.

The classroom teacher *can* be a positive factor in helping LD/ADD students overcome their learning difficulties. However, for most teachers, that is a goal for the future. Such a level of expertise is not likely to be attained quickly because it requires observation, demonstration, instruction, practice, and experience. To be realistic, the teacher must have this as her first objective: to see that no damage is done to LD/ADD students within the classroom.

Some readers may be insulted by the implication that classroom teachers harm these children. Nevertheless, it is a fact that needs to be explored. For years, teachers have done all the wrong things in their attempts to make LD/ADD pupils learn successfully. They have punished, badgered, shamed, and bribed. Their actions were based on frustration and a sincere desire to help. Mainly, however, their actions were based on ignorance.

> During first grade, Marcie's mild learning disability made it hard for her to learn to write. Her messy papers were always dog-eared and torn from all the erasing. Since her high intelligence made it possible for Marcie to succeed in all other areas of her schoolwork, the teacher assumed the sloppy papers were caused by laziness. She made many attempts to motivate the child. Most of them were harmful, but one was devastating.
>
> Before an end-of-the-year penmanship test, the teacher tried to inspire her class by holding up two examples of student writing. One paper was perfect. Lovely, rounded letters marched precisely across the page. The other paper was ghastly. The children snickered at the ugly, heavy black marks sprawling above the lines and around the splotches and holes. The example of "what we don't want our papers to look like" was Marcie's work.
>
> The public ridicule hurt Marcie so deeply that she turned off—and not just to writing or that teacher or that class. She turned off to school in general. Once she was past the third grade, her slight learning disability caused her no further problems. But Marcie never regained an interest in learning. Her high intelligence was channeled into mischief and defiance. The pursuit of boys, drugs, partying, and truancy made a

four-year high school into a five-year project. Then it took her six years to squeeze through a four-year college.

If that one teacher had only understood the real cause of Marcie's poor penmanship . . .

We teachers smile and say, "Well, yes, but that was thirty years ago. Nobody knew anything about learning disabilities back then. There was no such thing as ADD!" We think things like that don't happen anymore. We believe we know better now. Do we?

The following two incidents happened in the 1980s.

Freddie, a third-grader, was diagnosed as LD and provided therapy in a resource room. By late April, the youngster was making good progress but was still far behind the other students in his regular class. The psychologist, the LD teacher, the classroom teacher, the principal, the social worker, and the parents all agreed that repeating the third grade was definitely in the boy's best interest. The child accepted the plan with calm optimism. He believed another year in the third grade plus continued LD therapy would give him his first real chance for success in school.

Everything was fine until the last day of school. As Freddie's teacher handed out the report cards, she announced where each child would be the following year. Her roll call went something like this: "Johnny will be moving upstairs with the fourth-graders. Peter is moving this summer. He'll be in the fourth grade in his new school in Denver. Lucinda will be upstairs in the fourth grade. Freddie will be staying right here in the third grade with me. Paula will be . . ." When a student asked why Freddie would be staying in the third grade, the teacher casually replied, "You know that Freddie didn't do very well this year." The children snickered. Embarrassed, Freddie fled the room in tears.

Repeating no longer seemed like a chance for success. Staying in the third grade had been made to look and feel like punishment.

Walter's learning disability was diagnosed after his second unsuccessful year in the seventh grade. Public Law 94-142 had been in effect for several years, but the school system in his small hometown did not have any LD teachers. During the summer, Walter was given private therapy in a nearby city. In the fall, the private lessons continued, and an LD consultant was brought in to work with his school. All the boy's teachers cooperated fully. As they developed an understanding of his special learning problems, they eagerly made the kinds of adjustments that would help him succeed.

Reading was the only class where Walter continued to fail. But with his particular learning disability, that seemed understandable. The LD consultant and the reading teacher had several conferences. Both believed that every reasonable adjustment had been made.

It was mid-December before anyone realized that Walter would have been passing his reading course if it hadn't been for the weekly vocabulary tests. One look at the weekly word lists showed the reason for Walter's failure. The boy was reading on a low sixth-grade level. He had no dictionary skills, no study habits, and no self-confidence. His short attention span and distractibility made it impossible for him to concentrate long enough to complete assignments that required more than just a few minutes of thought. The reading teacher had adjusted all his work to fit his level of ability. Yet she had continued to assign him the regular vocabulary list. Every week, Walter was expected to look up and memorize thirty multisyllable words that he couldn't even read! The boy's inability to complete the assignments and the failing grades he made on the weekly tests ruined his grade average. He flunked his reading course.

The teacher did not see the part she had played in the boy's failure. In discussing the situation with the LD consultant, she confidently explained, "I think Walter needs the challenge of doing at least some of the regular work, don't you?"

Not if it makes him fail!

Even with the experience gained since the mid-1970s, when PL 94-142 and its strict guidelines for an appropriately modified education for exceptional students went into effect, many teachers are still ignorant about the role they play in creating situations where LD/ADD youngsters are bound to fail. The Individuals with Disabilities in Education Act of 1990 (IDEA) was supposed to eliminate the ineffective elements of PL 94-142 and assure every child an appropriate academic environment within the regular classroom. Such lofty ideals look impressive on paper but are extremely difficult to bring to reality.

> Ricky had a severe learning disability coupled with a very troublesome attention deficit disorder. In addition to the extreme difficulty he had learning to read, he had a lack of organizational skills that kept him from succeeding with even the simplest homework assignments. In grades one through four, an LD specialist worked with Ricky daily in the resource room. A big portion of their time together was devoted to keeping the youngster organized enough to reliably complete normal homework requirements.
>
> In 1995, Ricky moved up to middle school, where the LD/ADD support services he had found so helpful were no longer available. In the fall IEP conference, the youth's teachers were warned about his extreme forgetfulness and his profound organizational limitations. His instructors agreed to closely monitor a time-and-materials management system that was set out in elaborate detail in the year's educational plan. Through close supervision, the boy's problem with organization was not going to be allowed to prevent him from learning satisfactorily and making good grades.
>
> After eight weeks of phone calls and conferences, all but one of Ricky's teachers got the homework system fine-tuned so that it worked effectively. However, in language arts and social studies, the boy was accumulating a huge string of failing grades. Even though she was not fulfilling her commitment to play an active role in the boy's organizational system, the language arts teacher repeatedly called the child's parents to complain about lost and uncompleted assignments.
>
> The mother talked, explained, and came to the school for conferences. Claiming that she *was* carrying out her responsibilities for monitoring homework assignments, the teacher made no change in her practices and continued to penalize her student for failure to faithfully produce home assignments. In desperation, the family hired a consultant to work with the school. Although that one teacher was clearly out of compliance with the requirements of Section 504 of the 1990 IDEA, nothing changed. Even the possibility of lawsuits and due-process hearings did not lead to a resolution of the prob-

lem. By midyear, Ricky's parents were so discouraged that they gave up and told their son they had tried everything and nothing more could be done!

The above stories are not examples of uncaring, incompetent teachers. They are typical of situations occurring in classrooms every day. Teachers are just beginning to learn how to deal with students who have a learning disability and/or an attention deficit disorder. And as beginners, they make mistakes. It takes time to break away from the old habits and attitudes that have harmed LD/ADD youngsters for years.

Teachers are idealists. They want to leap from total ignorance to wonder-working wisdom in one bound. They don't seem to realize that before they can be part of the solution, they must learn how to stop being part of the problem.

Developing New Ways of Thinking

Before classroom teachers can begin to help their LD/ADD students, they need to look below the surface to find the real causes of the children's failure.

Traditionally, teachers have believed that success in school depends on only two factors: mental ability and motivation. Thus, it is assumed that any normally intelligent child who wants to learn can learn. The only possible causes for failure are stupidity and laziness. Such an old-fashioned, simplistic view makes it impossible for teachers to deal effectively with LD/ADD pupils.

At the end of fourth grade, Tommy's teacher told his parents that he hadn't learned a thing that year. The boy had done all the reading and passed all the tests, but he hadn't turned in a single piece of written work. All the B's and C's on his report card merely reflected what his teacher believed he would have gotten if he'd done the work.

The family and the school agreed that the boy was spoiled and did only what he liked to do.

In an attempt to remedy the situation, Tommy's parents enrolled him in a private school, insisting that he repeat the fourth grade. Since the youngster scored well above grade level on all the admissions testing, the headmaster was determined to place him in the fifth grade.

As a compromise, Tommy was given a two-week trial period in the private school's fourth grade. Unless there were problems during the probationary period, he would be moved up to fifth grade.

By the end of the first week of school, Tommy's total lack of motivation was apparent. Several strong courses of action were considered, including psychiatry. Since everybody was convinced that Tommy's problem was a matter of laziness, the youngster was not referred to the LD specialist for testing.

On the routine learning-disabilities screening given to all fourth-graders during the first month of school, Tommy scored very poorly. When the matter was discussed with his teacher, she talked openly about the child's lack of interest in doing any of his schoolwork: "For all I know, the kid could be allergic to pencils. I don't know how he does it, but that boy has wangled his way out of every single writing assignment we've had." She tapped a stack of papers and snorted, "Ten days of school and I haven't gotten him to write anything more than his name!" She shook her head in resignation and concluded, "Never before have I had a student I believed was basically lazy."

A time for testing was arranged. As the LD specialist departed, the teacher called to her, "Ask Tommy why he doesn't do his work. You know what he'll say? 'I'm lazy.'"

Testing revealed that Tommy had an IQ high enough to place him in the genius range. That was not surprising. It was obvious the youngster was bright.

Much to everybody's amazement, the test results also explained Tommy's lack of motivation. It wasn't that he didn't *want* to write, the boy *couldn't* write. Although he was an excellent reader, he couldn't tell whether letters were written backward or forward. Even though he was a fourth-grader with an IQ over 140, there were letters of the alphabet that he couldn't produce in either manuscript or cursive writing. Tommy had a severe writing disability.

If a youngster's good mind has not been recognized, limited mental ability may be considered the cause for his learning failure. When it is believed that a child is doing the best he can, there is no reason to search for alternatives that might improve the situation.

In the second week of the fall semester, Jerry was added to my seventh-grade remedial-reading class. The boy's records showed that he had "barely average" intelligence. Without analysis or additional testing, that verdict was accepted.

Jerry was an industrious young man and wanted very much to please. But the results of his efforts were meager. On classwork, homework, tests, and compositions, his grades were barely passing. Jerry found vocabulary-development activities especially difficult. When the weekly list of words gave him trouble, he'd grumble, "I don't see why I have to learn all these big, fancy words."

Throughout the seventh grade, Jerry's complaints and slow rate of progress were pretty much ignored. Since limited mental ability was the cause of the boy's difficulties, there seemed to be no reason to investigate further. It was assumed that whatever his problems were, they couldn't be helped.

Jerry's special instruction in language arts was extended into the eighth grade. In his second year in the special class, the youth showed some surprising insights not typical of a child of his intellectual ability. At first, his flashes of intelligence were attributed to increased maturity.

One incident was particularly puzzling. Jerry and I were walking to class together. As we sauntered past the science lab, a little glass orb shaped like a light bulb with a whirling silver pinwheel inside caught our eye. Jerry had never seen a radiometer before. Fascinated, he stepped near the window to have a closer look. The minute his shadow blocked out the light, the spinner stopped turning. Amazed, he looked at me and asked, "Why'd it stop?"

I grinned. From my own high-school physics class, I knew the mechanism's movement was caused by the heat of the light being absorbed and reflected. But Jerry needed the chance to figure that out for himself.

As I stood there in silence, Jerry reasoned his way to a solution with amazing speed. He immediately recognized that his shadow acted like an "off" switch. He then jumped in and out of the radiometer's light supply while analyzing aloud.

"The light makes it spin. . . . When it's without light, it stops. . . . The black sides go away from the light and the silver sides race toward it. . . . It must be some way of proving that black absorbs heat or light and silver reflects or repels it. . . . That's it! That would mean that . . ." Jerry snapped his fingers and looked up at me with great excitement. "That would mean that if you reversed the black and silver sides on the arms of that little gizmo, it would rotate in the opposite direction!"

Startled, I took another look at the revolving wheel, then replied, "Yeah, you're right, it would. I never would have thought of that, but . . ."

With his new discovery still fresh, Jerry launched into a whole new course of investigation. "Do you think this is related to the greenhouse effect?" he asked.

That possibility led to some very interesting speculations from this eighth-grader. His exploratory thinking and skillful reasoning couldn't possibly have come from a youth with limited mental ability.

The school psychologist agreed to give Jerry an individual intelligence test. The resulting set of scores was astounding. The youth wasn't just "barely average." He wasn't even average. Jerry's IQ was over 125, well into the superior range! He had gotten all the way to junior high before anyone suspected his true mental ability. Because everybody believed he wasn't very bright, all of Jerry's teachers had accepted his lack of academic success without question.

Even to experts, a child's true intelligence can get hidden behind a learning problem. When intelligence and motivation are considered the only essential ingredients in success, the LD/ADD student cannot be understood. Blame the child for the failure or accept the failure as inevitable—neither attitude helps the struggling, frustrated student whose efforts are being doomed to failure by a learning disability and/or an attention deficit disorder.

When dealing with the LD/ADD students assigned to their regular classes, teachers are constantly challenged to deal with failure. To come up with realistic solutions to the academic difficulties these youngsters experience, teachers must learn to see beyond what appears to be lack of motivation or ability. They must learn to recognize lack of success in all its many guises. Whether camouflaged by a child's bad attitude, hidden by the teacher's desire to ignore the problem, or excused by absences, the "covers" that explain away failure must be removed. Teachers have to develop a whole new arsenal of techniques for solving students' problems.

Defining Success

Problem-solving techniques are useful only to those who know how to find the problems.

> In Miss Patterson's LD class, there was one hard-and-fast rule: everybody did his homework every night.
>
> No excuses were accepted, ever! First thing each morning, the completed home assignment had to be shown publicly. After each page was scanned for general appearance, a check went into the grade book. The work was rarely collected.
>
> There was no set punishment for those who failed to produce their homework. Once in a while, Miss Patterson blustered and made a few outrageous threats, but that was mostly for show. Day after day after day, like clockwork, forgetful, disorganized LD/ADD students came to class with satisfactorily completed homework. It was wonderful. The teacher was proud of them. They were proud of themselves. And their days started off great.
>
> Then Tony joined the class. Daily, after explaining to Miss Patterson why he didn't have his homework, he was sent to the back of the room to produce the pages that would allow him entrance to class. It normally took a few weeks for a new student to get into the habit of doing home assignments. Patiently, Miss Patterson waited for Tony to see the light.
>
> By the end of the third week, it was apparent that Tony was not about to change. The other students didn't like Tony—and neither did Miss Patterson. They resented the way he disrupted their morning routine. It didn't matter why he didn't have his homework; they were bored with his excuses and tired of his problem. Days no longer started with success and enthusiasm and optimism. The tone of the class's whole day was being ruined by this obnoxious new kid who couldn't get his act together. He was despised.

The idea of spending so much time straightening out one student was appalling. Bidding Tony farewell as he moved to another school district or back to the regular classroom was a vision in which his frustrated teacher took delight.

In an effort to restore serenity to the morning routine, Miss Patterson put a new homework procedure into effect for Tony. He was no longer allowed to launch into any explanation or protest at the time everybody else presented their work. If he had his done, fine. If he didn't, he was allowed one word: "No." Punishment and special arrangements were preset. Anytime Tony came to class unprepared, he had to give up his morning break to make up the work. This improved the situation marginally. At least Tony no longer missed a big chunk of reading class every day. And it gave his teacher a breather.

Tony quickly fell into the routine of doing his homework during morning break. Miss Patterson pretended that she had worked out a solution to her student's problem. After all, something *was* being done about it.

It was nearly a month before she saw the truth of the situation. Rather than solving the boy's problem, she had merely found a way to avoid dealing with it first thing every day.

Finally, in a conference with Tony's father, a real solution for the youngster's problem was devised.

It turned out that the youth had been faithfully completing his home assignments every night. His difficulty occurred in the mornings, when he was so foggy-headed that he never remembered to take his papers to school.

With the father's cooperation, a simple solution was devised. As soon as the boy completed his assignments, he folded up his papers and put them into his school shoes. Since he never forgot his shoes, he never forgot his homework anymore either.

Tony had gotten away with doing his homework in class because his teacher lost sight of what the *real* problem was. The basic issue was that Tony was not bringing in his homework daily. The disquieting influence he had on his class's morning activities was the *result* of his failure to do his home assignments. Miss Patterson's original solution was about as effective as the person who furiously swats flies in the kitchen while leaving the screen door wide open. Making Tony do his work during the morning break did *not* get him to fulfill the requirements of the assignment. By definition, homework is to be done at home. It is independent work. Having the youngster finish his nightly assignments during morning break did not convert failure to success.

But by taking the time to define success, the reality of Tony's situation was recognized immediately.

To define success, a teacher establishes a clear mental picture of what satisfactory work means in terms of a particular assignment. Degrees of failure and the myriad reasons for failure are of no interest at all. What requirements must be met in order for the student to fulfill the task successfully?

For every assignment, the definition of success should be clearly stated as part of the process of making the lesson plan. What constitutes success, though decided solely by the teacher, should not be kept secret from the students. If pupils understand the teacher's interpretation of success, they know what their own goals must be. Thus, a clear understanding of success establishes guidelines for both teacher and students. Always, the goal is *real* success, and nothing short of that will do.

In judging a pupil's work, one question clearly distinguishes between success and failure: did the child meet the requirements of the assignment? Reasons, excuses, and extenuating circumstances will be considered later. At this point, the only allowable answers are "Yes" and "No." Success means satisfactory work, done according to the directions, turned in on time. Anything less than this, no matter what the reason, is not success.

Discovering Patterns of Failure

Once a student's lack of success has been recognized, it's important to see how it relates to other aspects of his learning style. When a child fails in a particular task, there is almost always a thread that links it to other failures. This connection can usually be discovered by fitting the unsatisfactory performance into the broader picture of other assignments of a similar nature. This process is much like the mathematical procedure of finding a common denominator.

In classroom situations, the pattern of an LD/ADD student's failure is rarely glaringly apparent. Unless a child's lack of success is deliberately investigated, the common denominator is seldom detected. In dealing with one pupil out of a class of thirty, or a single student out of five full classes per day, teachers must not expect to instantly recognize these patterns as they develop.

After two years in a self-contained LD class, Harry was placed in a regular seventh-grade classroom. The junior high's LD teacher provided the continued therapy he needed. She also worked closely with Harry's teachers. In every subject, the youth's work was adjusted so that success was realistically attainable.

Once a month, all of Harry's teachers met with the LD specialist. At these conferences, the youngster's progress was discussed, his difficulties analyzed, and any necessary corrective measures undertaken. Month after month, Harry was passing all his subjects. The boy's teachers were delighted with his success.

Then, in mid-December, Harry's English teacher announced, "I don't think there's any way for the boy to pass my course this semester."

Harry's other teachers fell silent. Finally, one of them asked, "How is that possible? He's been doing fine for over three months."

The English teacher shrugged her shoulders. "This late in the term, it's highly unlikely that he'll be able to make up all the work he has missed."

After a few minutes of general confusion, Harry's English grades were placed on the blackboard. Week after week, the boy's work and attendance were satisfactory—except for Wednesdays. For the first four Wednesdays of the semester, the LD student had an F; on the last eight, zeros indicated that he'd been absent.

"What in the world do you do in there on Wednesday?" the science teacher teased.

"And how come he misses all *your* Wednesday classes and he never misses *mine*?" the math instructor queried.

Harry's English teacher continued, "We have a quiz every Wednesday. It's our weekly test on spelling, vocabulary, and anything else we've been working on." She paused, sighed in resignation, then concluded, "For weeks, I've been giving Harry zeros, expecting him to come in for makeup tests. It's only in the last few days that I've realized he's gotten so far behind that it's impossible to make up all the tests he's missed."

There was immediate speculation about the youth's English class avoidance tricks. There were questions about notes and excuses and permission slips. Several of those present wanted to launch an investigation into Harry's absences, and the counselor agreed to look into the matter. Although it offered an intriguing opportunity for detective work, the teachers realized such action would be unproductive because, instead of solving the problem, it would merely place the blame on the child.

Everyone agreed that there was definitely something about the weekly English quizzes that made them impossibly difficult for Harry. Pressuring the youth to make up the work seemed pointless. It was decided that the English teacher would do the best she could to help the boy salvage the rest of the semester—and to make sure he was in class on Wednesdays. It was hoped that with a little luck, Harry could pass his English course with a D-.

Things did not turn out well for this seventh-grader. Harry flunked the course. His failure was *not* inevitable—it was caused by an English teacher who did not recognize the significance of a series of zeros.

No one had become alarmed by Harry's situation because the problem was not interpreted as failure. Most of the marks in the grade book were zeros, not Fs. Right up to the end of the semester, the issue looked like a matter of making up work caused by absences. Harry's problem was never identified; thus, it could not be corrected. If the requirements for success had been clearly defined, if the pattern of failure had been noticed and investigated, the seventh-grader's impending disaster would have been obvious. The youth needed to get at least 70 percent on the weekly English quiz. Was he succeeding? No. Every Wednesday, the simple truth could be seen as it was entered in the grade book: Harry was *not* successfully passing the weekly English quiz.

Sometimes, the full failure pattern can't be uncovered without checking with the child's other teachers. Does he neglect *all* his homework? What kind of work does he do successfully in other classes? Former teachers and cumulative folders also offer important clues. Maybe this isn't the first year this child has failed to produce a single book report. In looking for patterns of failure, teachers must not overlook parents as a superb source of information.

> From September to Christmas, twelve-year-old Cal was one of the best-behaved students in his class. His cooperative, cheery disposition made him a natural leader in his self-contained LD classroom. Despite his severe learning disability, the boy could always be counted on to put maximum effort into his schoolwork.
>
> In early January, Cal started horsing around in class and ignoring his work. Soon, he began neglecting his homework. No matter what his teacher did, his attitude continued to deteriorate. Something was terribly wrong.
>
> The records showed a pattern of good grades fall and spring, but bad attitude and lots of trouble every winter. His teacher couldn't find a clue as to why.
>
> Cal's parents came in for a conference. As soon as the teacher explained the difficulty their son was having, the boy's mother revealed the whole pattern. "There's nothing to worry about. It happens every year." She chuckled. "We're between seasons—and that boy lives for football."
>
> Without his favorite sport to burn off frustration and the excess energy associated with his attention deficit disorder, Cal was miserable. Fortunately, he used track as spring training for football. "Between seasons" lasted only from January to mid-March. When track season started, Cal returned to being a pleasant, highly motivated student.

Most failure situations do not require massive investigations involving parents, other teachers, and cumulative folders. Usually, the teacher's own records provide all the information required.

Analyzing the Task

Defining success and finding patterns of failure lead to a clear understanding of a problem. In analyzing the task, attention shifts to finding a solution. This process breaks an assignment into its component parts so that it can be determined which specific elements must be altered in order for the student to succeed. By carefully studying the troublesome task, the teacher bridges the gap between investigative procedures and corrective measures.

Ralph was a very bright eleven-year-old with a disability in writing and spelling. He did satisfactory work in a regular fifth-grade class and was usually excellent in arithmetic. His LD teacher was surprised when the boy's regular classroom teacher sent home a progress report to warn the family that Ralph was on the verge of flunking math.

In a conference with the parents and the LD specialist, the math teacher explained, "I can't get him to do his homework. I've tried everything. I've kept him after school, I've sent notes home, I've talked to him until I'm blue in the face. He's got a million excuses." The frustrated teacher pulled out his grade book. "Look at that string of zeros!"

One-third of the final grade would be based on homework. Ralph was indeed in trouble.

Anytime an LD specialist hears the statement "I *know* he can do it," a warning bell goes off. Immediately, the specialist wants to examine the pattern of failure. In response to the math teacher's insistence on the student's capability, the LD teacher asked, "What kind of homework do you give?"

The teacher offered a casual reply. "Oh, the usual. You know, a page or two of problems, maybe six or eight story problems." It was apparent he thought this line of investigation silly.

"The assignments that he did do," the LD teacher persisted, "what kind of problems were they?"

The math instructor referred to his record book. After running his finger along the column of scores, he looked up with a puzzled furrow in his brow. "Story problems." The teacher paused, stared at the grade book in disbelief, then added, "Nobody likes story problems. Even the best math students have trouble with them." He shook his head. "Those are what Ralph does *well*—those and tests."

The LD specialist asked, "What do tests and story problems have in common?"

The arithmetic teacher snapped his fingers with instant

understanding. "Writing! You don't have to do much writing." Excited with his insight, he explained, "Two whole pages of story problems is seldom more than twelve examples, fifteen at the most. But two pages of practice problems—you're talking about at least thirty-five, forty, maybe over a hundred examples to be copied out of the book and worked." With mounting enthusiasm, the teacher realized that the same reasoning applied to Ralph's success on tests. "There's no copying on tests. He does fine on tests because all he has to write is the answers."

With Ralph's writing disability, it was a terribly long and painful process to copy rows and rows of problems out of a book. It wasn't that the boy didn't want to work the problems. It was just that he couldn't force himself to go through the agony of all that copying.

The solution to Ralph's dilemma was easy. His teachers got him an old, beat-up copy of the math text and let him write his answers in the book. If such a book had not been available, they could have resorted to a daily trip to the copy machine.

Sometimes, a whole class or an entire school has a problem. When that situation occurs, the search for a solution involves the same analyzing process as that used on an individual.

At a newly founded private school for LD and ADD youngsters, complaints about the quality of homework were frequently heard in the faculty lounge and at teachers' meetings. With a "can you top this" sort of humor, teachers swapped horror stories about the outrageous excuses students gave for failing to satisfactorily complete home assignments. Forgot which page, did the wrong page, left the book at school, left the book home, forgot which book, lost the book, couldn't remember the directions, didn't follow the directions, didn't know there were directions. The list seemed endless.

But on analysis, there was an obvious common thread: in a school for LD and ADD children, *all* the students were disorganized. The youngsters needed a systematic remedial program to teach them organizational skills. To do this, the content of the nightly assignments had to be set aside while the children learned to manage the logistics: copy it down, carry it home, bring it back.

When the common denominator is found and failures are neatly linked, teachers sigh, "Oh, of course. Why didn't I see that before? It's perfectly logical—every time this is assigned . . ."

In analyzing specific tasks, teachers should look for the aspects of an assignment that would make success impossible for particular LD/ADD students. Once those elements are recognized and isolated, the work may be altered.

It's always tempting to analyze the child, then blame him as the cause of the failure. "If she changed her attitude, I'd be able to help her." "When he learns to copy his assignments down accurately, he'll quit having all these problems with homework." With such an approach, the investigator gets trapped in nonsolutions. Creative, positive problem-solving techniques are based on recognizing the child himself as a given.

We can't change children directly. We can change assignments and books. Children alter their behavior in response to success and failure.

Training Students to Succeed

The human animal forms habits quickly. All of us develop routine methods for doing everyday tasks, and keep many of them for life. Unfortunately, the fact that the brain habituates does not always work in our favor. We develop bad habits. Children with a learning disability and/or an attention deficit disorder often make a habit of failure. Once caught in that trap, they become helpless victims. To lead them back to success, a retraining process is necessary.

Those who are working to learn a new skill struggle and make mistakes. When parents put training wheels on a child's first bike, they create a situation where a new activity can be practiced without much risk. After repeated experience in the controlled environment, the new skill makes a lasting imprint on the memory. Then it can be performed in any setting.

Retraining LD/ADD students requires a similar process. In order to lead failing students to develop new patterns of behavior that will enable them to learn successfully, modifications must be made to normal teaching procedures. At first, "training wheels" have to be put on the thoughts and actions of LD/ADD students to prevent them from "falling over." Once they get the feel of academic achievement, they begin to believe themselves capable of learning. With this new view of themselves, they can recognize their accomplishments and feel that they have earned them. By controlling circumstances so that children experience a long series of classroom triumphs, teachers give them a chance to make successful learning a habit. Children with a learning disability and/or an attention deficit disorder need more than academic achievement. They have to come to see themselves as having the power to create success.

Expecting Success—And Getting It

When my daughter, Liz, was thirteen, our family went through the upheaval of divorce. We moved and I returned to teaching. During this difficult time, the stress took a heavy toll on Liz. She was caught stealing at school and got into some really serious trouble. The principal insisted that counseling was necessary, but Liz refused to cooperate. With a heavy heart, I enrolled her in a different school.

The situation looked bleak. The new school didn't seem to make much difference. Liz's attitude didn't improve.

To help me deal with the stress that my daughter's behavior was creating, I started working with a counselor. In addition to providing me with encouragement and guidance, the counselor taught me to make "mental movies." In my imagination, I watched my daughter come home from school smiling and heard her tell me how happy she was with her life. It was a short scene that lasted only about a minute. It felt wonderful. I used it every week in my counseling session, and I watched it every night before drifting off to sleep. I knew the scene was not even remotely related to the present reality, but "seeing it" made me feel better, so I continued to use it.

Gradually, the situation improved, and I used the mental movie less and less. After a year or so, I forgot about it.

In the eleventh grade, Liz transferred to an art school. In addition to a full schedule of regular academic classes, she took six art courses every semester. She was a very busy teenager.

One day, Liz came home from school with a big, lumpy brown blob with a gaping mouth and two bulging eyes; she had made it in pottery class. It looked like the head of a very ugly fish. Liz explained, "The teacher told us to make an animal that represents ourselves." Shoving the thing toward me with pride, she added, "This is me."

My heart sank. If that ugly brown thing represented what my daughter thought of herself, we were in deep trouble. As I reached to take it, Liz laughed, "Yes, that's me. Happy as a clam."

I nearly dropped the wondrous work of art. Then, to my surprise, Liz told me how much she loved school. Word for word, gesture for gesture, she stood by our front door and played out the exact scene I'd created in my imagination years before.

Such an event didn't fit with my view of the way the world works. I had experience with the power of prayer, but I couldn't understand how rejoicing in a success not yet attained could have helped create such dramatic results. So I looked for research that could explain my daughter's miraculous change of attitude. As an LD teacher, I had many students who needed a similar transformation. If there was scientific evidence to prove that some process similar to this simple "mental movie" technique could make a difference in my classroom, I was willing to try it.

I quickly discovered that many studies have shown that expectations have a strong effect on outcomes. One that is particularly well known to educators and psychologists was done by efficiency experts at Western Electric. In a series of experiments at the company's Hawthorne Works in Cicero, Illinois, every attempt to increase productivity achieved positive results. Turning the lights up increased productivity. So did turning the lights down! Such puzzling outcomes led to the realization that researchers tend to get the results they expect, a phenomenon now known as the "Hawthorne effect."

In the 1960s, a huge government-funded project equipped

classrooms with the best of everything so that teachers could test a variety of techniques and materials to determine the best method for teaching reading. Some classes made more progress than others, but no one instructional approach stood out as the most effective. A method that worked well for one teacher didn't necessarily work well for others. The key factor turned out to be the teacher's expectations. The project, called the "Twenty-seven Studies," led to a simple but fascinating conclusion: if the teacher believes in the method she is using, it will work for her.

In the 1970s, Robert Rosenthal, a developmental psychologist at Harvard University, studied expectations that are based on faulty information. He selected a group of average students and told their teacher they were gifted. Although the youngsters were no different from their classmates, their teacher expected them to do superior work—and they did just that.

In the "Hunter Point Studies," teachers were assigned deliberately mislabeled classes. Teachers who thought they had the top group led students to make excellent progress despite the fact that the pupils had never before been high achievers. Likewise, children who'd always been in the top group made the small amount of progress appropriate to their teachers' belief that they were low achievers.

It is frightening to know teachers have such a powerful effect on students—especially when no one ever tells them how to control their expectations.

This is the day of "at-risk" students. Large numbers of children are *expected* to fail. They enter classrooms labeled *LD, BD, ADD, EMH, TMH*. Teachers may fight students' problems with determination and have some hope for success, but everybody *believes* these students are likely to become dropouts, not graduates.

Two questions arise. How can educators look at a student who has all the signs of continued failure—poor grades, lack of basic skills, no motivation, bad attitude—and expect success? And how can the student himself expect to succeed?

Teachers need a simple way to gain control over their attitudes. For those who intend to lead LD/ADD students (and a host of other "exceptional" children now placed in regular classrooms as part of "inclusion") to success, a reliable method for building positive expectations is essential.

For the beginner, a very effective method is available through collage-making. Whether the focus is on an entire class or just one or two students, the whole process takes only a few hours, can be done at home, is both pleasant and inexpensive, and offers an easy way to replace expectations of failure with pictures of success. Attempts to help LD/ADD students are pointless if continued failure is anticipated. Some people see collage-making as too simple to be taken seriously. But those who actually give it a try are almost always so amazed by the results that they dare not attribute the success to such a ridiculously easy technique. For those who are determined to change their attitude toward LD/ADD students so that academic success is expected, collage-making is a good first step.

Picturing Success

1. Gather materials, including colorful magazines with lots of pictures, rubber cement, scissors, and a sheet of poster board. Other supplies like ribbon, sequins, and buttons might be useful but are not necessary. Schedule about two hours in a quiet environment for the activity.

2. Go through the magazines and cut out pictures of what successful students look like. Find words and scenes that evoke thoughts of good grades, enthusiastic learners, peaceful classrooms, happy children. Gather illustrations that represent teachers and students having a fabulous school year. Arrange the pictures on the poster board and glue them into place.

3. On the back of the completed collage, write a *very brief* description of what each picture represents. Give the piece a title, then sign it and put on the date.

4. Hang the collage where it will be seen daily. Don't try to explain it to others. When asked about it, say that it's a picture of current goals.

5. Over a period of three to six months, look at the collage often and feel the warm glow of success that would be experienced if all the pictures came true.

The ideal time for collage-making is the beginning of a school year or semester. It can also be useful when dealing with students who are experiencing special difficulties. Realistically, it is appropriate anytime an educator wants to create the positive expectations that open the door to success.

After a teacher has made a few collages and seen how they actually work, she can teach the process to an entire class. Once introduced to the research findings, most students are eager to learn how to take charge of their expectations. It could be the most important thing they ever learn in school.

Ask the Specialist

CHAPTER 7

YEARS AGO, I TAUGHT A REGULAR FOURTH-GRADE CLASS. Students were constantly pulled out of my room for band, safety patrol, student government, private counseling with the school psychologist, hall monitor duties, and so on. "There's *never* a time when I can teach my whole class," I protested through gritted teeth. Bolting the door to keep the intruders from snatching my pupils was a frequent temptation. Reason told me that most of these activities were beneficial to the students involved. Yet in my heart of hearts, I resented *anything* that removed even one of my children from my room.

It took years of classroom experience before I understood that my attitude was not unique. Most teachers feel possessive about their students. "I want *my* students in *my* classroom where I can teach them *myself*." Teachers rarely put it into words, but an outsider can feel their antagonism when passing through the classroom door. Once, a spunky first-grade teacher actually did bar me at the door to her room. With a broad grin and playful tone of voice softening the deadly serious look in her eyes, she said, "Don't you dare come into *my* classroom." For three years, she prevented me from "messing around" with her students. This lady was unusual only in that she openly expressed the possessiveness that all teachers feel.

Any person who enters a classroom for *any* reason is stepping into the teacher's territory. To those who enter her domain, she issues an unspoken warning: "Don't you dare come in here and tell me how to run my class. You don't know as much about any of these children as I do. You couldn't possibly care as much about these children as I do." Her suspicious attitude forms a barrier to effective communication.

The teacher whose territorial instincts make it impossible for her to open the door of her classroom to specialists, and to open her mind to the advice only they can give, will *not* be able to give LD/ADD students the help they need. More than that, any teacher who cannot develop trust and cooperation with special education teachers who work inside her classroom will penalize herself as well as her students. Those who intend to maintain a healthy learning environment while providing appropriate modifications for LD/ADD children need strong support from therapists and specialists. The teachers who get the most meaningful assistance from these experts are usually those who radiate an inviting, open-minded attitude of welcome to all who enter their domain.

Classroom teachers occasionally have contact with specialists from outside their own school system. But most often, they work with LD teachers and psychologists who are part of the staff of their own school. Whether a child is being helped by a private therapist or a specialist from within the school system, the teacher needs to develop a collaborative professional relationship with the person involved. The expert will occasionally ask for information or request permission to observe the student within the regular classroom. For the most part, however, specialists have much to offer and ask very little in return. They have the knowledge that can make classroom success possible for the LD/ADD child. Most of them share this information freely.

If we are going to make the model of "inclusion" work for youngsters who have a learning disability and/or an attention deficit disorder, classroom teachers need to confer with specialists for three reasons: to solve problems that are preventing the student from succeeding; to make major decisions about therapy, program, and placement; and to report progress and adjustments of the program. Most of the exchange of information between experts and classroom teachers will take place in conferences of one of the following types.

Types of Conferences

THE NONCONFERENCE OR QUICKIE

Teachers feel that conferring with specialists usually takes three times as long as necessary. Experts aren't deliberately long-winded. They believe that educating the public is part of their job. Thus, for every two minutes of advice they give, they try to provide ten minutes of theory. In many schools, there is a standard joke: "Ask an LD specialist what time it is and she'll tell you how to build a watch."

For the sake of efficiency, classroom teachers need ways to get experts to present their advice in five minutes or less. The "nonconference" can do exactly that. It is ideal for those common situations in which the teacher needs help with one specific student, the specialist knows the child, and there is one particular problem to be resolved.

The quickie has three basic rules: catch the specialist when she has only a few minutes, don't sit down, and state your question immediately.

The secret of success of the nonconference is to control the setting. In the lunch line, over morning coffee, while reading the announcements on the faculty bulletin board, when passing on the stairs—anywhere paths "happen" to cross, that's the setting for the nonconference. It can work if the classroom teacher breezes into the specialist's room but does not sit down. It shouldn't be attempted if the specialist happens to be in the teacher's classroom. That can lead to a situation best described as being "trapped."

When the timing and setting are right, the teacher should make a direct approach. General openings such as "How's it going?" and "Do you have a minute?" should be avoided. They lead in the wrong direction and waste precious time. The idea is to dive right in. Name the child, describe the problem, ask for suggestions—in thirty seconds or less. "Jim Bolton is having trouble learning to multiply two-digit numbers. He says he gets confused about where to put the numbers he gets for answers. I tried the ones-column, the tens-column, and the hundreds-column routine. It made things worse. Will you give me some ideas on how to help him get it straight?" Chances are, the specialist will take a minute to offer three or four suggestions. And the nonconference will be successfully concluded.

There is, of course, the possibility that the specialist will say, "I don't have time right now." In mastering the technique of the quickie, teachers must guard against interpreting "Not now" as a brush-off. That reply should merely lead to something like "Will you think about it and give me some suggestions when I see you at lunch tomorrow?" The nonconference cannot conclude with an answer of "No." It either ends with a solution or sets a time when the matter will be discussed.

THE TELEPHONE NONCONFERENCE

In getting advice from busy specialists outside the school, the telephone quickie can be a great timesaver. The trick is to catch the person whose opinion is wanted. Secretaries and messages can ruin the technique's effectiveness.

To make the telephone nonconference work, an introductory step must be added. "Dr. Stafford? This is Mrs. Olson, Bobby Kline's teacher at Lake Hills Elementary School. You have Bobby on medication for his allergies." Before stating the problem and requesting help, the teacher must be certain she has clearly identified herself and the child in question.

Those who try the quickie over the phone find that many experts will not give answers off the top of their heads. In refusing to provide the instant information the teacher wants, they politely say something like "Let me check my files and get back to you." When faced with this response, the teacher merely moves to a concluding step in which she and the specialist agree on the method by which they will get back in touch with each other. Leaving a message on the teacher's answering machine is ideal, provided there is a mutually accepted time frame. If the response doesn't come within forty-eight hours, a repeat call is appropriate. The telephone quickie almost always succeeds in eliminating the need for a time-consuming formal conference.

THE SMALL FORMAL CONFERENCE

This conference is "small" in three ways: only two or three people are involved, only a few problems are discussed, and the time limit is thirty minutes or less.

The beauty of this type of conference is its flexibility and casual tone. Though a formal, businesslike atmosphere is necessary (applying all the techniques discussed later in this chapter), the teacher who requests the meeting should approach the specialist with an attitude of "I need a little advice."

The small conference has one unique advantage: it can be squeezed into any of a number of time slots in the school day. The psychologist and the LD specialist might join the classroom teacher for lunch in the workroom. A specialist and the teacher might confer in the classroom before the students arrive in the morning.

It is through the quickie and the small formal conference that the classroom teacher can get the routine expert guidance to make her work with LD/ADD students successful.

THE FORMAL CONFERENCE

The standard one-hour conference is appropriate for making a routine report on a student's progress over a whole semester or year. It is also appropriate for those times when there's a big problem. Any formal conference concerning an LD/ADD child includes the parents, the LD teacher, and all the classroom teachers who work directly with the student. It rarely involves fewer than four people and often includes other specialists as well. Because they cover so many topics and involve so many people, formal conferences require firm leadership. The suggestions made later in this chapter will be especially useful to teachers participating in a formal conference.

THE MAJOR PRODUCTION

This conference is big and very official. It is called when radical action—like settling major disagreements or working out large adjustments in a child's program—is needed. In some situations, this type of conference is required by law.

Major conferences almost always include several high-level officials from the school system, the parents, classroom teachers, the psychologist, the LD specialist, any other specialists who work with the child, and the principal of the school. It is not unusual for them to also include an assistant superintendent or two, lawyers or outside experts brought by the parents, a social worker, doctors, representatives from the special education department, and others. It can get to be quite a crowd. Rarely is the child's classroom teacher expected to provide leadership for such a large production. She is, however, expected to be a very active participant.

Conference Guidelines

All of these conference situations place heavy demands on teachers. Workshops, teacher training, and education courses rarely prepare teachers to understand their role in such meetings, whether as leader or participant. Yet with today's approach to providing services for special education students through "inclusion," it is essential that classroom instructors develop techniques that make it possible for them to communicate effectively with experts. The following suggestions should help.

1. Use and respect home-court advantage.

Except in the case of a major production, the person who initiates a conference usually assumes the role of leadership. Even when acting for a large group (as in a formal conference involving psychologist, principal, specialist, parents, social worker, and classroom teacher), the one who makes the arrangements can assume she'll be expected to preside over the meeting.

The leader's first duty is to issue a clear, specific invitation, naming the child and giving the purpose, the time and place of the meeting, and the time limit. For instance, a classroom teacher might approach the LD teacher this way: "I need to talk to you about Bobby Kline's math. Can you come by my room for about twenty minutes at three o'clock on Wednesday?"

At the conference itself, the person in charge must open the meeting by restating its purpose and time limit, then see that things progress smoothly toward that goal. The advantage of having initiated the conference lies in the fact that the leader gets to bring up the topics she wishes to discuss. The other participants are allowed time, but not equal time.

Obviously, the classroom teacher is not always the one to request or set up a conference. When that is the case, she must respect the other person's right to assume command of the situation. In the role of participant, the teacher is expected to bring appropriate records and materials to the meeting. If Amanda Miller's problem with spelling is to be the topic, the teacher should bring the spelling book, the grade book, and samples of the girl's work. She should also bring the materials needed to explore some of her own concerns about Amanda.

Whether acting as leader or participant, the teacher should employ creative problem-solving techniques as discussed elsewhere in this book.

2. Talk about a specific child.

Even in meetings set up to discuss a particular child, experts sometimes end up presenting a broad explanation of their particular field of special education. This is fine for a lecture but is not appropriate for a conference. Teachers who seek general knowledge can read a book, attend a workshop, or take a course.

To keep discussion centered around a particular student, teachers should ask questions about *only* that student. Don't ask, "Why do LD/ADD youngsters get mixed up when given a whole page of questions to answer?" Do ask, "Why does Joe get mixed up when he has to do a whole page of math problems?" It is up to the conference leader to keep the proceedings focused on the one student whose problems are being considered.

3. Ask specific questions.

Teachers also ought to ask questions that deal with particular aspects of the child's behavior. Experts cannot help in the problem-solving process unless teachers supply them with clear explanations of a student's difficulties and show examples of the work involved.

Questions like "How do I get Billy to do his math?" and "Why does Billy have so much trouble doing routine spelling homework?" force specialists to talk in general terms. "Why" questions are particularly likely to lead to long, theoretical explanations.

Specific questions and statements give experts an opportunity to produce creative solutions suited to a particular child. "Billy has trouble with several types of exercises routinely assigned as spelling homework. Here are two of his papers showing the difficulty he has when told to break words into syllables. Here's one of his typical unsuccessful attempts at alphabetizing." Notice that the teacher specifies the areas in which she feels help is most needed. It is her judgment, her evaluation of the situation, that leads the expert in a productive direction.

4. Ask for *many* possible solutions.

Specialists are famous for coming up with brilliant solutions that are totally impractical. They often appear to have little knowledge or concern about the teacher's tight schedule and heavy work load.

There is a simple way to avoid this dilemma: never ask an expert for *the* solution to any problem. To be on the safe side, it's best not to ask questions that even imply that only one solution is acceptable.

Sample A

Teacher: You've explained why Joe's spatial disability makes him get confused when confronted with a whole page of math problems. What do you suggest I do to make it possible for him to get his math done in spite of this difficulty?

Specialist: I recommend that you assign him the exact same work but present it to him in a different way. If the class is doing a worksheet, give Joe the same worksheet, but have his cut up so that he sees only one example at a time. If the class's assignment is a page in the arithmetic book, have Joe do the same page and number of problems, but have his problems cut out of the book or written on file cards so he looks at only one at a time. (At this point, the teacher decides this expert is a crackpot not worthy of her attention. The solution proposed is superb—for a one-to-one tutorial school charging twenty-five thousand dollars a year. A classroom teacher in a public school needs a solution that is less time-consuming. But any teacher who tries to tell the specialist this is squaring off for a real battle. The secret is in rephrasing the question.)

Sample B

Teacher: You've made me understand why Joe's spatial disability leads him to get confused when confronted with a whole page of questions or math problems. Would you suggest five or six things I might try in order to make it possible for Joe to be successful with such assignments?

Specialist: You might try taking a file card and cutting a "window" in it about the size of a postage stamp.

On a page of math problems, Joe could use the card to reveal just one problem at a time. It would take a little experimentation with the size of the hole and getting him to use it effectively, but it could work. Or you could try ways of folding his paper so that everything but what he's working on is folded back out of sight. (By now, the teacher is enthusiastically taking notes.) Or maybe get him to put a ruler under the row of problems he's doing and use a blank piece of paper to cover the part he's already done. Another approach would be to assign Joe a partner. One of your really good students could probably get his own work done while still helping Joe. For instance, with math, let's say you're going to allow the class twenty minutes to do a sheet of problems. Since you know Joe's partner can do the work in ten minutes, you get him to help Joe while he does his own problems. Give the partner a stack of file cards. Have him copy a row of problems, one to a card, for Joe. While Joe works the first row, his partner does the same on his own paper. Or give the partner a piece of carbon paper to go with the stack of file cards. As he copies the problems for himself, he can make a copy for Joe, one to a card. (At this point, the teacher is totally confident that she can indeed help the child. She's not only armed with several techniques she can try out right away, but the expert's suggestions have given her some good ideas of her own as well.)

Most specialists can produce an incredible number of solutions for every problem that comes up. Teachers should encourage them to do exactly that. A wide variety of possibilities allows the teacher to choose the one she believes most practical for her. Also, it leaves several ideas to fall back on if the one selected doesn't work as hoped.

It's important to note that both samples above involved the same expert. When asked for "the best way," "the right way," "the recommended way," or even just "a good way," most experts come up with *one* idealistic solution. When asked for "five or six ideas," "a list of suggestions," or "several possible solutions," they usually generate a string of suggestions, at least one or two of which is practical.

5. Get answers in language you understand.

The more highly trained and narrowly specialized the expert, the less likely she'll speak simple English. Those in the field of learning disabilities and attention deficit disorder employ terminology from psychology, neurology, psychometry, linguistics, and so on. LD specialists not only speak in this "medico-psycho babble," they *think* in it. Because it's the accepted lingo in their department, campus, or clinic, it's the language they work in. Unless they've had a lot of recent experience with classroom teachers, they think their jargon is understood by every person in the teaching profession.

No matter how profoundly wise the expert's advice, the teacher who can't understand it can't use it. The minute a teacher gets lost in a specialist's terminology, she should tactfully ask for a translation. A simple "Could you explain that in more simple terms?" or "Would you explain what you mean by that?" usually suffices. In asking an expert for further clarification, it's especially helpful to ask how-to questions.

> **Sample**
>
> Specialist: Jim's tendency to perseverate can work either for you or against you. I suggest you find ways to use it to his advantage.
>
> Teacher: How could I do that with spelling? And what do I need to do to make it work for him with math?

When how-to and what-to-do questions are asked, the emphasis shifts to action, and puzzling terminology gets translated into words that describe observable behavior.

6. Get answers that are practical, rather than abstract or theoretical.

Experts often speak in broad terms, expecting their listeners to fill in the details or apply the basic concept to reality. Teachers must learn to beware of abstract answers that sound useful because they're phrased in simple English.

> **Sample**
>
> Specialist: Be sure all of Joe's work is presented to him in such a way that he sees only one question or one problem at a time.
>
> Teacher: Could you give me some examples of how I can do that?

In fighting abstractions, the key word is *examples.* When lost or in doubt, ask for examples.

7. Know the classroom teacher's role in helping LD/ADD students.

When a student with a learning disability and/or an attention deficit disorder is diagnosed, given remediation, *and* kept in a regular classroom, his progress is a *group project.* The psychologist offers advice and supervision based on tests and other forms of formal evaluation. The LD teacher uses specialized instructional techniques to address the child's specific deficits. The classroom teacher, guided by the psychologist and the LD specialist, helps the youngster succeed in the classroom in spite of the learning problems.

The specialists help the LD/ADD child overcome his limitations. The classroom teacher accepts the LD/ADD student as is and works around his limitations. By adjusting the work and not the child, she strives to teach him the skills and subject matter offered in her class. To be effective, she must think of herself as part of a team and view her responsibilities accordingly.

Ask the Child

CHAPTER 8

WHEN FRUSTRATED BY A CHILD'S LACK OF SUCCESS, adults tend to ask unanswerable questions. "What did you do a dumb thing like that for?" "Where on earth did you get that crazy idea?" "When are you going to learn to do this the right way?" "Who told you to do it that way?" "Why didn't you follow the directions?" "How many times do I have to tell you?" Unanswerable questions force the child to accept blame. They prevent him from seeking real solutions. The confession "I did it wrong and it's all my fault" settles the issue. It closes the door to further exploration.

Within each student is the information that can explain the failure. The youngster himself knows more about his problems than anybody else. A technique must be developed to unlock this rich source of information. When a student fails at a particular task, the frustrated teacher needs to ask questions that encourage the child to participate in the search for the cause of the failure.

Preventive Questioning

Every time a teacher prevents failure, she saves herself time, energy, and exasperation. Thus, before assigning a task that might cause an LD/ADD student difficulty, she should take preventive measures. The files, the LD specialist, and past experience can all supply guidance. Often, it's easier to consult the youngster himself. This should be done in private, of course.

> After years of teaching eighth-grade English, Mrs. Roberts knew which aspects of her course created problems for learning-disabled students. When Scott, an LD fourteen-year-old, was assigned to her class, she immediately began using preventive questioning in order to help him avoid academic disaster.
>
> On Friday of the second week of school, Mrs. Roberts assigned the year's first vocabulary test. As the students filed out of the room, she asked Scott to remain after class.
>
> Mrs. Roberts held out a copy of the week's vocabulary words as the puzzled student approached her desk. "I just want to take a minute to ask you about the vocabulary list," she explained. "Can you read these words?"
>
> After glancing at the paper, Scott gave her a suspicious look, then answered hesitantly, "Yeah, sure . . . Why?"
>
> To hear them tell it, eighth-grade boys can do anything. Just to be sure, Mrs. Roberts replied, "Let me see how you do on these. Read the first five for me."
>
> The boy tried but needed help with each of the five. When he finished, he let out a sigh of relief.
>
> The youth's valiant effort made Mrs. Roberts smile with approval. "Tough ones, huh?"
>
> Scott nodded.
>
> "How good are you with a dictionary?" the teacher asked.
>
> The youngster responded instantly. "I know how to look up words." Shuffling his feet, he stared at his teacher as he waited for her next question. When none came, he fumbled for further explanation. Mrs. Roberts's expectant silence made him uneasy, and he didn't come up with anything else to say.
>
> To move the discussion to a different angle, the teacher asked, "Have you got a dictionary at home?"
>
> "Yes."

"Scott, I don't want you to tackle this whole long assignment tonight. How about if you do the first five words? Do you think you could look up that many in one evening?"

The adolescent seemed torn between truth and bluster. He swallowed hard, then mumbled, "Yeah, I guess so."

That wasn't the positive response the teacher was seeking. Instead of considering this a done deal, she questioned further. "Realistically, how many of these are you going to have time to finish tonight?"

The youth stared at the list in silence. He knew that with enough time and determination, he was *capable* of completing the assignment. The question in his mind was whether or not he could get himself motivated enough to attempt something so thoroughly unpleasant. It would take a pretty high level of commitment just to remember to take the book home.

To help her student analyze the requirements of the task, Mrs. Roberts repeated the directions she'd given in class. "You'll have to find each word in the dictionary, write down the word, show how the dictionary breaks it into syllables, and copy down the first definition." Measuring off a chunk of air with her thumb and index finger, she indicated the amount of writing likely to be needed for each word.

When Scott did not respond, his teacher helped him picture the completed task by describing the paper he would have to turn in the following day. "I don't want you to make a commitment you can't live up to," she explained. "Five words would take quite a bit of writing. Probably close to a page." There was no doubt about it—to this teenager, a whole page of written work would be a gigantic task.

Still, Scott did not respond.

"How many of those words can you look up all by yourself tonight?"

Reluctantly, the boy replied, "Two or three?"

"Two at fifty points apiece or three at thirty-three points each—which will it be?"

"Three. I'll do three."

"Okay." The teacher nodded as she wrote that number by his name in her assignment book. Looking back at her pupil, she asked, "Do you want to pick them? Or do you want me to?"

"Read me the first five words again," the boy requested.

Mrs. Roberts complied.

"I'll take *exuberant* and *mediate*," Scott announced. "I like the sound of them." Looking at his teacher, he grinned. "You pick the third one."

"Okay, I'll pick *intuition*. That's a good quality to have. I think you have lots of it." The teacher checked the three words they'd chosen, then handed the list to Scott. "What are you going to do with those three words tonight?"

Without hesitation, Scott replied, "I'm going to look them up, break them into syllables, and write down the first definition."

The teacher knew how unreliable Scott was with homework and didn't want the student's lack of organizational skills to get in the way of his following through on his good intentions. Without any tone of condemnation or condescension, she asked, "What do we have to do to be sure you don't forget to take the book home?"

The boy had a simple solution to that. "I'll write them on a file card and put it in my pocket. That way, if I forget the book, it won't matter."

"Good idea! I'll even supply the file card and write them out for you."

As she handed Scott his vocabulary list, Mrs. Roberts glanced at the clock and drew the discussion to a close. "You've got one minute to get to your next class. I'll give you an excuse so you'll have time to stop at your locker or get a drink."

Note in hand, Scott waved from the door. "I'll see you tomorrow—*with* my three words."

Including the time it took Scott to struggle through reading the five words, the discussion took less than five minutes.

When using preventive questioning, the teacher should have a particular assignment in mind. And she must seek four pieces of information *before* making the assignment:

1. Is the student capable of doing work of this level of difficulty?

2. Can he handle the amount of work involved?

3. What can be done to make sure that his lack of organizational skills won't prevent him from succeeding?

4. Will he be able to get himself motivated enough to actually attempt the work he has agreed to?

The wise teacher takes none of these issues for granted. Her attitude is one of "Can you do this?" She also points out potential pitfalls, creates preventive measures, and says, "Show me." All four of these elements stand out clearly in the example of Scott's first vocabulary assignment.

1. The teacher found that the words were far beyond the boy's reading level.

2. Since she wanted to give him the challenge of trying them anyway, she reduced the assignment to an amount *he believed he could handle.*

3. She did not consider hemming and hawing and shuffling feet to be positive responses, but kept negotiating until the boy said, "Yes, I can do that."

4. Without belittling the boy for his absent-mindedness, she made sure that he had a specific plan to guard against his disorganization. The teacher did not stop until the student made a firm, confident commitment.

If the preventive questioning worked, Scott could be expected to succeed in looking up three vocabulary words each night and passing the weekly test covering the words he had studied. Lack of success on the homework *or* the test would make it necessary for the teacher to apply problem-solving techniques.

Questioning to Solve Problems

Every time failure occurs, an analysis of the situation is essential.

Teachers will sometimes wish to pursue their investigation alone, in the manner described in other chapters of this book. Often, however, it is wise to include the student in the problem-solving process.

To incorporate the child as a full participant in an investigation of his failure, the teacher must establish the appropriate tone and provide strong guidance. It is her responsibility to lead the student step by step through an analysis of the task that gave him difficulty. In exploring a frustrating situation, the student is likely to get emotional and express anger or shame. Teachers who maintain an investigative, open attitude that reflects compassion and respect find it possible to remain calm even when a student gets upset.

To open the discussion, the teacher needs to state the problem and ask the child a specific question that will lead to an exploration of the failed assignment.

Example A

"Scott, you didn't pass the vocabulary test. You got 60 percent. What in the world went wrong?"

Here, we have an honest opening statement of the problem. But the question that follows is unanswerable and vague.

Example B

"Scott, you did so well on the vocabulary test. Sixty percent is almost passing. What do you think we could do so you can do even better next time?"

Here, we have failure covered with syrupy praise to make it look like success. Such statements encourage a child to hide from the truth and prevent even the best problem-solving techniques from being effective.

Example C

"This week's vocabulary test didn't work out as well as we'd hoped. You needed 10 more points to pass.

> What were the things that made the test hard for you?"
>
> Here, we have an honest statement of the problem without any attempt either to criticize the student or gloss over the lack of success. The well-phrased opening question should lead to a productive search for the cause of the difficulty.

Since the teacher is to guide the analysis, she must be careful to keep the search progressing until *real* causes are found. Children often prefer taking the blame ("I didn't study enough") to admitting a cause they're ashamed of ("I couldn't read the words").

> After three years of intensive LD therapy, Stewart confidently launched into his first year of high school. The fifteen-year-old was optimistic about his new school and his chance of success in its college preparatory program.
>
> Although his previous academic problems were documented in his records, Stewart and his parents hoped his new teachers would not discover that he had a learning disability and an attention deficit disorder. The ninth grade was to be the time when Stewart stopped being different.
>
> The first few weeks of school went beautifully. Stewart used all the tricks his LD therapist had taught him. He stayed organized. He worked diligently to be sure he didn't get behind. He forced himself to follow directions and produce papers that were neat. He double-checked all his work for the types of errors he was prone to make.
>
> The youth's efforts paid off handsomely in all his classes but one. Halfway through the first marking period, Stewart's parents received a notice warning them that their son was failing algebra.
>
> When asked about the situation, Stewart snorted, "The teacher's a creep. She wears her hair in a bun and has these weird little glasses. And she always wears the same ugly brown dress." He shuddered dramatically. "I can't stand to go into her room."
>
> Astonished, the youth's father asked, "Are you going to flunk algebra because you don't like the teacher?"
>
> "No. I want to drop the course," Stewart replied.

The family could not seem to get to the bottom of the issue. Every time the subject was brought up, the failing student went into a tirade about "that disgusting teacher."

Stewart's parents had a conference with the algebra teacher. From what they could see, the lady seemed normal enough. She felt the problem was in Stewart's attitude. "He did his homework for the first two weeks of school, found it difficult, and quit trying," she explained.

Looking surprised, Stewart's mother asked, "You mean the problem is that simple?"

In slow, even tones, the algebra teacher said, "Students who don't work don't learn." Pointing to her grade book, she summarized the facts. "Stewart hasn't completed a single assignment successfully since mid-September. He hasn't passed any tests since then either."

Although the conference lasted more than an hour, Stewart's algebra teacher was of no help in identifying the student's problem. The parents had to look elsewhere for assistance.

After calls to the principal, the guidance counselor, and their son's former LD therapist, the boy's parents enlisted the help of Mrs. Pratt, the high school's LD teacher. She hadn't had any personal contact with Stewart. But once the details of the youth's difficulty were explained to her, she agreed to check into the matter.

Mrs. Pratt had a brief chat with each of Stewart's teachers, checked the records, conferred with his former LD teacher by telephone, asked his mother a lot of questions, and then called the boy himself in for a conference. Mrs. Pratt introduced herself to Stewart and quickly made him comfortable with the fact that she was going to help him straighten out the problems he was having in algebra. "I've talked to everyone else involved, and now I want to hear what you have to say." The woman stared straight at Stewart and, with a no-nonsense attitude, asked, "What is going on in algebra?"

"I'm flunking, I guess," the boy replied.

"I'd say that's a pretty fair summary of the situation," Mrs. Pratt said. "And can you give me any clue as to *why* you're flunking?"

"Because the teacher's a jerk." Stewart paused, then added, "And I don't do any of the work."

"So I've heard." The LD teacher nodded calmly. "I understand you have no trouble getting homework done for your other classes. How is algebra different?"

The pupil snapped, "I like all my other classes."

Ignoring Stewart's flippant attitude, Mrs. Pratt pursued her questioning. "Is it that you forget or just never get around to your algebra homework?"

The student responded in a soft voice, "No. I just don't do it." Stewart gave a heavy shrug and shook his head. "There's no way to please her, so why bother?"

"No way to please her?"

Stewart did not elaborate.

Mrs. Pratt tried a different approach. "Can you do the problems?" she asked.

With instant certainty, Stewart answered, "Yes, I sure can. I made a B in prealgebra last year. It was my best subject."

"Without any difficulty?"

"Without *any* difficulty!" Stewart nodded emphatically. "I did all my work. I did good on tests. I got good grades." As an afterthought, he added, "I like math. I thought prealgebra was great."

"What's so different this year?" the LD specialist asked.

As Stewart paused to reflect, the enthusiasm drained from his face. He sighed, then responded flatly, "The teacher."

Since the youth kept coming back to this subject, Mrs. Pratt pursued it. "How does the teacher stop you from succeeding?"

Stewart sneered, "I could do the work if she'd let me do it my way."

"What's wrong with the teacher's way?" she probed.

Stewart's voice intensified as his frustration mounted. "The way she makes us do it, I get mixed up," he said.

Mrs. Pratt countered, "What are some of the things that make you get mixed up?"

"All kinds of stuff." The agitated student used choppy gestures to emphasize his words. "She's got her own way of doing algebra—and it doesn't make sense!"

From the increasing level of Stewart's excitement, Mrs. Pratt knew they were on the right track. "What kinds of things do you have to do when you do it *her* way?"

"She's got a lot of dumb rules about how your paper has to be set up. She's got rules about everything. No talking. No gum. No leaving the room. Everything has to be just so."

"And you can't do that?"

The boy made no reply.

The LD teacher cocked an eyebrow, tilted her head to one side, and queried, "So right answers aren't enough?"

"For this crazy lady, getting the right answer is just the beginning. Then you have to move it over and put it in her stupid 'answer column.'" The teenager snorted. "The woman is so lazy she won't look to find your answers right there where you worked the problem. Oh, no, she's got to find all her answers in a nice neat row down the side of the page." The boy snarled out a few vulgar names, then set his lips in a rigid line and fell into silence.

Unruffled, Mrs. Pratt pursued her line of investigation. "Getting the answers into the answer column gives you trouble?"

"Gives me trouble?" The student's eyes narrowed, his back stiffened, and his fists clenched. "That woman and her answer column are driving me crazy. I *hate* her."

"What happens when you do a page of algebra?"

"I get knots in my stomach just thinking about it."

"But suppose you actually did a page of problems—worked them?"

"I'd get them all right, but she'd mark them all wrong."

"Why?"

"Because I'd forget to copy the answers into the stupid, idiotic answer column." As an afterthought, Stewart added, "Or I'd get them out of order or the numbering would be wrong."

In a gentle whisper, Mrs. Pratt asked, "Or you'd copy them down wrong?"

As though confessing an atrocity, Stewart replied, "Yes," then closed his eyes and let his head drop to his chest.

"And then you feel foolish . . . and stupid."

"And embarrassed," Stewart muttered without looking up. "The teacher makes such a big deal out of it. When she gives my paper back, she holds it up and announces to the whole class, 'Too bad you didn't follow the directions.' She makes a big public display of the baby who's too dumb to get all the little numbers in a neat row." It was obvious the boy had experienced some very humiliating moments.

Knowing they had finally gotten to the bottom line, Mrs. Pratt gently explained that the inability to copy accurately was a common problem for those with a learning disability and/or an attention deficit disorder. Gradually, Stewart calmed down. He found it reassuring to see that someone understood how frustrating it was to make mistakes on a task as simple as copying.

Before proposing some possible solutions, the LD specialist asked one last question: "If you didn't have to bother with the answer column, what grade would you get in algebra?"

"An A," the youth fired back without hesitation. Grinning, Stewart then modified his boast. "I could get a B, easy."

With an understanding of the problem, Stewart's teachers were finally in a position to start working on some real solutions.

Leading a student through such an analysis never follows any neatly organized script the teacher might have in mind. Children give surprising responses that make it impossible to pursue a planned sequence of investigation. But if the teacher persists in asking leading questions and lets the student get angry without growing irritated herself, she can keep the search moving in a productive direction.

Including the child in the problem-solving process helps the student as well as the teacher. It fosters a relationship of mutual trust. It gives the youngster a model of effective troubleshooting techniques. By working as partners, the pupil and the instructor assume joint responsibility for the success of the learning process.

There are times when this straight-from-the-shoulder approach is ineffective. Teachers need to be wary about *forcing* a youngster to face the facts about his learning disability or his attention deficit disorder. The attempt to impose an attitude of openness and honesty may drive a child away. This is especially true of adolescents. They will talk about specific difficulties they are experiencing and ways to resolve the problems, but many of them refuse to be labeled or singled out in any way that implies they are "defective." To a teenager, it is so important to blend in and look like everybody else that almost all special assistance is resisted or even rejected outright. If forced to make a choice, an adolescent will choose failure—to which he is accustomed—rather than allow himself to be made to look different.

By the time LD/ADD youngsters are thirteen or fourteen, the failure pattern is so deeply ingrained that they can't *imagine* themselves succeeding in school. Any teacher who insists that it is possible for them to achieve academic success will simply not be believed. Thus, in working with students in junior and senior high, it is frequently necessary to be discrete to the point of subterfuge.

The straight-from-the-shoulder approach is also inappropriate for students who have not been officially identified as LD/ADD. By law, classroom teachers are not qualified to diagnose or categorize those they suspect of having a learning disability and/or an attention deficit disorder. Yet it is their responsibility to recognize a pupil's learning style and make the kinds of adaptations that will maximize academic achievement. In such cases, it is wise to avoid any hint of labels and stay focused on specific difficulties that can be overcome.

Adjustments must sometimes be made without ever discussing the matter openly with the student. When the situation demands such an approach, the teacher must rely on information gathered by closely monitoring the youngster's level of success and then make appropriate changes.

Ask the Parents

CHAPTER 9

THE PARENTS ARE IN THE KEY POSITION that determines whether or not an LD/ADD child finds success. Teachers, doctors, psychologists, specialists—they come and go. Only the mother and father have responsibility and influence all through a youngster's schooling. They can undermine all the professionals struggling to help their child. They can also create a home environment that is so rich and rewarding that no amount of professional ineptitude damages their offspring. A teacher who does not fully appreciate the role of the parents will not be able to do much lasting good for an LD/ADD child.

Teachers' traditional attitude toward parents is that the farther they stay away from the school, the better. Educators who apply this approach to parents of LD/ADD children are depriving themselves of a very valuable resource.

Mothers and fathers rarely use fancy terminology or refer to standardized test scores. Yet to the teacher who will listen, they can provide a vast amount of useful information. A particular student's problems may be new to this year's teacher. But they're not new to his parents. "He never could understand borrowing and carrying. If he uses his fingers, that sometimes helps." Parents may not know much about educational theories, but they almost always have a good idea of what will work with their youngster.

There are two dangers involved in seeking the advice of parents: they'll tell the teacher more than she ever wanted to know about their child, and they'll try to get the school to make special adjustments that are totally impractical. Neither of these obstacles is insurmountable. Through careful management of conferences, a teacher can gain the information she needs from parents and also avoid becoming entangled in situations that prevent cooperation and communication. The following recommendations will help teachers use conferences as an effective means of working with parents.

Dealing with Both Parents

Mothers may have a job that requires careful planning around a tight schedule, but they can usually be relied upon to make the necessary arrangements for a meeting during regular school hours. However, unless there are major problems, fathers rarely are asked to appear. That is a big mistake.

One-parent conferences put the attending parent in an awkward position. And they cheat the absent family member out of information. No one can go to a meeting on someone else's behalf. It's impossible for others to fully explore all the questions that are of interest to someone who isn't present. It's impossible to give a full report that adequately describes all the topics that were discussed. The teacher's attitude, the appearance and atmosphere of the classroom, and other such impressions can only be gained by being there. It is not fair to expect one parent to act as the family's sole representative in dealing with the school. If two parents live in the home with the child, then two parents should come to the school for conferences. (In the case of divorced parents with joint custody, all of the adults with parenting responsibilities need the opportunity to gain firsthand information through conferences. This definitely includes stepparents and other adults who live with the youngster and supervise his activities. Sometimes, this requires two conferences—one for the father's household and another for the mother's. Such duplicate conferences can place a burden on the school, but it is imperative that all who share the duties of child care and homework supervision be well informed on the youngster's educational status.)

In order to get parents to attend a conference, teachers must make it clear that the presence of both of them is strongly desired and arrange to be available at a time convenient for the parents to come to the school together. Any parent willing to give up a lunch hour or take time off from work is entitled to the full cooperation of the teacher. It is sometimes necessary to reschedule an entire school day in order to free a teacher for an important conference. Such things as swapping gym or library periods with another class, getting an aide to supervise lunch, or trading planning periods with a teacher who's willing to act as a substitute can create the free time the teacher needs while still providing a creative, well-supervised environment for her class.

Speaking Plain English

Technical terminology intimidates and confuses parents. Even simple words such as *structure* and *reinforcement* have specialized meanings among educators. Leave the lingo to the Ph.D.'s. To talk with parents about real children, use real words.

Setting a Time Limit

Keep in mind that in conferring with parents, you are talking about one of their favorite subjects—their child. With the slightest provocation, they'll whip out the baby pictures and tell how cute he was on his third birthday. Proud parents, desperate parents, almost all parents are eager to share a vast array of information about their precious offspring. Parents of LD/ADD children are especially prone to going on for hours about all the trouble they've had getting help for their youngsters. Accounts of their struggles deserve patient understanding. A time limit, however, helps keep these situations from getting out of hand.

The time limit should be clearly established in the note or conversation used to schedule the appointment. It is wise to mention it again at the beginning of the conference. Then it is the teacher's job to set a pace that will allow discussion of all the desired topics within the time allotted.

In the case of phone conferences, the time limit should be specified before ever bringing up the subject that prompted the call. "Mrs. Watson? This is Miss Carling, John's teacher. I need to talk to you for about five minutes. John is having a problem with his math homework." If a longer conversation is desired, use the time limit to make sure the call is not causing serious inconvenience. "Mrs. Watson? This is Miss Carling, John's teacher. Do you have time to talk for about fifteen minutes?"

In addition to giving the teacher a degree of control over the situation, the time limit helps create the businesslike tone that is essential in all conferences.

Establishing an Atmosphere of Mutual Respect and Trust

In every conference, the teacher's first goal is to develop effective communication. This is achieved through words and actions that make parents feel comfortable and optimistic. Parents must be led to an understanding of their role as full partners in a project concerning their child.

Conferences are almost always held in schools. That is the teacher's territory. Inside these institutions of learning, principals and teachers are in charge. They are powerful authority figures.

Very few adults *ever* get over their fear of teachers. They come to school full-grown, successful, even rich and influential, yet they are afraid they will be criticized for some flaw in the way they're raising their child.

> When my own son, Alex, reached his senior year in high school, he had the legendary Mrs. Spalding for physics. The lady was notorious for being a tough, no-nonsense teacher

who could make the most unruly eighteen-year-old cower in terror.

Daily, Alex regaled me with accounts of what went on in physics class. He didn't seem afraid of Mrs. Spalding. But he and I were both fascinated with the methods she used to tyrannize students.

A typical incident involved a boy suspected of breaking the dress code.

"'You got a tie under that sweater?'" Alex squawked in imitation of his teacher.

Pausing, my son explained, "Jeff *had* a tie on. You just couldn't see it under his sweater. He *knew* he wasn't going to get in trouble, but before he could say anything, old Spalding grabbed him by the front of his shirt and shoved him up against the wall."

Pretending to have Jeff by the throat, Alex set his face in a menacing glower. "Then she shoves her nose right up into his face and says, 'You forget to wear a tie to *my* class and we'll have to play house—you'll be the door and I'll slam you.'"

I gasped. "That woman sounds dangerous."

My son shrugged. "Nah, most of it's just bluff."

My eyes were probably as big as saucers as I shook my head and warned Alex, "Listen, kid, if you ever get in trouble with that woman, I am *not* coming to school to bail you out." I was deathly serious.

I knew that teacher couldn't hurt me. But deep down inside, I wanted to avoid meeting her at all costs. Whatever opinions she might have had about me as a mother, I definitely did not want to hear them.

During that entire year, I never set foot in Alex's school. If Mrs. Spalding had called me in for a conference, I'd have been terrified.

Parents have to be treated gently. It must be understood that they enter the classroom feeling nervous and apprehensive. They are afraid they're going to be blamed for something they're doing in the upbringing of their child. They fear they will meet resistance instead of cooperation, condemnation instead of help. Until the teacher demonstrates otherwise, she is thought of as an adversary. Thus, it is up to the teacher to demonstrate her confidence in their ability to work together as equals in the best interest of the child.

By understanding the advantage she holds by the mere fact that she is "the teacher," it becomes possible for an educator to find ways to put parents at ease.

It is wise for the teacher to go to the door to meet parents as they enter the room. This makes them feel they are welcome guests in her classroom. It is appropriate to greet them in the formal manner of shaking hands and addressing them by their surnames. The parents will need time for a moment of light chitchat and some browsing around the room. As they scan bulletin boards and other display areas, they will enjoy hearing about interesting projects, especially those involving their child. Most parents like to be shown their youngster's desk. Some even like to take a look inside. Even after previous successful meetings have established an attitude of trust, the teacher should begin every conference by allowing a few minutes for the parents to survey the classroom and become comfortable with the environment.

The seating arrangement is vitally important. Sitting behind a desk is like sitting on a throne—it is a position of authority. Those who must perch on small, uncomfortable chairs pulled up alongside the seat of power are made to feel like underlings. The teacher who conducts a conference from behind her desk adds all possible weight to the idea that she is the superior in charge. Unless there's some reason to keep parents "in their place," it's best to arrange the seating so that everybody feels like an equal. This can be achieved by pulling together a cluster of student desks. Conferring around a worktable can be effective if the family and school personnel don't sit facing each other like opposing teams. At all costs, an us-versus-them feeling should be avoided.

The larger the conference, the harder it is to organize the seating so that the parents don't feel they're being ganged up on. In a "major production," it is likely that the classroom teacher and the LD specialist will be the only ones with whom the parents are acquainted. A room full of strange faces usually makes parents feel pretty badly outnumbered. In such situations, those who are known and trusted by the family should be seated near them. Since she is the one most deeply involved with both the parents and the child, the classroom teacher is always the one responsible for making her student's family as comfortable as possible in conferences.

As participants arrive for the meeting, they need to be introduced to the parents with a brief explanation of how they fit into the child's educational activities. Usually, the family has had some past experience with those attending, if only from phone conversations, written reports, and formal communications. If the gathering includes more than three or four unfamiliar faces, parents will find it difficult to keep all the names and job titles straight. In such situations, nametags or place cards can be a great kindness.

As soon as all the participants have arrived and the parents have been given a few minutes to get acclimated, the teacher should get everyone seated and assume the role of discussion leader. The first order of business is to state the purpose of the meeting and the time limit. The issues that need consideration should then be named. Having a list of specific questions at hand is essential.

Sample

Teacher: There are three things I need to talk over with you: the weekly vocabulary tests, math homework that isn't getting done, and some behavior problems John's having in the lunchroom.

Mother: We want to talk about that math homework, too. Nobody in our house can ever seem to figure out the directions.

Teacher: Then John has been trying to do it?

Father: Trying? The whole family has been trying. But those directions . . .

Teacher: Yes, they are sometimes confusing. But once John *does* understand what he's supposed to do, does he have trouble with the assignment?

Mother: Not usually. At least if he does, we don't

hear about it until he's done and shows us his paper.

Teacher: What happens when nobody can figure out the directions?

Father: Oh, that's a mess. John usually gets so upset he goes in his room and locks the door. We've had some horrible scenes.

Mother: When he gets really riled up, he ends up not doing any of his homework.

Teacher: That explains several things that have been puzzling me. I can see that the math has really been causing some problems.

Father: Not as many problems as we got with his older brother. Now, Paul . . .

(At the first opportunity, the teacher brings the talk back to the subject of John.)

Teacher: Well, let's see if we can figure out a way to solve John's difficulties. In order to understand and follow directions, a student has to pay close attention to details and keep the elements of a sequence in the right order. Because of his learning disability and his attention deficit disorder, both of these tasks are things John does not do well.

Father: Maybe you could write out an explanation of the directions for *us*. Then, once we know what he's supposed to do, we can explain it to him.

Teacher: I think it would be better for John if we could find a way for him to do his math homework by himself.

Mother: You mean you're going to get us out of the homework business?

Teacher: Absolutely. You've already passed the fifth grade. Now, it's John's turn.

Father: Maybe if you'd go over it with him one extra time before he leaves school . . .

Teacher: That sounds like a good idea. I can take a minute to review the directions with him. I could even have him work the first problem to be sure he understands. Do you think it would help if I wrote my home phone number in the front of his book? Then, if he forgot what he was supposed to do, he could call me.

Mother: That's a great idea. That would get us out of the math entirely.

Teacher: Then we agree. I'll give John some extra help with the directions. And from now on, if he has trouble with his math, he's to call me.

Father: Right. And we'll keep out of it.

Teacher: Now, as to the difficulty with the vocabulary tests. So far this semester, we've had four weekly tests. John has succeeded in passing only one. . . .

Parents need a clear description of what their child has to do in order to succeed. "Every Friday, the children get twenty minutes to do a matching test with their vocabulary words. They have to get a grade of at least 70 percent to pass." At this point, the wise teacher will show the parents the test in question. Once the mother and father see the actual work that caused their youngster difficulty, they can usually come up with helpful insights.

It is important to notice that by being specific and honest, the teacher keeps control of the conference. She accomplishes this by knowing exactly what she wants to discuss, stating the problems clearly, explaining what is needed to achieve success, and keeping conversation focused on the desired subject.

Thinking of Several Possible Solutions

After the cause of the difficulty has been discovered, the teacher and the parents need to explore the possible ways the problem might be resolved. Then, from this list of possibilities, one can be selected that is mutually agreeable.

Parents do not have to take the needs of an entire class into consideration. The teacher does. It's up to the teacher to see to it that all special commitments made are practical for the child *and* for his classmates. Sometimes, in the process of exploring a problem, parents come up with unworkable suggestions (as did John's father in asking the teacher to send a special explanation of the directions for his math homework). These need not cause alarm. In any problem-solving session, most of the proposals are discarded. They are merely part of the thinking process. Unrealistic ideas are never given further consideration after a practical and effective solution is found.

Giving the Parents a Turn

Long conferences should allow time for parents to bring up subjects they wish to discuss. The teacher needs to turn the floor over to the mother and father with a clear statement of her intentions. "We've discussed all the topics that have been concerning me. We have about ten minutes left. Are there any things you want to talk about?" Notice that even here, the time limit is stated along with the invitation.

Parents often have an amazing awareness of how their LD/ ADD child's mind works. Psychologists and specialists can offer knowledge gained in a few hours of intensive formal testing. The mother and father can offer insights gained through the intimacy of family living and long years of personal experience. They are a tremendously valuable resource that must not be overlooked.

PART 3

Developing Creative Child Management Techniques

CHAPTER 10

THERE ARE TWO STANDARD STYLES OF DISCIPLINE: old-fashioned strict and modern permissive. Neither is effective with LD/ADD children. Rigidly following traditional rules and enforcement procedures does not acknowledge and accommodate their differences. Strict disciplinarians hurt them with harsh, inflexible controls that offer no understanding or compassion. Yet giving LD/ADD youngsters complete freedom does not recognize their special need for firm guidance. If the classroom teacher does not create a setting that puts limits on them, they will not make up for the lack by imposing control on themselves.

LD and/or ADD students need a "structured environment." Yet the art of establishing one is generally unknown. The highly organized classroom got sacrificed in the 1920s as part of the process of shifting to our modern, flexible style of child management. Most of our present-day educators have never been exposed to the carefully controlled schoolroom. The techniques involved in creating one have not been passed on through instruction or example.

This chapter and the next will explore ways to develop a structured environment. Through discipline and careful classroom management, the teacher can get students with a learning disability and/or an attention deficit disorder to be cooperative and attentive. Only then can they learn.

Prevention Is the Key

Effective child management is based on prevention and praise. When a teacher thinks ahead, a crisis is not allowed to develop. By carefully setting up the conditions, a teacher can "trick" the child into good behavior, which is immediately recognized and rewarded. Bad conduct can almost always be predicted and counteracted before it materializes. Danger can be foreseen by knowing the child as an individual, recognizing situations that lead him into trouble, and keeping attuned to his varying moods and attitudes.

> A psychologist was called in to observe Jimmy, an LD/ADD second-grader. His teacher suspected that his "impulsive behavior" might be a sign of an emotional problem.
>
> For more than an hour, the specialist sat in the classroom waiting to see Jimmy do something "impulsive." The child did nothing that could even be classified as strange. He stayed in his seat and kept to himself. He didn't get much of his work done, but he didn't cause any trouble either.
>
> By the time Jimmy's reading group was called to the front, the psychologist had about given up on observing anything significant. It didn't seem likely that something noteworthy would happen, but she did want to hear him read.
>
> Jimmy grabbed a chair in the middle of the reading circle. After the usual commotion of getting seated and organized, the lesson began. The children took turns reading aloud. Jimmy had his book open and followed along. With each new reader, he sat up more rigidly in his chair. As his turn drew nearer and nearer, he began to fidget. He shuffled his feet and glanced at the other children. Then the little girl on his immediate left began her page. Jimmy was next.
>
> With no warning, Jimmy jammed his elbow into the ribs of the boy sitting to his right. In the scuffle that followed, the victim's chair flipped over backward.

Leaping to her feet, the teacher shouted, "Jimmy, go back to your seat and stay there!" Then she bent over to comfort the youngster who had been attacked.

Jimmy did as he was told. Once back to his place, he put his head on his desk and remained in that position until reading period was over.

In talking to the psychologist later, the teacher said, "See what I mean? He does something like that in the reading circle every day!"

"Can he read?" the specialist asked.

"How should I know?" the teacher snorted. "He never lasts long enough to get a turn. I never get to hear him."

This seven-year-old child was outwitting his teacher daily. She was failing to prevent the continual disturbance he was causing. And worse yet, in handling his bad behavior, she was rewarding him instead of punishing him. Getting out of that reading circle was exactly what Jimmy wanted. He hated oral reading.

Many preventive measures were possible in this situation. Any of them would have saved Jimmy's victim from injury, spared the teacher the time and energy needed to resolve the crisis, and gotten Jimmy to do his reading. The youngster's oral reading could have been done privately one-to-one. Or he could have been called on first to spare him the mounting anxiety of waiting. Or he could have been required to participate in all the activities of the group except reading aloud. Or he could have been seated at the end of the row with an empty chair separating him from anyone he might harm. Or he could have been allowed to select his passage in advance so he could practice it before reading it aloud in the circle. Or he could have been put in a group that used a book he could read more easily. The possibilities are all but endless. Rather than trying to stop Jimmy's bad behavior, the teacher needed to focus on preventing it entirely. She needed to change the situation into one in which the boy could succeed. Jimmy would still have been different. But he would have felt proud of his satisfactory reading and good behavior. His teacher's praise would have been a pleasant reward.

And the cycle of failure and misconduct would have been reversed. Jimmy would still have been getting special attention, but it would have been positive and satisfying.

1. Call students by name.

Prehistoric man believed that his name was magic. The person who knew his name had power over him and was feared.

Deep down inside, we still feel that way. We do rude things to strangers that we would never consider doing to someone with whom we are even remotely acquainted. It's not safe to break the rules in front of even one disapproving person who can find us later for criticism, punishment, or revenge.

There is safety in anonymity. As long as no one knows who you are, you can get away with almost anything.

Believing that one person gains power over another merely by knowing his name sounds like primitive superstition. It's not. It's a basic part of human nature.

> Some neighborhood children were using my apartment building for war games. I was out of town while most of this was going on. When I returned home, my neighbors told me all about the horrible teenagers who had invaded our building. Ducking in and out of corridors and doorways to shoot at each other with BB guns, they were a real menace. Our peaceful environment had been turned into a battle zone.
>
> Tenants who caught the culprits in the act yelled, "Go play somewhere else!" or lectured, "Those guns are dangerous. You could put somebody's eye out." Such encounters didn't discourage the combatants.
>
> One day, several boys were on the front porch of the apartment house when I came back from doing some shopping. Although I knew the boys didn't live in the building, I felt no suspicion about this blue-jeaned bunch of twelve- and thirteen-year-olds. Most of them scampered off the porch as I approached with my first load of groceries. One darted into the stairwell and bounded up the steps; his partner stayed at the bottom and peeked around the corner of the open door. The boy standing guard had a pellet pistol. And I knew him.
>
> As I fumbled to get my keys out of my purse, I looked

> the make-believe soldier sternly in the eyes and said, "Richard, you take your friends and your guns and get out of here."
>
> He didn't say anything, but his eyes told me he'd heard. He turned and raced up the stairs.
>
> I didn't say anything more or take any further action.
>
> In the time it took me to unload my car, the youths peacefully departed. The war games in my building never resumed.
>
> The power of the name—out of five or six children, I knew *one* by name. I knew where he lived. I was acquainted with his mother and sister. If he didn't cooperate, I had the ability to find him. My knowing who Richard was meant his friends couldn't remain safely anonymous either. If informed of the group's behavior, Richard's mother and sister could have gotten on the phone and shared the news with the families of the others.
>
> No threats or actions were necessary. I had the power to make all their lives unpleasant. Knowing that one name gave me power over the whole group!

The official use of legal identification is based on this same principle. When the highway patrol pulls a car over, the first thing said is "Let me see your driver's license." The nature of the offense is not stated until after the driver's identity has been established and called in to headquarters. People in authority remove the safety of anonymity before taking action. Passports, application forms, references, license plates, dog tags, check-cashing policies, library cards, social security numbers, credit cards—the power of the name is an active principle among us. If I've got your name, I've got the edge.

Smart teachers make it the first order of business to learn each student's name during the opening days of school. It is the basic requirement behind all effective systems of child management and discipline.

When used wisely, the ability to call every student by name is more than a protective device. Using someone's name gives that "personal" touch that communicates caring, intimacy, and love. Any child who is addressed as "little boy with the blue shirt in the back row"—or worse yet, "young man"—knows that his teacher can't possibly understand or care about him. She doesn't even *know* him. It is impossible to feel that other people know us in the fullest sense if they don't know our name.

A great deal of etiquette is concerned with the proper use of a person's name. Titles show respect. Use of surnames is businesslike; it maintains distance and formality. Calling someone by his first name shows familiarity; it implies, "We are friends." We are all sensitive about what we are called—or not called. Children get upset when someone calls them names. So do adults. Ph.D.'s become irate when not called "Doctor." The way a person uses our name has a powerful effect on us.

> LD/ADD children frequently have trouble remembering my name. As often as not, they call me Stevenson instead of Stevens. Sometimes, I correct them. Usually, I just let it go.
>
> I once had an eighth-grade student who called me Stevenson as a deliberate form of disrespect. With defiant eyes and a malicious grin, Carl would say, "Good morning, Mrs. Stevenson," as he brushed by my desk on the way to his seat.
>
> Always, I politely replied, "The name is Stevens."
>
> Without even looking at me, Carl would grunt, "Right."
>
> It was like small skirmishes in a war. Every day, the youth took a shot at me. He started every class with a little victory at my expense.
>
> One day, I thought of a way to return the fire.
>
> Carl's last name was Kudlinski. Most people found it difficult to pronounce, but it had never caused me any trouble. When Carl entered the room that day and shot out his customary greeting, I answered with a broad, sweet smile, "Good morning, Mr. Kudlinskovich."
>
> My improvising on *his* name did not sit well with Carl at all. He fumed in silence for most of the class.
>
> I don't know if the youth ever forgot about it or forgave me, but he never played games with my name again. Hearing his own name deliberately mispronounced had been a painful, personal insult.

What a teacher does with pupils' names sets the tone for their whole relationship. If allowed to be nameless, students remain distant. No bond of trust can be developed. Children are expected to remember and correctly use their teachers' surnames as a form of respect. It causes resentment and hostility when the teacher does not extend the same courtesy in return. It is illogical for teachers to expect cooperation and respect from students whose names they have never bothered to learn.

For those who teach self-contained classes, getting to know 30 pupils is not a particularly difficult task. For those who have five or six classes a day, mastering 150 to 200 names is an awesome undertaking. For those who teach music, art, or physical education, learning 300 to 500 names seems impossible. And for those who substitute teach, the task seems downright ridiculous. Yet the greater the number of pupils, the greater the importance of being able to call each one by name. Art, music, band, and physical education are the classes that most often turn into a "zoo." That's not merely because they are less structured than other classes. It's also a result of students' being allowed to remain anonymous. Any teacher carrying such a massive student load cannot know them all by name and therefore forfeits control.

Nametags, seating charts, and place cards solve the problem easily. For physical-education teachers, a carefully kept record of batting order and position played can serve the same purpose. Seating charts are not conspicuous and do not inconvenience the children, but they do impose a certain degree of regimentation on the class. Nametags allow for a free-flowing environment, but students usually dislike wearing them. Place cards hanging from the front of the desks offer a reasonable combination of flexibility and convenience. Most students will cooperate with a system based on nametags or place cards *if* they are allowed to make their own as an expression of their personality.

Some teachers prefer memory courses, get-acquainted games, or other devices. Any gimmick is fine, but the objectives are always the same: getting to know the students and being able to call each one by name, *fast*.

2. Make realistic demands.

Everyone has limitations. The perfectly rounded person capable of fulfilling every expectation simply does not exist. There are lots of grown men who can't sit still and lots of perfectly normal mothers who have trouble remembering where they put the car keys. Teachers have pet peeves, subjects they hate to teach, responsibilities that require the use of skills they don't have, and days when they're sure that there must be an easier way to make a living. No one can live up to all the ideals and hopes of self and others.

In establishing a code of conduct to be imposed on their students, teachers must set high but *achievable* standards. Unrealistic goals do not inspire; they overwhelm and kill motivation.

By demanding only what is possible, old-fashioned discipline can be tempered by modern respect for the child as an individual. In setting up reasonable expectations, the teacher must make the student's uniqueness the main consideration. Yet once the rules have been established, the disciplinarian's firm enforcement methods provide the consistency upon which a structured environment is founded.

Setting standards is an especially difficult task when dealing with students who have a learning disability and/or an attention deficit disorder. It's hard to tell what is impossible for them. Things they can't do usually look like things they could do if they really tried. This is further complicated by their on-again, off-again pattern. Things they could do yesterday are not necessarily possible for them today. Teachers find it a constant challenge to recognize LD/ADD students' limitations and make appropriate adjustments.

It is vitally important that the standards of behavior demanded of LD/ADD children be realistic. They become overwhelmed very easily. They handle frustration poorly. Expectations that they cannot meet produce dramatic and devastating effects. For them, it must be one day at a time, gradually building and growing from one accomplishment to another. They can achieve our loftiest goals if we lead them forward one step at a time.

I once had an unruly self-contained LD class of fifth- and sixth-grade boys who always wanted to play football during their physical-education period. But they couldn't run more than a few plays before someone started a fight, which then erupted into a free-for-all.

When the fists and foul language started flying, they were brought back to the classroom to sit out the rest of the period in silence. The longest lecture they ever got was "You may play football. You may not fight."

After a series of these abruptly abandoned games, the boys asked permission to set up rules to prevent fights. They wanted to stay outside for the full physical-education period. The self-imposed regulations improved the situation so that fighting broke up their game no more than two or three days a week.

The children had one simple goal: getting that full gym period.

I had only one objective: no fighting.

The boys revised their rules and struggled to referee more justly. Their determination gradually produced acceptable playground behavior almost every day. By January, individual outbursts were no longer triggering brawls. The no-fighting rule was enforced by assigning offenders two to five minutes in the penalty box. Flashes of anger grew rare. The boys often went a whole week without having even one student sit out part of the game. Day after day, the children refereed their own games and settled their differences peaceably as I sat on the sidelines enjoying the fresh air.

During February, our class started a behavior modification program to perk up classroom performance and study habits. The boys needed to find a realistic reward to buy with the points they would be earning. The first suggestions were the usual jokes of "How about a color TV?" and "You could take us to the beach for a week." Then, one by one, the boys came to agreement. They wanted to go out and play football for the last part of their twenty-five-minute lunch period.

I protested immediately. "That means I'll have to give up part of my lunchtime to come out and supervise."

"No, you won't. We can take care of ourselves," they countered.

I reminded them that in September they had been the only class in school that couldn't make it through five minutes of football without getting into a fight and being brought in. Despite their changed behavior, there was still a long list of reasons why twelve rowdy boys might end up in trouble if left unsupervised on a playground full of children.

They held their ground. They were willing to work for the privilege, but they wanted a chance.

The behavior modification plan was so demanding that it seemed unlikely the prize could be attained in the three months left of the school year. Just to be on the safe side, I requested the principal's permission. A brave but wise man, he advised, "Be sure they've really earned it, then let them give it a try."

With a juicy incentive, the program began. February and March flew by. The boys' classroom performance and behavior were fantastic. The points mounted rapidly. Their goal was reached before the end of April!

As the day of reckoning approached, I warned the principal. He stood his ground courageously. I was tempted to back down.

When it came time for the big payoff, I shuddered as my class left me in the lunchroom and headed out the door. It was all I could do to finish eating and calmly walk back to the classroom. My mind kept flashing pictures of blood and mayhem. I could just see some angry teacher charging down the hall dragging one of my boys by the scruff of the neck.

But nothing happened. The students did fine. They raced back to the classroom the minute the green flag appeared in the window to signal them to come in. With proud smiles of satisfaction, they hurried to their seats and prepared for work.

For six solid weeks, the boys earned the privilege of going outside after lunch every day. Never once did they abuse it. It was such a remarkable accomplishment that the principal took the time to come to our classroom to compliment them on their outstanding behavior.

They had achieved something special—one tiny step at a time. There had been no lofty hopes of making them models of good sportsmanship. All of us had goals that were short-sighted and totally selfish. I was determined to eliminate fights during gym class. They simply wanted to stay outside and play.

By aiming at a level of good behavior they *could* attain, these LD/ADD youngsters worked their way from one small victory to the next. Each new objective was difficult but

> possible. Every small success had a reward. At the end, totally by accident, they stumbled into achieving what had originally been impossible.

LD/ADD youngsters will turn themselves inside out to accomplish a goal that means something to them. They crave success. No objective is too high if they are convinced they can succeed with the step that is required today.

Teachers should have impossible dreams—but keep them to themselves. They should tell the children only that part of the goal they can achieve today, then let successes build one on top of another.

3. Don't ask senseless questions.

In a classroom, the teacher is in charge. When a student's behavior needs correction, this authority must be communicated. This is easily achieved through body language. The teacher raises herself to her full height, squares her shoulders, sets her face in an expression of sternness, levels her gaze at the offender, and speaks the official word.

If the disapproval is expressed as a question or in a questioning tone, the air of authority is destroyed.

"John, will you please put that toy away and get back to work?" What if he refuses? Such questions give the child an option. Good behavior is *not* optional. Discipline does not offer the student a choice about whether or not he will live within reasonable standards of conduct. If rephrased without the "will you," the above request could even be delivered in a gentle tone of voice and include the word *please* without compromising the teacher's authority.

Unanswerable questions are a still more destructive form of teacher communication. They kill the effectiveness of discipline the moment they are spoken. They remove the tone of authority *and* make the student uncomfortable. "John, why are you still playing with that toy when I told you to put it away ten minutes ago?" How can the child respond without getting himself into further trouble? There is no acceptable answer. The child is caught in a power play designed to humiliate him. There's a huge variety of these cruel unanswerable questions available to those who love to make a child squirm. All of them are unethical. They are meant to trap a youngster and make him feel ashamed and powerless. Children resent them bitterly.

> David's year in the ninth grade got off to a bad start. He wasn't getting as much special instruction and assistance as he needed for his severe learning disability. The classroom teachers at his new school didn't understand how to work with him. Although he'd been the hero of his junior-high football team, his new coach didn't appreciate his talents and disliked his attitude. As the youth's frustration mounted, his allergies flared up and forced him to miss a lot of school. Daily trips to the doctor for shots made him miss most of his first-period class every day. By early October, things were a mess.
>
> Accustomed to working closely with her LD son's teachers, David's mother repeatedly called the school to request a conference with all of the youth's instructors. But her pleas fell on deaf ears.
>
> The situation grew steadily worse. The football coach made life miserable for the boy. David got fed up and gave up all involvement in sports, took up with a new crowd, and became a serious discipline problem at home. He hated the world and everybody in it. His frantic mother knew the whole mess stemmed from her son's extreme frustration in school. But try as she might, she could not get any cooperation from administrators who had the authority to help.
>
> In midwinter, David got arrested. The offense was quite serious, but the juvenile court was merciful because he was a first-time offender.
>
> At David's trial, it came out that he had a severe learning disability and an attention deficit disorder and that the school had refused to cooperate with his mother's request to bring a private specialist to confer with his teachers. The judge probed for all the important details, then issued a stern order to one of the court officials: "You call the lawyer for the school system the minute we're finished here. You tell him to get in touch with this boy's principal to get a conference set up within the next twenty-four hours—or I'll see him here in my court tomorrow."

After so many months of useless attempts, David's mother got to meet with his teachers by court order. The meeting was well attended. Crowded around two conference tables were the principal, the assistant principal, the guidance counselor, the LD teacher, two high-level administrators from the school system's Department of Special Education, several other administrators, David's probation officer, the youth himself, his mother, and an outside LD specialist. Only one teacher came! And the football coach was conspicuously absent!

For more than an hour, the educators took turns defending the system and blaming the youth for his lack of success. From their point of view, everything possible had been done to help the boy; all the problems and failures were his own fault. Over and over, David was told, "You have a bad attitude. Until you change your attitude, there's nothing we can do."

The condemned teenager sat there in silence. When accused of chronic and deliberate tardiness, he did not defend himself. Yet every one of his thirty-six tardy reports had a doctor's excuse.

After everyone had thoroughly berated the boy, it was decided that the school didn't need to make any changes on his behalf.

The principal had sat through most of the meeting with narrowed eyes and firmly set lips. At this point, he took the floor to lead the conference to its conclusion. A hushed silence fell over the room as he talked with cold authority to his troubled student. "David," he began, "I want you to look around this table at all these people here."

The boy glanced up briefly, then returned his gaze to his hands.

After a long, dramatic pause, the principal continued, "Son, there are a lot of people here, busy people who have important work to do and very full schedules. All of these people had other things they could have been doing this afternoon—but they're here." Again, he paused to let silence add impact to his words.

The color was rising in David's face. He did not look up.

The principal leaned on the conference table to stare at the student. "David, I want you to answer one question for me: why are all these people here? You think about that for a minute, then tell me. Why are we all here today?" The man sat back in his chair and let the room fall into a thick, uncomfortable silence.

All eyes were on David. His face was glowing red. As he slumped forward with bowed head, the muscles of his cheeks twitched with the energy holding his jaws clenched and his features rigid. He knew exactly what he was supposed to say. But he couldn't bring himself to do it. He also knew the truth of the situation. But he didn't dare speak it. Instead of shouting, "You're here because you didn't care enough about me to have a meeting until the court ordered you to do it!" he lowered his head further and said nothing. When the principal repeated the question and forced a response, David said, "I don't know."

He felt an indescribable hatred toward the man who had tormented him with that unanswerable question. At that moment, David detached himself from any further cooperative dealings with "the system." Drugs, truancy, larceny, prison—he chose to get his education in ways that demonstrated his total loathing for those in authority.

Whenever a student is asked a question, it should be mutually understood that the response will be heard open-mindedly and given genuine consideration. Questions should be used only to lead, guide, and help. They can be a great tool in developing understanding.

When we create situations where it is dangerous to speak the truth to authorities, we kill a child's faith in the system.

4. Avoid lectures.

LD/ADD children are immune to lectures. They live in the world of the senses. They are action-oriented. Avalanches of words just roll right by them. Many children with a learning disability and/or an attention deficit disorder get lost in long speeches. Logic, analysis, reasoning, looking at the past, presenting abstractions—none of these fits with the way their minds work. Lectures turn them off. Any method of child management that relies on long verbal explanations is not likely to work with LD/ADD youngsters. Long, logical, complex monologues which eloquently explore the significance of the rule that has just been broken are a form of punishment. They are boring. For most children, boredom is very unpleasant. But it doesn't produce changed behavior. Most students think of a lecture as "paying the price." To them, it's an unspoken agreement: "I'm willing to listen to your speech in return for getting to do what I want."

> Gentle, soft-spoken Miss Blackham did her student teaching in my self-contained LD class. She had never been around children before. All her ideas about them came from books. Miss Blackham really believed she could manage an LD class without ever raising her voice or putting her foot down! She thought that the only truly effective method of discipline had to be based on developing understanding. In a discussion, she told me, "Correcting bad behavior is merely a matter of getting a youngster to understand why some action is offensive. Punishment should never even be necessary." The young lady shook her head and concluded, "Once a child knows *why* he's supposed to act in a particular way, he'll do it on his own."
>
> It made a great theory.
>
> In practice, it didn't work so well. Miss Blackham was very conscientious about applying her method of child management. Yet the children walked all over her. They didn't take her discipline seriously.
>
> One morning, I was grading papers in the back of the room while Miss Blackham taught the reading lesson. She and the students were playing a phonics game she had spent weeks designing.
>
> From her position in the front of the room, the student teacher couldn't see that Marty, one of the boys in the back row, was busily mutilating one of the exquisite players' cards she had crafted. I walked over to the youngster to investigate.
>
> The boy looked up at me, rolled his eyes, shrugged his shoulders, and whispered, "Boy, am I going to hear about this one, huh?" We both paused to think about what the student teacher was going to say.
>
> Marty already *knew* he was doing wrong. As far as he was concerned, the detailed explanation Miss Blackham was going to give him was nothing more than a boring lecture. Knowing it was coming did not do a thing to help him control his behavior.

As a means of rewarding success or good behavior, the lecture doesn't work very well either. Praise that is too lavish makes children feel embarrassed.

> Elaine, an intern, was working one-to-one with fifteen-year-old Jack. The boy was extremely self-conscious about his poor reading and needed lots of encouragement. His young teacher tried to recognize all of his small successes and reward them.
>
> But Elaine thought praise had to be in the form of a long, gushy speech. "Jack, I'm so proud of you. You just read that page with almost no mistakes. Your reading has gotten so much better. It's really wonderful to see you make all this progress. . . ." The intern poured out paragraphs of approval.
>
> Each extravagantly applauded success made Jack more uncomfortable. With a look of agony, he sank lower in his chair and glanced at me out of the corner of his eye.
>
> The long lecture was terribly embarrassing to the teenager. Success was actually causing Jack pain!

Whether correcting or praising, it's wise to use as few words as possible. Keep it specific and brief. Success needs to be recognized and appreciated. "Paul, that was outstanding lunchroom behavior. You stayed in your seat, kept your voice low, and ate like a gentleman. Good job." Corrections are best made with similar exactness and brevity.

5. Avoid threats and promises.

We've always been told, "Don't make a threat if you don't intend to follow through." That's decent advice. But it's only a partial truth. Yes, if a specific threat is made and a child persists in the objectionable behavior, it is important to carry out the pledged action. Promises must be honored in the same way. If a student is promised something as a reward, the teacher must follow through regardless of how much she regrets having made a foolish offer.

Since the teacher's word must be treated as a solemn bond, it's better not to make threats or promises in the first place.

I had gotten tired of my students slouching, clomping, shuffling, weaving, shoving, tripping, stumbling, and straggling down the halls. No matter what I tried as an incentive to get them to change, they continued to look like some ragtag band of thugs.

One day, after an especially ghastly procession from the lunchroom, I exploded. Snorting with fury, I concluded my tirade by giving up on them in disgust. "I quit!" I shouted. "It's hopeless. You guys *can't* walk down the hall like gentlemen. I give up. If you're ever going to learn to walk like gentlemen, the army will have to teach you."

The students had a surprising reaction to my statement that they were hopeless cases. Although they still looked guilty and ashamed, most of them drew up taller in their seats and squared their shoulders in defiance.

After a long silence, spunky Bobby looked me right in the eye and asked, "What'll you give us if we can?"

"Nothing," I snapped. "Because you *can't*! Even if you really *wanted* to look sharp in the halls, you guys don't know how!"

I was being deliberately insulting, but the class ignored it completely. Bobby cheerfully pursued his idea of striking a bargain. "A trip to the Soda Shoppe to get one of those nine-dollar twenty-three-scoop sundaes?"

"I wouldn't buy you slobs an ice cream cone," I sneered.

Following Bobby's lead, Larry took over the negotiations with a revised proposal. "Next Friday, after one week of being great in the halls, you take us to the Soda Shoppe. We pay the nine dollars ourselves."

They had trouble with spelling and math, but they sure knew how to wheel and deal.

But it was pointless. I was convinced that outside the four walls of our classroom, it was not possible for them to act like gentlemen. My anger was gone as I gave them my honest opinion. "It'll never happen. You guys are kidding yourselves. You've never even been *decent* in the halls. What makes you think you can act *excellent*?"

With wide eyes, Larry asked, "Deal?"

"It'll never happen," I protested.

"Maybe we'll have a miracle. Deal?"

Smugly certain of their failure, I nodded. "Deal."

There's little need to describe the gory details. For one solid week, those twelve-year-old monsters were angels. Other teachers commented on their fantastic behavior. The principal even noticed their conduct in the lunchroom and the halls. I wanted to wring their adorable, well-mannered little necks.

They brought money. They brought permission slips. They knew I'd keep my word. And they knew I'd hate doing it.

Despite the fact that I felt foolish, I had to explain the situation to my principal and get his permission to take my class off the school grounds. After telling him how I'd gotten myself into such a mess, I concluded, "I climbed out on this limb and they are in the process of gleefully sawing me off."

The principal chuckled, then offered a piece of wisdom from his years of experience as an educator. "There is a certain perversity in children that makes them delight in watching teachers eat their words." Then he kindly gave our outing his blessing.

I was too embarrassed about our frivolous field trip to ask anyone to help with transportation. It took all afternoon Friday for us to walk to the distant ice cream parlor and back.

Living up to rashly made promises is more than an inconvenience. It makes students lose confidence in their teacher by proving she can be manipulated. Children always think they can outwit the teacher. But every time they actually do so, they lose respect for her.

Threats are equally dangerous. They do damage even if they never have to be carried out. The teacher undermines her authority every time she gives dire warnings of what will happen if some particular behavior continues. Since she is reacting with words and not action, she is postponing. Putting something off until later communicates weakness. It implies that the person in charge prefers not to deal with the problem.

References to a higher authority are often included in threats. "One more crack like that, young man, and you're going to the principal's office." This is a doubly destructive tactic. The hope is that the misbehaving youngster will be impressed by the power of the person to be called upon if the need arises. But the main message is "I can't make you behave." An authority who has that attitude will not be taken seriously. She shows children that she doesn't really expect good behavior. And she gives youngsters a clear-cut choice. By announcing the penalty in advance, the teacher indicates her belief that the offensive actions might continue. In dealing with children, it's dangerous to make them think bad behavior is expected. More often than not, they live up to expectations.

Threats and promises weaken the teacher's position by shifting the power of choice to the child. If the student knows the cost of his actions in advance, he can make his own decision about whether or not he'll cooperate. Acceptable conduct has been made optional. By forgoing the trip to the Soda Shoppe, my class could have continued to clomp around the halls in their preferred sloppy fashion.

Suppose Todd is sitting in the back of the room making loud twanging noises with a rubber band and the teacher tries to correct him by saying, "Young man, you stop making those noises or you'll get an extra row of math problems added to your homework." For only ten extra minutes of homework, Todd can buy the right to disrupt the class, demonstrate his power over the teacher, and prove he's one tough, defiant dude. To him, it might be worth it. For a few minutes, he can have control over his teacher and earn the admiration of his peers.

Children with a learning disability and/or an attention deficit disorder often have a strong defiant streak. Many of them are officially classified as "oppositional." Any behavior management system that lets them *choose* between the desired action and some predetermined consequence will not work. They watch for opportunities to say, "No, I won't—and you can't make me." And they know they're right. Somehow, they have figured out "the system." They know that as long as they're willing to pay the penalty, they can do anything they want. That knowledge gives them an alarming amount of power!

Promises and threats are intended to trap the child. Usually, they put the child in control and trap the teacher.

6. Make rules broad.

To make a child management system effective, it is essential that *all* the rules be enforced vigorously. This requires determination and constant vigilance. Because of limitations on time and strength, wise teachers make as few regulations as possible. They conserve their energy. They do not waste their ammunition on minor irritants. Either an issue is important enough to warrant strong, consistent action or it's insignificant enough to be ignored. Teachers need to pick their issues carefully and establish only those regulations that can be wholeheartedly enforced.

By defining major categories of conduct, it's possible to set up broad, easily understood, totally enforceable rules for classroom behavior.

One major area requiring firm regulation is property rights. If you don't own it, don't touch it without permission from the owner. This plain statement covers all those awkward situations where students protest, "I was only going to borrow it" or "I didn't mean to lose it" or "It was already cracked before I got it." This one rule eliminates the need for a host of smaller ones: you may not go into anyone else's desk; you may not take anything from another person's locker; you may not get materials out of the cupboard without permission; you may not remove anything from the teacher's desk; you may not borrow anything without asking the owner's permission; you may not use the tape from the supply closet. Without strict, broad guidelines governing respect for others' property, a teacher can run herself ragged playing policeman.

Another needed category of rules centers around maintaining a quiet classroom atmosphere. Students must understand that they will not be allowed to prevent others from getting their work done. This can be attempted through a set of regulations covering spit wads, whispering, humming, roaming the room, using the pencil sharpener, throwing paper airplanes, slamming books, calling out to the teacher, and so on. Or it can be viewed as one rule: no one has the right to disturb his classmates.

The single-regulation approach allows teachers to determine

the areas in which they concentrate their energy. And by strictly enforcing basic rules, teachers can back off on matters of less significance. There is no sound reason for the guilty conscience caused by letting a child get away with something. Some issues are better ignored. Teachers often disturb their whole class in the process of correcting a student who wasn't bothering anybody. Classroom tranquility should not be broken by loud calls of "Harry, get back to work." The child who is snoozing or quietly amusing himself does not require immediate correction. Unless a student's actions are causing a disturbance, teachers are wise either to ignore the infraction altogether or to postpone criticism and correction until it can be whispered to the offender privately.

Praise must not be neglected. Broad rules are especially good for providing increased opportunity for praise.

> Chuck was the bully of the entire school. He was famous for blackening eyes and bloodying noses. The big, muscular youth with the bad temper was in my eighth-grade LD group. In addition to his learning disability, Chuck had a severe attention deficit disorder and was extremely defiant.
>
> At the beginning of the year, the students set up regulations to govern class conduct. The rule forbidding fighting merely said, "I will respect the physical well-being of others." I wasn't at all sure Chuck would abide by such a gently stated regulation. Brawling teenagers are usually thought to need a tougher discipline policy.
>
> On the last day of school before Christmas vacation, one of the other boys in the class made a crack about the shirt Chuck was wearing. The remark was both crude and totally uncalled for.
>
> Chuck and I both responded immediately. He leaped to his feet with his fists clenched. I called to the youth who had offended him, "Joe, I will talk to you in the hall." Not sure what Chuck would do, I walked to the door and held it open—waiting.
>
> Joe's eyes darted between his infuriated classmate and me. A moment of electric silence filled the room. Then Joe turned and walked toward me at the door. Chuck let him leave unmolested.

After the issue was settled, apologies sincerely offered and accepted, I had a brief private exchange with Chuck.

Anybody with Chuck's quick fists could have found dozens of ways to get back at Joe. But they all fell under our one broad rule. It was with real pleasure that I complimented the notorious troublemaker. "Thank you for respecting the physical well-being of Joe. I know you could have taken him apart. I'm glad you didn't."

The big, burly youth grinned. It was probably the first time in his life that he'd gotten recognition for *not* hitting.

In selecting broad categories of rules to govern their students, teachers make a commitment to strictly enforce a basic code of conduct. But they also free themselves from getting excited over picky misdeeds that don't really matter. For most classrooms, effective child management can be maintained with ten rules or less.

Broad regulations are especially useful when the teacher is governing the conduct of LD/ADD children. If it is a cosmic law that all students must stay squarely seated at their desks, the hyperactive youngster cannot obey. But if the rule emphasizes not disturbing classmates, the overactive child is free to kneel, stand, crouch, lounge, or perch as long as the movement doesn't bother others. Broad regulations give the teacher and her pupils the latitude to accommodate individual differences while still living by the rules. This type of child management system provides the unusual blend of extra structure and extra freedom that children with a learning disability and/or an attention deficit disorder need.

7. Use imaginative rewards and threats.

By strictly adhering to a system of preventive measures, a teacher can get children to abide by a few broad rules. But merely avoiding anonymity, impossible demands, senseless questions, lectures, and threats is not enough. The teacher needs new weapons. She must have surefire tactics that put authority into her words. Day in and day out, the teacher needs to communicate, "I am in charge of this class. If you misbehave, you have to answer to *me*."

It's much easier to get children to *want* to behave than it is to *make* them behave. Thus, the mainstay of the teacher's disciplinary arsenal should be incentives, reminders, and motivators that focus on the positive. Rather than warning about the bad, talk about the good. Don't caution, "Anybody who starts a fight on the playground will get sent in." If that is the rule and everybody knows it—and the teacher is faithful about enforcing it—no warnings are necessary. Instead, emphasize what is desired: "Children who play according to the rules will get the bonus of a pleasant smile from a happy teacher." Teachers should find a phrase that speaks to students about their high expectations and their pleasure in the children's success. Mr. Custiss was the best disciplinarian in our school. When he turned his class loose for recess, he'd beam with love over his little flock as he made a simple request: "Make an old man happy—play nice." The children rarely disappointed him.

Through properly devised motivators, children are reminded that it *is* possible to please the teacher. They are told how to do it in a given situation. And they're given a reason for wanting to cooperate.

Teachers can add depth to their incentives through the offer of ridiculous rewards. Children find it fun to hear, "Good lunchroom behavior will get you your very own Saturn rocket for the weekend." The outlandish promise really says, "You'll do it because I say so." But it says it nicely, with good humor and no confrontations. It eliminates the need for bullying or pressuring.

> I was always very strict about homework. Every student had to do all his homework every night. Failing to complete the nightly assignment was simply not allowed.
>
> Every once in a while, some student would pester me about my policy, asking, "What's in it for me?"
>
> Sometimes, I bored such protesters with a truthful "You get an education, you get my approval, you get a check in the grade book, you get the acceptance of your classmates, you get to feel good about yourself. . . ."
>
> Other times, in response to the proverbial question

"What'll I get if I do my homework?" I'd respond, "How about a trip to Europe?"

Most children understand the message behind offers of outrageous prizes and threats of ridiculous punishments. They know that the teacher has offered them something that's fun to dream about but far too fantastic to expect in reality.

Offering a ridiculous reward is usually a two-step process. First, state the real goal clearly and simply: "You act like gentlemen during the assembly, with no horsing around in the auditorium, and . . ." Second, tack on some wildly extravagant prize: ". . . your tickets to the Super Bowl will arrive in the next mail." In the daily routine of child management, this technique can be used regularly. Silly as it sounds, it is a powerful preventive disciplinary measure.

It isn't always possible to focus on the positive. Sometimes, a situation is too grave for the offer of any type of reward, whether serious or in jest. When disaster appears imminent, it's time for the ultimate weapon: "the Fonz technique."

The 1970s situation comedy *Happy Days* featured Henry Winkler as "the Fonz," a tough-guy high-school dropout with a heart of gold. He was the smallest of all the youths in his TV gang, but he always got his way. He never hit anyone. He never whined. He never bullied. Yet his friends would do anything for one small sign of his approval. Everyone, adults and teenagers alike, treated the Fonz with respect. Everybody wilted at the slightest indication of his disapproval.

How did he do it? What gave him control over those around him? It was probably the result of his absolute honesty, his total consistency, and the power of the outrageous threat.

No one *ever* crossed the Fonz and got away with it. He was *never* too busy to stop everything and demand respect. He always stood firmly on his own authority. He never looked to someone else to protect his interests. The Fonz never said, "If you do that again, I'll tell your mother." Whenever his rights were threatened, he reacted, "Whoa. That ain't the way you treat the Fonz."

When firm action was required, he relied on wildly absurd threats such as "How would you like to see the parking lot upside down?"

This technique has been known for years, though it never seems to be taught anywhere. Those teachers who discover its effectiveness are usually operating on pure instinct. Some teachers have tried everything else and turned to it in desperation. Since everyone has a sense of the absurd, the technique is equally effective with all children. It is ideally suited to those with a learning disability or an attention deficit disorder, children who don't respond well to logic or verbal reasoning, and strong-willed youngsters who tend to be defiant.

To adults, these threats sound humorous to the point of being downright silly. But students of all ages take them very, very seriously. Despite the fact that I never laid a hand on students, my pupils all believed that I had left a trail of little corpses behind me in my previous years of teaching.

Some people complain that this tactic can be emotionally damaging. But as long as the wild threats are not graphically ghoulish and are balanced by equally enthusiastic—but real—praise when appropriate, youngsters will not be harmed. If the outrageous threat damages a teacher-child relationship, it's being used incorrectly.

> I used my first wild threats on a regular self-contained fourth-grade class. Throughout the year, I worked to perfect the technique that was making such an amazing difference in the behavior of my students. As a beginner, I made a few mistakes.
>
> One day, Jack was horsing around and ignoring his assignment. The big, tough farm boy was preventing three reading groups from getting their work done. His antics were also distracting the youngsters working with me up front.
>
> As one group returned to their seats and another prepared to come forward, I walked over to Jack's desk. The boy was so engrossed in his activities that he didn't notice me approaching. Out of the blue, he heard his teacher's voice snarling, "You stop disrupting this class or I'll rip off your arm and beat you with the bloody end of it."
>
> Stunned, Jack turned to me, gaped in horror, then burst into tears.

Although I apologized immediately, my conscience still bothers me. I learned my lesson the hard way at a child's expense. The object is to stop bad behavior, not to shock and terrify. Go gently. Don't employ surprise attacks. Avoid blood and gore.

Miss Green was an absolute master of the outrageous threat. This loving lady was always in control of her exceedingly difficult class of thirteen- to fifteen-year-old LD students. Nothing escaped her notice. Her students couldn't get away with anything. She was equally lavish with wild threats and real praise.

In walking by the door of Miss Green's room, my class and I once overheard an open confrontation between this fantastic teacher and a student recently assigned to her class. The big, gangly youth was angry about something. In his rage, he squared off in preparation to attack Miss Green.

The statuesque lady raised herself to full height and glowered into the boy's face. "Honey, you hit me and there'll be two of us on the floor." Pausing, she cocked her head and narrowed her eyes. "And I promise, *I'll* be on the top!"

The student dropped his fists, stared at the ground for a second, and returned to his seat.

A word of caution is in order. For that tiny minority of youngsters who have a verbal-processing problem that makes them unable to understand metaphoric language, this technique is not appropriate. Such children appear naive and very gullible. They will believe *anything*. When the teacher offers a new color TV for a passing mark on a spelling test, they tell their mother they're working hard so they can win a prize. They can't tell joking from straight factual information. Their peers tend to pick on them. They usually have serious social problems because they can't tell a compliment from a put-down. They'll run to the teacher in terror because some kid has threatened to knock their teeth out. When a classmate makes a cutting remark like "Oh, great idea, smart guy," they think they're being praised; they hear only the words and miss the sneer in the voice and the disapproval in the body language. To these "literalists," outlandish punishments are accepted as truth and cause confusion and genuine fear. For such children, the use of absurd promises and outrageous threats is to be avoided.

> It's traditional to announce the ground rules on the opening day of school. In my brief speech of dos and don'ts, I always included one wild threat: "Don't *ever* touch my desk. That is *my* property. You touch my desk and lightning will strike you dead!"
>
> Once or twice a year, the warning needed repeating as some student's hand hesitantly reached forward to borrow a pencil or a piece of tape. "Touching that desk is very dangerous" was always enough of a reminder.
>
> This one outrageous threat produced wonderful benefits. My purse could hang casually on the back of my chair without ever being touched. Stopwatches, keys, Red Cross money, and other objects of interest to children remained safe while in open view on the top of my desk. And best of all, the students adopted the same respect for private property among themselves. No one *ever* went into another person's desk—including the teacher. Among the students in my class, there was great trust and mutual respect. We knew there were those among us who might filch something under other circumstances. But within the four walls of *our* classroom, private property was absolutely safe. We deliberately created an island of trust in a world of uncertainty. We took tremendous pride in the fact that in *our* classroom there were no thieves.
>
> All of this grew out of a ridiculous threat that affected students' behavior as if they took it seriously. What would I have done if some child ignored the rule about the sacredness of my desk? I don't know. In thirty-seven years of teaching, it never happened!

Standard classroom discipline is not very effective with LD/ADD children. Punishments don't stop them. Rewards don't lure them. Choices and consequences bring out their defiant streak and eat up huge amounts of time without changing them. Even the hottest new methods rarely impress them.

"The Fonz technique" is particularly useful with students who have a learning disability and/or an attention deficit disorder. Due to their tendency to be "oppositional," they hate to be bossed around. Child management systems based on punishments and rewards usually lead to lots of confrontations and open defiance. Many LD/ADD youngsters find the proddings of teachers, parents, and other authority figures to be very irritating. Though they are forgetful and disorganized, they resent gentle reminders intended to help them fulfill their commitments to do household chores or schoolwork. Even when the action suggested is the very thing they themselves had just decided to do, they refuse to cooperate and choose to do something else!

> Steve was in the academically gifted program in the fifth grade. His attention deficit disorder was so severe that even with large amounts of medication he found it impossible to sit still and pay attention for more than a few minutes. His writing disability was so troublesome that he despised all tasks that required picking up a pencil. And he found math an aggravating jumble. But Steve had a wonderful attitude. He was highly motivated and very much wanted to please.
>
> He had a terrible time with homework. Between his problems with organization and his hatred of writing, he found completing home assignments a nightmare. His parents had been deeply involved in his nightly study sessions for years and did everything they could to help. The older Steve got, the more he resisted their assistance. With an impish twinkle in his eye, this bright fifth-grader told his teacher, "The best way to get me to do my math homework is for my mom to tell me it's time to do my spelling."
>
> This ten-year-old child had noticed that his defiant streak made him want to do just the opposite of what his parents and teachers told him.

Since LD/ADD children are extremely sensitive about criticism and get their feelings hurt very easily, any technique that points out their faults is likely to lead to defiance, sulking, withdrawal, and damage to their already shaky self-esteem. When the outrageous threat is used to correct behavior, these pitfalls can usually be avoided.

Those who have a learning disability and/or an attention deficit disorder usually have a vivid imagination and a well-developed sense of humor. They are quick to point out the absurdity of everyday situations. They love to tease and make jokes. They are famous for their wisecracks and often become the class clown. When "the Fonz technique" is used to enforce discipline, LD/ADD children gleefully picture outlandish punishments and act as though they believe there is real danger that the wild threats will be carried out. Apparently, this shift into pretending draws attention to the absurdity of the threats and lets the change of behavior become a mere side effect. There is no loss of face, undesirable behavior is changed, and everyone ends up smiling.

Outrageous threats must be recognized as more than a mere warning. They act to caution the child against continuing a specific activity, but they also make it clear that the misconduct is not going to be tolerated further. For most children, wild threats carry such a strong message of disapproval that they actually function as a form of punishment.

Like most people, children are afraid of anger. They do not want to see what might happen if the teacher loses control of herself and flies into a genuine rage. Those who paddle, send notes home, and expel students from class are usually the least effective disciplinarians. Those who use outrageous threats reveal a tiny corner of themselves that serves to remind students that an angry human being can be very unpleasant and cause a lot of pain.

For most situations, a swift, simple "No, you may not do that" is sufficient. For those occasions when a blockbuster is needed, the wild threat can be powerful. Extravagant threats and promises are effective methods of communicating an attitude of total confidence. The words and body postures are merely ways for the teacher to act out her inner conviction that she has the power to manage her class. Such inner certainty is the foundation of effective discipline.

Enforcement Procedures

No matter how carefully practiced, preventive measures go only so far. The unexpected happens. Children misbehave. There are times when the teacher must take *real* action. In applying disciplinary measures, there is always a threefold purpose: to stop the child from persisting with the offensive behavior, to punish the youngster for the misconduct, and to prevent recurrence of the misbehavior.

It must not be assumed that punishment changes behavior. Disciplinary procedures encourage youngsters to stop using unacceptable patterns of action, but they do not teach more appropriate behavior. New habits are established through success and praise. Thus, true child management goes far beyond setting up rules and enforcing them through punishment. It must also include leading children to adopt new patterns of conduct. Good discipline does not eliminate bad behavior—it replaces it with good behavior.

To be effective, the punishments and rewards that comprise effective discipline must be administered in accordance with the following four rules.

1. Punishments and rewards must be immediate.

Discipline must be in full operation at all times and places. A child's bad behavior must be recognized, stopped, and punished immediately.

When faced with a misbehaving student, the good disciplinarian does not make a choice about whether or not to take action. There are no options about when and where to make a move. The time is always *now*, at the moment of the misconduct. The place is always *here*, at the scene of the crime. All youngsters know that there are certain situations in which they can get away with almost anything. If there's ever a place children will do something obnoxious, it will be in a public setting where the teacher will be too embarrassed to take action. Or it will be at a moment when the teacher is too busy to take action. On such occasions, children feel it's safe to ignore the rules. But if punishment is immediate, such carefully timed misconduct will not happen more than once.

In the case of public misbehavior, the immediate part of the discipline involves getting the offender to a private place. The long arm of the teacher might tap the pesky child on the shoulder and guide him toward an exit. "Step out into the hall" might be quietly whispered. The message can be delivered silently by motioning with the hand. There must be no shouting. No scene. The offender must be removed so that his problem does not become a problem for others. In this way, the disciplinary action begins immediately. Since it is vital to act quickly regardless of the setting, smart teachers determine an appropriate private area for such disciplinary emergencies when first entering unfamiliar territory.

The same principle holds true for rewards. If a child is trying to establish a new pattern of behavior, his first successes must be recognized and applauded no matter when and where they occur. The praise does not have to be elaborate, but it does have to be genuine and specific. Often, a wink, a smile, a nod, or a victorious thumbs-up will do.

There is a tricky aspect of praising immediately. If not timed carefully, the reward can interrupt the desired behavior and stop it from continuing. Generally, it's best to hold the compliments until the good conduct has reached its natural limit.

> Charles often brought his youngest daughter, Rhianna, to Quaker meetings. With this charming little three-year-old on his knee, cradled against his chest, he would sit in the silence of the gathering. Sometimes, Rhianna would sit quietly for ten minutes. Occasionally, she'd last for nearly half an hour. No matter when his daughter got restless, Charles would carry her out of the room triumphantly while whispering compliments on the length of time she was able to sit still. They would then play together in a nearby area where the little girl's need to move and chatter did not disturb others. There was no such thing as failure. When she reached the limit of her ability to remain quiet, she was praised and rewarded immediately. Rhianna loved to come to meetings. Her presence was always welcome. For a three-year-old, she could remain serenely quiet for an amazing length of time.

Providing immediate correction and punishment is usually easy. Rewarding success tends to be more complicated and usually requires experimentation and a number of compromises.

2. Rewards must be pleasant, punishments must be unpleasant.

Youngsters are often rewarded with things they normally try to avoid. Old-fashioned teachers used to say, "You be good and get all your work done and I'll let you sit up here with me during story hour." Little children found that very appealing. But the offer struck terror into the hearts of all youngsters beyond the third grade. Older students carefully guarded against being too good, lest they face the embarrassment of having to sit on the teacher's lap. The teacher's idea of a reward seemed like sheer torture to most students.

Lots of things done as punishment don't seem even mildly unpleasant to children. Mothers hiss at youngsters who wiggle in church, "You sit still and be quiet." When the fidgeting continues, the child is taken outside. The kid wins! He was misbehaving because he didn't want to be trapped on a hard pew in a stuffy room listening to a boring sermon. He wanted out. What did his unacceptable behavior get for him? It got him exactly what he wanted!

It's not at all unusual for teachers to misjudge a situation and end up rewarding bad behavior.

> A small group of fifth-graders was working with me in the LD resource room. Much to my surprise, the students were finding the day's lesson difficult and boring. Their usual cooperative attitude disappeared. Wiggling, snickering, and horsing around replaced any serious attempt at paying attention. Unable to get them on the right track, I finally gave up in frustration. "Breaktime. We're going outside for ten minutes. After everybody has run off all the wiggles, we'll come back in and try this again."
>
> The little group bounded gleefully onto the playground. The time off felt good to me, too. Smelling sweet spring air was infinitely more pleasant than struggling to teach syllabication rules.

> We returned to the resource room refreshed and free of tension. As the students took their places, the significance of our break dawned on me. Wisely, I had bailed out of a losing lesson plan. But foolishly, I had rewarded my students for bad behavior.

Discipline does not have to be physical in order to be unpleasant. It's possible to administer a truly ghastly penalty without ever laying a hand on a child.

> When I was in high school, there was a Spanish teacher who hated gum chewing. Every year, she warned her students of the bizarre fate that would befall them if they chewed gum in her class.
>
> Those few students who got caught with gum in Señora Lepley's room became the laughingstock of the school. For weeks, they were reminded of how foolish they looked as the Spanish teacher marched them up and down the halls meting out her version of justice.
>
> Armed with a paper bag and a sharp pencil, the rule breakers were led to each of the dozens of drinking fountains in the building. The criminals used the pencils to spear those awful wads of used gum that collect around the drains of public drinking fountains. One by one, from fountain to fountain, they stabbed the gooey blobs and dropped them into the bag.
>
> That feisty little Spanish teacher couldn't have been more than five feet tall. But her crusade against chewing gum humbled even the toughest teenagers. Señora Lepley's gum-spearing expeditions were unusual because they horrified *everybody*. There was never a youth who found the activity even mildly tolerable. For adolescents, any public humiliation that makes their peers laugh at them is excruciating.

Very few punishments are considered unpleasant by all students. Little girls aren't necessarily bothered by being put in time-out; they don't always dislike being forced to sit still. For most little boys, enforced periods of inactivity are agony. Overweight, unathletic types hate running laps. The agile or hyperactive think such strenuous exercise is fun. Those who are good at amusing themselves can even get pleasure out of sitting alone in the cloakroom. Yet for most youngsters, being shut in a closet would be so terrifying that the teacher could be accused of child abuse. One child's delight is another child's torture.

All-purpose rewards and penalties are not nearly so effective as those specially selected for a particular child. In choosing an appropriate disciplinary action, the teacher should take the child's behavior patterns into consideration. Something intended as punishment must not end up providing fun time. To have the desired effect, penalties must be easy, safe, and definitely *not* enjoyable to the child. Likewise, rewards must bring pleasure.

3. Discipline must be consistent.

Discipline that is on-again, off-again encourages a child to analyze the situation and adjust his conduct accordingly. With haphazardly enforced standards, the youngster does not develop an attitude of consideration for others. He becomes devious, one of those clever little brats who sizes up the teacher to figure out how much he can get away with. Sneaky children are not born that way; they are created by adults who enforce discipline inconsistently.

Children are persistent. If there's the slightest chance of getting the payoff they desire, they'll keep trying. But they're not stupid. If a particular action *always* results in an unpleasant experience—if discipline is applied consistently—they quickly give up and move on to something else. Youngsters never persist in tempting the law of gravity. As toddlers, they fall off the couch a time or two. At five, climbing trees or riding bikes produces a few more falls. Before they enter school, painful experience has proved that gravity is always in effect. And they totally accept that fact.

Parents and teachers usually apply absolute enforcement only in areas of their personal pet peeves.

> Many students with a learning disability and/or an attention deficit disorder find that chewing gum enhances their ability to concentrate. Like any other repetitive, rhythmic movement of the mouth, it acts to integrate the nervous system so that it is easier to sustain attention. Improbable as it

> sounds, a number of my students have found that chewing gum while reading radically improves their comprehension!
>
> Gum chewing has never bothered me. But most schools have rules forbidding it. Year after year, I compromised with the system. Discrete, inoffensive use of gum was allowed in my classroom. Nothing messy, noisy, obnoxious, or damaging to property was tolerated. The preferences of administrators and other teachers were respected. Any student who chewed gum in my class dropped it in the wastebasket before leaving the room. Within the four walls of my domain, I not only allowed gum, I provided it.
>
> My tolerance for gum chewing had one important limitation. I find the sight and aroma of grape-flavored gum repulsive. I can smell the stuff clear across a room. Students weren't allowed to bring grape gum into my room. The only child who ever tried it was immediately whisked out to the hall to dispose of the offending wad and the rest of the pack he had stashed in his pocket.
>
> The appearance of my students and classroom gave clear evidence that my policy was strictly enforced. There were no blobs stuck to the bottoms of seats and desks. No one blew bubbles or made loud cracking noises. The aroma of grape flavoring was never present. Yet it was not unusual to see several sets of jaws rhythmically working on a piece of gum. The rules were consistently enforced and obeyed.

Being consistent about praise requires some careful maneuvering. It is important that children's successes be recognized. But the way achievement is rewarded should vary. As a youngster first starts behaving in a desired way, he should get something special for every success. The first time a student does his homework, he should get something like a star on a daily chart, an extra two minutes of computer time, or some other small privilege worthy of being considered special. As the new conduct grows into a habit, the reward should be decreased in size and frequency but should still be used for encouragement. When the stars and chart are retired, the reward might shift to something weekly, like five minutes of extra art time for every five days of satisfactory homework. After the new pattern is established, the routine recognition given anyone else for the same behavior is enough—

with an occasional added word of praise.

All children who are doing what is expected should be frequently rewarded with praise. Students who faithfully do their homework night after night should get a private word of recognition every once in a while. As Fred turns in his assignment for the 103rd consecutive day, a personal comment is appropriate: "Fred, you still have a perfect record! Never ever have you failed to do your homework. Reliability is a very good quality. Nice job." Simple recognition does a great deal to maintain desired behavior. But note that in some situations, it is wise to keep such comments private. Public praise for academic success can damage a child's social status!

Adults rarely provide punishments and rewards with relentless determination. If total consistency were applied to all child management measures, the results would be revolutionary.

4. Discipline must be understood.

When students accidentally do something good, they're likely to get complimented. With no notion of whether the praise was for their sunny smile, neat paper, cooperative attitude, good posture, or correct answers, they grin sheepishly and mutter, "Thanks." But in not understanding what they did that was so good, they have no chance of deliberately repeating the behavior and earning another pleasant reward.

The same thing happens with punishment. "Stop that!" carries almost no information. Most LD/ADD students could probably stay out of trouble if they'd just stick to amusing themselves quietly at their desks. Very few of them ever figure that out. It never occurs to them that most of their problems are caused by continually disrupting the class. And teachers never tell them. What seems obvious to the adult in charge is often not even faintly apparent to the child.

> Eleven-year-old Penny had emotional difficulties in addition to a severe learning disability and an attention deficit disorder. The child had no social skills at all. Everybody dis-

liked her constant whining. Both in her neighborhood and at school, this thoroughly unpleasant little girl was a discipline problem and had no friends.

Penny's parents had taken her to counselors and clinics. Over the years, the youngster had been exposed to tennis, swimming, dancing, horseback riding, tap-dancing, cooking, sewing, rock collecting, and rock climbing. She had been given lessons in piano, guitar, clarinet, crafts, and art. At various times, she had been a member of the YWCA, Girl Scouts, 4-H, church choir, and school band. She had been sent to camps and special schools. None of these activities suited Penny. Always, she dropped out within a month.

Just when it looked as if Penny was destined to spend her life alone watching TV, eating, and having tantrums, some neighbors went on vacation and asked her to baby-sit their guinea pigs. Reluctantly, the girl's parents agreed to let her try it.

Much to everyone's amazement, Penny was totally conscientious about caring for the guinea pigs. She did the feeding, watering, and cleaning of cages without even being reminded.

During the last week in Penny's care, one of the females produced a large litter. Since the young baby-sitter was unprepared for such an event, she had to consult the library and a pet shop for advice. When the neighbors returned to reclaim their furry little rodents, Penny proudly presented them with a healthy and greatly enlarged group of pets.

As a reward for a job well done, and with the blessing of her parents, Penny was given a pair of guinea pigs from the litter born under her care.

Gradually, the girl's attitude changed. Her interest in guinea pigs gave her something to be proud of and something to talk about. She found that other children listened to her. Some of them even came over to Penny's house to play with her pets. A few children seemed to like her. For the first time in her life, Penny had friends and playmates.

There was an equally dramatic improvement in the situation at school. Penny's attitude toward her work and her classmates gradually showed a change. The girl's new confidence helped her gain increasing success in every area.

As Penny became well known for her talent with guinea pigs, her growing collection of pets was featured in a newspaper story. In the aftermath of the excitement caused by the article, the young celebrity commented to her parents, "Now that I have guinea pigs, everybody wants to be my friend." The girl did not understand the real reason for her popularity.

Wisely, Penny's mother and father began a program of praising their daughter for the cheerful, cooperative attitude that was making her acceptable to those around her. Every act of kindness or generosity was recognized and praised. At every opportunity, Penny was made to see that she now had friends because she had learned how to *be* a friend.

At fifteen, Penny's interest shifted from guinea pigs to boys and a more mature social life. But the lessons she'd learned through her pets remained unchanged. With or without guinea pigs, Penny had become an interesting, attractive, thoroughly pleasant young lady.

Teachers need to be careful that a student sees a clear connection between his behavior and the punishment or reward that results. Youngsters with a learning disability and/or an attention deficit disorder are particularly prone to missing the cause-and-effect relationship between their actions and any disciplinary measures that follow. Unless the behavior that prompted the penalty is pointed out to them, they are apt to feel like misunderstood, innocent victims of an unjust system run by hateful adults who are out to get them. And many of them carry that attitude into adulthood.

Such failures of communication are easily avoided by a simple statement. With direct eye contact or use of the child's name, the teacher should name the broad category that covers the present conduct. "Bob, you are disrupting the class." "Carol, stop that whining." "Lester, thank you for being so helpful." It is usually appropriate to add a brief description of precisely what the child did to prompt the teacher's reaction. "Ted, you are disturbing the class with your humming." "Jeff, you were very helpful in art class today. Thank you for cleaning all the brushes." Whether positive or negative, the statement should be specific and brief. Prolonged praise is embarrassing. Lectures about bad conduct are boring. The object is to see that the child understands the cause-and-effect relationship between his action and the praise or punishment that follows. He must learn to recognize his ability to create pleasant or unpleasant responses in those around him.

An organized system of punishments and rewards can lead youngsters to a change of behavior. For this to happen, children need teachers and parents to set the example, to treat them with respect, and to guide them in making wise choices that lead to pleasant payoffs. They count on us to see possibilities, then set them up as goals. They rely on us to make objectives clear, then break tasks into sequential steps that can be faced one at a time. They look to us to monitor their progress so they can make the adjustments that lead away from failure and toward success. And then, at the end, as they smile in victory, shouting, "Wow! See what I did!" they need us to confirm and celebrate their success.

Adjustments in Classroom Management

CHAPTER 11

ONE CHILD WITH A LEARNING DISABILITY and/or an attention deficit disorder can keep a classroom in constant uproar if nothing is done to counteract his trouble with attention, organization, time, and social acceptance. In these areas, the youngster does not have the ability to control and change his own behavior. Teachers have to deal with these problems by adjusting his environment. Careful classroom management can prevent the LD/ADD student from becoming a strongly disruptive influence.

Students with a learning disability and/or an attention deficit disorder usually find the normal hum of classroom activity extremely distracting. Even such tiny, unavoidable sounds as turning pages, shuffling feet, and whispered conversations catch their attention and draw their minds away from schoolwork.

When left to their own devices, LD/ADD students tend to use background music to filter out normal environmental noises. They usually like to play the radio, the stereo, or the television when they want to concentrate. They also find it helpful to work in an area where they can spread out, move around, and be comfortable. Body postures other than sitting up straight at a desk help them to "get into" what they are doing. Standing at the blackboard, kneeling on the floor, leaning back in a chair, perching on a stool, pacing around the room, or hunching over a workbench, a countertop, or a drawing table—any position that increases whole-body involvement is likely to help these youngsters pay attention to their work. When studying at home, they tend to prefer spreading out on the dining-room table or sprawling on couch, bed, or floor.

By taking note of the modifications these youngsters provide for themselves, teachers can make adjustments in the classroom environment to help LD/ADD students overcome many of their difficulties with paying attention in class. In a carefully controlled atmosphere, the LD/ADD pupil has his best chance for successful learning.

Distractibility and a short attention span are major causes of the LD/ADD youngster's classroom disasters. The child who is not paying attention to his work is usually doing something else. And as often as not, that something else produces noise or movement that disturbs the rest of the class.

Thus, the teacher's first objective is to establish firm limits on the LD/ADD student. His difficulty with focusing attention must not become the entire class's problem.

Finding the Right Spot

Regardless of age, LD/ADD students usually have an attention span significantly shorter than that of their classmates. Because their periods of concentration are so brief, they frequently look up from their work and check on what's going on around them. If there is something interesting nearby, it captures their attention so that they never return to their work.

> Claude was an extremely bright, extremely active first-grader. He loved school; he loved people. He was curious

about everything. First-grade work should not have been terribly difficult for Claude. His learning disability was mild, he was getting excellent therapy, he was on stimulant medication, and he very much wanted to learn.

But in the classroom, the youngster never got his work done. He barely even got started on most of his schoolwork. "He's off in the clouds," his teacher complained. "Staring off into space. He just won't get down to business. The boy doesn't even try."

The LD specialist spent a morning in the classroom observing Claude. Just as had been recommended, the boy was seated at the end of the front row next to the teacher's desk. Unfortunately, this location placed him beside an aquarium and a row of windows that provided a fabulous view of a busy playground.

Claude wasn't "off in the clouds." Every time his attention broke and he looked up, there was something fascinating going on in the fishtank or on the playground.

It took several moves to find the right spot for this wide-eyed first-grader who found everything interesting. One seat provided a neighbor who enjoyed fooling around with him. Another was so close to the door that he kept watching the activity in the hall. Finally, when seated off to the side by a blank wall, with two studious little neighbors and no interesting animals or vistas nearby, Claude found his ideal location. His surroundings were so boring that schoolwork was the most interesting thing available.

Everything in the LD/ADD child's environment competes for his attention. And extreme distractibility makes his focus very fragile. Even among highly motivated LD/ADD students who develop adequate study skills, difficulties with concentration cause lifelong problems.

For the teacher, the trick is to seat pupils with a learning disability and/or an attention deficit disorder where there is little of interest to hold their attention when it's not focused on schoolwork. A seat in the front of the room is often best. This limits what's in the student's line of vision. Instead of seeing a whole room of interesting bulletin boards plus thirty or more active bodies, he sees only the front third of the room, the blackboard, and a few classmates. If the pupil is situated on the extreme left or right side of the front row, distractions can be cut to a minimum. However, front-row corner seats present special problems which must be taken into consideration. Areas of heavy traffic and frequent activity should be avoided. If the teacher's desk, the wastebasket, and the pencil sharpener are on one side, the LD/ADD child should be on the other. When the choice is near the door or near the window, the door is usually the less distracting of the two.

College students with a learning disability and/or an attention deficit disorder almost always have less trouble paying attention in class when seated in the front of the room and off to one side. When seated in the middle or back of a lecture hall filled with two hundred or three hundred students, they notice every person—what they're wearing, what they're doing, where else they've been seen around campus—and little attention is left for watching the instructor, listening to the presentation, and taking notes.

In young children, this tendency to notice everything going on around them can be a tremendous handicap. For those few who simply cannot screen out the sights and sounds around them, any class of more than six or eight students makes concentration totally impossible! No amount of medication, classroom modification, or one-to-one instruction can enable them to tune out the other students and keep their minds on their schoolwork. Such children can make a shambles out of a tranquil classroom. With "inclusion" the law and small LD classes rarely available, parents of these highly distractible youngsters are faced with the choice between homeschooling and private school. Leaving severely distractible children in regular classrooms is far too destructive to the child—not to mention to his teacher and his classmates—to be given serious consideration.

Some LD/ADD students should *not* be placed in the first row of a classroom. For those who are hyperactive and those with serious behavior problems, sitting in front of an entire class makes them actors with an audience. When the distractions that disturb them are limited, they become the distraction that disturbs everyone else. This must not be allowed.

Overactive children—whether medicated or not—wiggle, bounce, tap, twist, hang out of their chairs, wander around the room, and race to the teacher's desk. Most of the time, they are playing with something in their hands. Almost always, they are in motion. Medication often helps them *contain* their excess energy, but as a general rule it is pointless to try to *control* their level of activity. The most effective approach is to limit their territory.

Hyperactive students usually are least disruptive if seated at one end of the back row. This location also provides them the extra amount of physical freedom they need. Rather than wasting her time and energy trying to keep such youngsters in their seats, the teacher can concentrate on confining their activity within reasonable but specific bounds. It is effective to give such youngsters an adjusted set of rules: "You may move freely about this area of the room, provided you do your work, don't do anything dangerous, and don't disturb others." The exact limits of their territory should be made absolutely clear. With young children, it may be necessary to mark off their space with a chalk line or a strip of tape so they know exactly where the boundaries are. This approach enables a teacher to exert a reasonable amount of control over hyperactive pupils. But it will work only if the adjusted rules are strictly enforced.

It is also helpful to give these wiggly children something to play with in their hands. They almost always bring an item from home to fill this purpose, but it is usually a toy that is so much fun that it demands all their attention and keeps them and their neighbors from work. A piece of modeling clay, a big rubber band—anything they can twist and squeeze without distracting their classmates—can help them sit still and focus.

For testing, a private place is almost always essential. The Individuals with Disabilities in Education Act of 1990 requires that solitude and quiet be provided for students of all ages who are officially diagnosed as LD and/or ADD (including those in advanced programs such as medical school and graduate school) when their difficulties with concentration prevent them from performing well on tests administered in the normal environment.

LD/ADD students who cause constant discipline problems should also be seated in the back. With them, the teacher's objective is to protect the rest of the class from the disturbances they create. Situating these youngsters in a corner of the back row has the effect of separating them from the other children. No one has to watch their antics, and there is only one neighbor to be disturbed.

For more complete separation, a disruptive boy can be surrounded by girls who will not interact with him. He should *not* be given the enlarged territory allowed the hyperactive child. And he should *not* be placed in some remote corner that isolates him entirely. (Although total isolation may be in the child's best interest, a teacher should not take this type of action without first consulting the LD specialist, the psychologist, the school's counselor, the principal, or some other administrator who is intimately acquainted with the legal ramifications of such actions under Section 504 of the Individuals with Disabilities in Education Act of 1990 and other current legislation that might apply. Any action that counteracts the general concept of "inclusion" can lead to serious legal difficulties.)

Children's preferences can be a great help in determining the ideal location and type of seating. The learning-styles research of Drs. Rita and Kenneth Dunn is also useful in analyzing the five environmental factors that must be considered when choosing an appropriate study locale.

1. Noise.

The noise level is of primary importance. For many pupils, deep concentration is so easy that they stay engrossed in their work despite even loud sounds. Very few LD/ADD youngsters have the ability to tune out the smallest background noises. It's usually difficult—and sometimes impossible—to provide the degree of quiet they need when there are other students nearby.

For those who can tolerate looking "different," sound-insulating earmuffs like those used at airports may be helpful. Earplugs and stereo headsets playing white noise offer the same benefits at less expense.

Many learners actually *need* noise in order to concentrate. Background sounds from a radio, stereo, or television help such students filter out the intrusive background noises that would otherwise disrupt their concentration. There is a growing body of evidence to suggest that certain types of classical music can be an aid to concentration and learning. For LD/ADD students who find music helpful during study sessions, a small cassette or CD player with a headset can be extremely valuable.

2. Light.

The amount of light in the work area can have a strong effect on concentration. Some students find that dim lighting makes them sleepy and sluggish, while bright light helps them stay alert. Others find that low light helps them feel calm and focused, while intense light makes them fidgety and nervous. Several studies have shown that poor readers and right-brain thinkers tend to prefer dim light for study. As might be expected, many LD/ADD students find it easiest to learn in a room with low-intensity lighting. Perhaps baseball hats should be allowed in classrooms as a socially acceptable form of eyeshade.

3. Temperature.

Personal preferences concerning room temperature vary widely. While some students fan themselves and complain of the heat, others seated nearby shiver. There is a limited temperature range within which the human brain functions well. When the classroom thermometer registers above eighty degrees, the mind becomes sleepy and sluggish; when the reading falls below the mid-sixties, discomfort disrupts serious thinking. Youngsters with a learning disability and/or an attention deficit disorder seem especially susceptible to extremes of cold or heat. Consequently, the teacher's personal comfort level shouldn't dictate what's right for an entire classroom. Students need to be taught to adjust their clothing according to the temperature so they can remain clear-headed and alert. It is essential that classroom temperature be monitored closely.

4. Seating.

Standard classroom seating isn't ideal for all pupils. Mozart wrote his music standing up at a high table. Others do their best thinking stretched out on the floor. Some can't concentrate unless they're in motion. While it's more convenient for the teacher to have the entire class sitting in chairs lined up in neat rows, LD/ADD students should be encouraged to explore alternate postures.

5. Oral stimulation.

Many people find that the machinery of thinking works best when accompanied by movements of the mouth. When concentrating, they chew on a pencil, smoke a pipe, eat, drink, chew gum, or bite their fingernails. Some experts believe that such activity "integrates" the nervous system. Although food and drink aren't normally available in a classroom, many youngsters with a learning disability and/or an attention deficit disorder could benefit from such intake.

> A former student of mine recently waited on me in the glove department of a local department store. As we exchanged news, Rose said, "You know, it's because of you that I graduated from college."
>
> This lovely young woman's flattering comment caught me by surprise. As a fifth-grader, Rose had experienced such severe problems with reading comprehension that I assumed she was going to have trouble just getting through high school. It hadn't occurred to me that she might actually make it through college. Unable to remember what I had taught her that proved so valuable, and eager to hear about my great skill as a teacher, I asked, "What did I do that was so helpful?"
>
> Rose replied, "You were right. That one trick you taught me made all the difference. I haven't had any more trouble understanding what I read."

> Trying not to show my confusion, I wondered what "trick" I'd taught her so many years earlier. Fortunately, Rose continued. "Yes," she said, "as long as I chew gum when I read, I have no trouble with comprehension."

The Dunns' learning-styles research makes it clear that some very small adjustments in the classroom environment can make a gigantic difference in a student's academic achievement.

Always, in selecting the ideal seat for an LD/ADD student, the teacher needs to look for a quiet spot with little traffic, a limited view, and few neighbors. The neighbors can be as important as the location. A youngster with a learning disability and/or an attention deficit disorder should *not* be seated near children who pick on him or tease him. Talkative students and those who fool around a lot should also be avoided. The LD/ADD child's distractibility is bothersome enough without noisy classmates nearby to make it worse. A seat beside a pleasant, quiet, good student can have a very steadying effect.

The "Good Neighbor"

"What page are we on?" "What row are we supposed to do?" "What were the directions?" A student with a learning disability and/or an attention deficit disorder has many such questions. Traditional classroom rules force him to either figure out such things for himself or go to the teacher for help. Figuring them out for himself seldom leads an LD/ADD student to successful completion of an assignment. Asking the teacher would be fine if the situation didn't occur so often. Constantly trotting up to the front embarrasses the child and becomes an inconvenience to the teacher.

The questions routinely asked by LD/ADD children can almost always be answered by any good student in the class. By choosing the right neighbor and carefully controlling an adjusted set of rules, the teacher can see to it that pupils with a learning disability and/or an attention deficit disorder have a ready source of information available right there at their elbow.

The teacher, the LD/ADD child, and the neighbor must all have a clear understanding of the special arrangements they're making to create a "good neighbor plan."

1. The two youngsters are allowed to talk openly and freely but *quietly* during class.

2. The LD/ADD student is not permitted to pester his neighbor or use the conversations as an excuse for socializing.

3. The "good neighbor" must maintain a cooperative, understanding attitude.

4. To make sure that the children understand the difference between a "good neighbor plan" and a partnership, the teacher must establish clear and specific guidelines. The youngsters must know what kinds of questions the LD/ADD student may take to his neighbor. "What does this word say?" or "Do the answers have to be in sentences?" would probably be allowed. "What's the answer to this question?" would definitely not be acceptable. The two children also have to understand exactly what kind of help the neighbor may provide. Is he to copy arithmetic problems from the book? Does he supply answers to basic questions such as "How much is 14 take away 6?" Is he responsible for reminding the LD/ADD child about capital letters and punctuation? There must also be a clear understanding of special situations when their talking will not be allowed. Does the policy remain in effect during tests? Does it apply only in one classroom or anywhere in the school?

Most LD/ADD students ask two questions repeatedly: "What's that word?" and "How do you spell ———?" They need to know where to turn for answers to these questions no matter what the situation. Most difficulties can be avoided if the full details are settled at the time the agreement is made.

By the fifth grade, Mike had overcome almost all of the problems caused by his learning disability. In most areas, he was a good student. He was especially patient with himself about his poor spelling. Whenever he got stuck on a word, he went quietly to the teacher to ask for help. But Mike did not deal with his copying problem so effectively. Copying things off the blackboard caused him serious difficulties. Every time he made a mistake, he got terribly upset. Erasing and correcting his errors made him furious. It got to the point where Mike caused at least one ugly scene every day.

In mid-November, a new boy, Tim, enrolled in the class. For no particular reason, the teacher gave him a seat next to Mike.

An outgoing child, Mike took it upon himself to help the new student get into the routine of the class. In hushed tones, he answered questions about the way the teacher wanted things done. He told Tim where to find supplies. Quickly, the two became friends.

Sometime in December, the teacher realized that Mike no longer had problems copying things off the board. He hadn't had one of his outbursts in weeks. She had no idea what had caused the change in her LD pupil but assumed it had something to do with sitting next to Tim.

One afternoon, right in the middle of a social studies test, the teacher caught Tim handing a note to Mike. Positive that the two boys were cheating, she snatched their papers away, demanded that Mike give her the note, and dragged the two criminals into the hall.

On the scrap of paper Tim had given Mike, there was only one word: *democracy*. Waving the evidence, the teacher challenged sternly, "Other than cheating, I can't imagine any possible reason for this note!" Her eyes flashed as she glared first at one boy, then the other. "I will give you gentlemen one minute to explain exactly what this note means."

Gulping and stammering, both boys tried to talk at once. "I asked him how to spell *democracy*," Mike muttered at precisely the same time Tim said, "He asked me how to spell *democracy*." Since it seemed unlikely that two children would tell the exact same lie simultaneously, the teacher heard her students out. Their stories fit perfectly. And they clarified several things she had found puzzling.

Mike and Tim had developed their own version of the "good neighbor plan."

> Tim explained simply, "Mike don't spell so good, so I help him sometimes."
>
> "And he copies stuff off the board for me," Mike added. Shrugging, he confessed, "That's how come I don't mess up and get so mad anymore."
>
> The teacher's broad smile made it easy to see that she approved of the system the two friends had devised. Her curiosity led her to ask her LD student one final question: "And what do you do for Tim in return?"
>
> Before the learning-disabled pupil could reply, his buddy cut him off. "He don't have to do nothin' in return. It's okay. He's my friend."
>
> In his own simple way, that eleven-year-old boy stated the whole theory behind the "good neighbor plan": when given an opportunity, most children will gladly help a classmate without expecting anything in return.

Selecting the right child to act as a helping neighbor can be difficult. It's often wise to let the LD/ADD student take part in the process. Sometimes, a rotating team of "good neighbors" is most practical. With that system, the LD/ADD pupil has a regular seat, and one desk immediately beside him is reserved for his special neighbor. Week by week or month by month, students rotate in and out of that seat. Regardless of the system used, only students who are willing to be an assistant should be considered for the role. Recruits have the wrong attitude. They tend to see their role as a chore rather than a privilege.

Time Limits and Schedules

Many children with a learning disability and/or an attention deficit disorder race through life at high velocity; they are *hyperactive*. Some slow-moving LD/ADD youngsters are referred to as *hypoactive*.

Regardless of LD/ADD students' preferred pace, time tends to slip through their fingers. Whenever they're allowed out of the classroom, it's unlikely they'll be seen again soon. A two-minute trip to the bathroom takes them five minutes—or often fifteen. For a short errand to the office or library, they'll be gone twice as long as seems reasonable. Much of this is to be expected and tolerated, but a few tricks can help.

Many teachers impose a time limit on students who leave the classroom for a trip to the lavatory, their locker, the drinking fountain, and so on. This is usually done with a sign-out sheet on which students record their name and the time they left the room. Since most LD/ADD children (of *all* ages) have a poor concept of time, this standard method doesn't always work for them. They seem to have no internal "feel" for time. With no mental clock to pressure them to move along, they use up the allotted time on a sightseeing trip through the halls. Those who have a watch and are willing to use it rarely have any skill at figuring out what time it will be when their time is up. More than their classmates, LD/ADD students need something to force them to hurry along on their errands.

The sign-out approach can work for an LD/ADD student if he uses an hourglass, a cooking timer, or a stopwatch instead of a clock. When leaving the room, the student takes the hourglass or timer from a shelf near the door, starts it running, and places it on his own desk. If he returns before the sand runs out or the bell goes off, he merely puts it back on its shelf and returns to his seat. If he's late, he suffers some standard penalty. With *all* types of students in grades one through twelve, this method gives the teacher a way to enforce rules governing how long pupils are allowed out of the classroom. It has two distinct advantages: it's no trouble to the teacher at all, and it does not single out LD/ADD children for special treatment. The time limits apply equally to all. For those youngsters who are repeatedly late with the timer, some other system must be devised.

> Brian was hypoactive; he was a chronic slow mover. If allowed out of the classroom, this pleasant eighth-grader stepped into a time warp and lost track of time altogether.
>
> The bathrooms and drinking fountains were right across the hall from my second-floor classroom. All my students could visit both and be back before our three-minute timer ran out of sand.

All my students, that is, except Brian. I tried letting him use a timer that gave him an extra two minutes to allow for his shuffling pace. I tried having him carry a timer *with* him so he could see the time running out. I even sent a student with him as an escort. Nothing worked. Always, he came dragging back shamefaced and late.

Much as the other pupils liked Brian, his delayed returns always prompted a few digs.

"Out there watching the girls, eh, Brian?" someone would tease.

"What'd you do, man, use the sink to wash out a few things?"

The jokes embarrassed the youth terribly. They were much worse than any punishment I'd have ever thought of. In desperation, I gave up. Unless it was a real emergency, Brian was not allowed out of the room.

The stalemate continued until a January day when Brian had a legitimate reason for leaving the room and I had an equally valid reason for insisting he be back in no more than five minutes. On an inspiration, I pulled my pocket calculator out of my purse, set its timer for four minutes, and shoved it into Brian's hip pocket. "When that beeper goes off, you drop whatever you're doing and run back to this room," I warned.

The boy grabbed a hall pass and scurried out the door as though carrying a bomb in his pocket. He completed his mission and made it back to class before the alarm even went off. I guess Brian didn't want the embarrassment of having people see him with beeping noises coming out of his jeans.

It takes a tremendous amount of patience to work around an LD/ADD child's nonadjustable pace. In most situations, the only answers are compromises that work around the problem.

Whenever the teacher takes her students outside the classroom, it is necessary to guard against the LD/ADD child's problem with pace. Like most other youngsters, he pushes and shoves to get to the front of the line. Yet once the group is on the way to its destination, that same LD/ADD child lags. If he's at the end of the line, he may get left behind altogether. This is particularly troublesome on field trips.

There are no surefire cures for this problem. A sturdy nametag (giving address and phone number for both home and school) is a necessity for young LD/ADD children being taken off the school grounds. A buddy system can also be effective in such situations. It is *not* wise to let LD/ADD youths be the last one in line at any time. If not kept under a watchful eye, the quick ones dart off to explore, while the slow ones become engrossed in something and stop entirely.

As part of their nonvariable pace, most LD/ADD youngsters have trouble shifting from one activity to another. "It's time for music." "Turn in your sentences and get out your dictionary." "Put away your math and go wash for lunch." The school day is full of abrupt changes. Some students develop a habit of pleading, "I'm not done yet." Others just ignore the requested action. LD/ADD students are particularly prone to causing trouble when concluding one activity and beginning another. In the first place, they frequently fail to complete their work within the period allotted. Also, their faulty concept of time makes it difficult for them to gauge how many minutes they have left for a particular activity. For them, the order to turn in their paper comes as a total surprise. No mental timer has made them aware of the looming deadline. If LD/ADD youngsters are not mentally prepared, they balk. Instead of making an agreeable, efficient change from math to reading, they keep right on with math, or begin horsing around, or stare off into space, or get angry and rip up their paper. Orders that come like a bolt out of the blue simply do not produce the desired responses.

The regular use of a five-minute warning can work wonders. Within the classroom, a simple "Five minutes left for the health project" can help the entire class get into the right frame of mind for the coming change. On the playground or in the lunchroom, the teacher can signal by holding up five fingers. Even homeschoolers have to deal with activity shifts and need to give advance notice to set the stage. Then, when the moment for the change arrives, everyone knows the time for action is *now*. No excuses are accepted. The five-minute warning makes it possible for a teacher to impose the added structure needed to get LD/ADD youngsters to live within some kind of schedule.

Dealing with Disorganization

The school day is a procession of varied activities requiring frequent transitions which pose no problem for most students. For LD/ADD children, each task shift provides a new opportunity for the mind to drift. Long after the new assignment has been given and the rest of the class has settled down to work, students with a learning disability and/or an attention deficit disorder can be found staring off into space—without ever having gotten out the necessary materials.

It isn't a matter of not doing good work. If left to their own devices, LD/ADD students don't do *any* work. They never get started.

Traditional methods of dealing with this difficulty can stimulate the child to action, but they rarely keep the situation from recurring. Instead of undergoing a lasting change of behavior, the child learns to wait for others to *force* him into motion. He doesn't learn techniques for self-monitoring and self-discipline. He has little chance to develop organizational skills, initiative, and independence.

Both student and teacher are damaged by continual conflict. The teacher's patient optimism wilts, while the youngster comes to view authority figures as enemies.

Standard corrective measures can make matters worse. Many of them deprive the student of an opportunity for real success with the work assigned. Removing the child from the classroom can solve the problem, provided that the alternate location is quiet and well supervised. But that is rarely the case in the cloakrooms, corridors, back corners, and office spaces that are readily available in today's schools.

Sometimes, in an attempt to force a pupil to get his work done, teachers unintentionally reward him for being unproductive in the normal setting. Teachers should abandon any efficiency-enhancing techniques that allow the youngster to get out of doing his work and have a great time while he's not doing it.

Truly effective solutions come from recognizing the root of the problem and making adjustments there. LD/ADD children are dreamers. That can't be changed. But it is possible to avoid or alter situations that send them off into the clouds.

A child with a learning disability and/or an attention deficit disorder almost always has trouble shifting gears and getting started on a new activity. A large part of this difficulty can be attributed to the fact that he is so disorganized. He doesn't get his book out because he can't find it. Or in the process of looking for it, he discovers some long-forgotten treasure buried at the bottom of his desk. Every time an LD/ADD youngster looks into his desk or locker, he takes a trip to never-never land.

Many problems can be solved by simply keeping the student out of his desk and his locker. His rummaging time can be limited to a five-minute period first thing every morning. Within that time, he must get out everything needed for the entire day. A schedule and a list of daily supplies should be taped close at hand for easy reference. For some LD/ADD children, a materials partner is necessary to help with the process of "getting it together" for the day.

While an LD/ADD child is learning to get control of time and supplies, it is sometimes best to have him keep all books, notebooks, and equipment on an open shelf or in a cabinet within easy reach. This eliminates the need for (and breaks the habit of) desk digging entirely. In extreme cases, a teacher can keep custody of all his materials. That sounds impractical, but it's actually more efficient than the repeated confrontations that develop when disorganization becomes a chronic problem for a student.

Smart teachers do not allow a child with a learning disability and/or an attention deficit disorder to take textbooks out of the classroom. They see that he has duplicate copies at home for use on homework and projects. It is also wise to monitor the LD/ADD student's inventory of school supplies on a regular basis so that pencil and paper are always available for use in class. Ideally, the pupil provides these materials and always has them with him.

Even with careful control, a backup system will be necessary. An old coffee can full of pencil stubs will usually suffice for emergency needs. No matter what measures have to be taken, make sure an LD/ADD youngster never has to leave the room to go in search of supplies. Sightseeing trips around the building take much more time than can be allowed.

Notebooks are a special source of difficulty. Unless some kind of system is forced upon them, LD/ADD students do their English assignment in their science notebook, leave worksheets at home on the kitchen table, and never have what they need with them in class. A notebook control system is absolutely essential if these disorganized youngsters are going to have the faintest hope of being properly prepared for class. The basics of such a system are outlined below.

1. For each subject, the child should have a separate spiral notebook with pockets for storing loose papers. Each subject has a notebook of a different color. For severely disorganized types, it is best if these notebooks never leave the schoolroom.

2. Two pencils should be kept in the notebooks' storage compartments. As they wear out or disappear, they should be replaced immediately.

3. A calendar and a schedule should be taped to the inside of the front cover of the notebooks. The student should use these to keep track of the regular routine as well as due dates for special assignments.

4. A small spiral notebook should be kept on the student at all times. In it are assignments and reminders about the things he's likely to forget. For young children and the extremely unreliable, the notations should be made by the teacher or a study buddy. As one of the world's absentminded types, the LD/ADD child needs to be taught how to compensate for his unreliable memory.

5. The student should carry a large loose-leaf binder from class to class. He should also take it home every night. It should contain the spiral notebooks for each subject and also provide a safe place for transporting papers, assure a steady supply of fresh paper, and give the student a place to store additional pencils. A calendar taped to the inside of the back cover should help keep track of due dates for projects, book reports, and other long-range assignments.

6. Other supplies that are absolutely necessary—rulers, erasers, ballpoint pens, a checking pencil, paper clips, etc.—should be kept in a zippered plastic pocket permanently fastened inside the loose-leaf binder.

This notebook control system does not require close cooperation between home and school. A teacher can use it without the help of parents. The family can set it up without involving the school. Either way, it takes at least six weeks of close monitoring to help the student develop the habit of using the system. During this break-in period, the entire binder must be checked daily, night and morning. At this time, missing items should be replaced, inaccurate notations corrected, and important messages made current.

Checks on a calendar in connection with some system of rewards can supply the motivation needed to get the student cooperatively involved. It also helps if the youngster adds personal touches in accord with his own tastes and interests. Stickers, artwork, monograms, and slogans can convert a distasteful form of discipline into a source of personal pride.

Be sure every piece of the binder is clearly labeled with the student's name, address, phone number, school, teacher's name, and grade. If misplaced, easily identified materials are likely to be returned.

Many LD/ADD students are highly resistant to setting up such a materials control system, yet they are the very ones who need it the most. If it is imposed by the authority in charge, designed by the youngster, and monitored closely with an enforcement system based on positive rewards, it leads almost all students to develop the desired organizational habits within six to eight weeks. With those few truly scatterbrained youngsters who are totally unable to develop orderly habits, teachers have to monitor the system for the entire year. That sounds like a lot of work—until the alternatives are considered.

If active supervision is not available for the first few weeks of this materials control system, it should not be started. This program can produce the desired behavior change *only* if the student is provided with the necessary materials *and* is systematically taught how to use them.

Controlling Distractions

Modern electronic equipment offers some amazing alternatives in controlling the distractions in the LD/ADD student's learning environment.

> Ed was in an individualized ninth-grade program with an open-classroom environment. Because of his attention deficit disorder, such a busy schoolroom was not ideal for him. His short attention span and high level of distractibility made it impossible for him to concentrate while other students were conferring with the teacher, using files, setting up filmstrip machines, building models, and so forth. Most of Ed's class time was spent chatting with his neighbors.
>
> When assigned a page of easy problems, Ed would ask permission to put on a headset and listen to rock-'n'-roll while he worked. He said the music helped him concentrate. Despite some early skepticism, Ed's teachers agreed to the arrangement. As long as the youth had rock music blasting through his headset, he was attentive and productive.
>
> Ed's teachers tried to think of a way to extend his success with concentration into other areas. But the youth could study to music only when the assignment involved easy, routine work. The sense of isolation produced by the headset made it possible for him to tune out distractions. But if he had to read or use language, the music drowned out his inner processing. After trying the headset in English class, Ed com-

plained that he couldn't hear himself think. The boy's teachers searched for some kind of music that would allow concentration during reading activities. Several types of soft, repetitive music were considered. Even the selections of Bach, Mozart, and Vivaldi suggested by study-skills experts proved to be a distraction rather than an aid. Finally, one of the teachers discovered a recording of the ocean. As long as this tape played, the listener heard only rolling breakers and crashing surf. The cyclic ebb and flow sounded so realistic that you could almost taste the salt in the air.

Ed loved it. He found that the gentle rhythms of the sea not only screened out all the distracting sounds of his classmates but also gave him a sense of calm. And he loved what it did for his concentration. Ed's family got him a Walkman to carry around from class to class. Other students heard about his special background music and began asking to try it out. By the end of the semester, at least a dozen students were using a tape recorder and headset as a means of improving concentration.

Through the use of a headset, the auditory level of a student's environment can be almost completely controlled. Distracting noises in the classroom can be masked by neutral, nondisturbing sound. Although many types of music produce the masking effect, research has shown that classical music, particularly Bach, actually enhances the brain's processing capacity. When selecting the music for a classroom Walkman or portable CD player, it's not a matter of matching the student's personal taste; the goal is to find the music that does the best job of building concentration.

Computers offer an even more powerful aid to overcoming distractibility and short attention span. Since they are so visually stimulating *and* offer tactile and kinesthetic involvement, they can rivet a student's attention to the screen and get him immersed in instruction. Youngsters with a learning disability and/or an attention deficit disorder often have a strong talent for computers. The languages and methods of processing make sense to them in a way that the world of written language does not. For many LD/ADD pupils, sitting down to mouse or keyboard triggers the "hyperfocus" mechanisms that make them get totally absorbed in whatever activity is on the screen. Since it produces a state that is the extreme opposite of their usual classroom distractibility, it can be helpful in all academic areas.

Avoiding Social Problems

Any student who takes more than his fair share of the teacher's time . . . any pupil who ruins the peaceful atmosphere of the classroom with strange or disruptive behavior . . . any child who gets away with ignoring rules, schedules, and assignments . . . any youngster who keeps the entire classroom in turmoil is resented and rejected by his classmates.

Thus, prevention must be the teacher's first line of defense against the LD/ADD child's social problems. Through careful classroom management and all the special adjustments discussed in this book, the teacher must help children with a learning disability and/or an attention deficit disorder succeed with their schoolwork. If they can do their math, they won't have the tantrums that make other children think they're weird. If they can finish their assignment on time, the others won't grow restless and angry because they're constantly being kept waiting for this one slow worker. Everything that makes it possible for LD/ADD students to function satisfactorily within the classroom makes them more acceptable to their classmates.

While using this indirect approach to achieve long-range goals, teachers need to be on guard against issues that require firm, direct intervention. "I don't want to sit next to her." "I don't want him on my team." "Does he have to be on our committee?" Statements like these hurt, but LD/ADD youngsters often feel a stronger level of rejection than is intended. As long as there is no name-calling or open ridicule, the issue is best treated as a social snub. For the offender, the routine lecture that a classroom is not a social club is appropriate. Then the matter should be dropped.

Rejection that includes name-calling and cruel teasing needs to be treated as a major offense. Just as a teacher does not allow anyone to call an African-American student a "nigger," an Oriental student a "slant," an Italian student a "wop," or a Jewish student a “kike,” she must not tolerate children calling an LD/ADD child “stupid” or “retard.” Such name-calling calls for strong, immediate corrective action.

Teachers need to keep in mind that children mirror the attitudes and behavior of the adults around them. If the teacher hounds and scolds a child constantly, the students in the class tend to do the same. If the teacher shows a lack of patience, understanding, or respect for a student, the other children follow her example.

Meg came to the LD resource room with a small group of her classmates from Miss Johnson’s fourth grade. The freckle-faced youngster was energetic, cooperative, and eager to learn. She had the short attention span typical of LD/ADD children her age. The girl acted just about like the other youngsters who came with her from Miss Johnson’s class. But the other children treated Meg as though she were different. They criticized her constantly.

“Meg, stop tapping your foot.”

“Meg, quit jiggling the table.”

The little girl’s classmates often corrected her for some small disturbance even when I felt she had done nothing wrong. The situation was very puzzling.

It was likely that Meg’s homeroom teacher knew why the other children picked on her. But Miss Johnson and I couldn’t seem to get together for a conference. While waiting for the meeting date we finally agreed upon, I kept watching for clues that could explain this group’s strange behavior.

A day or two before the conference, as the class wrote a dictated paragraph, Meg did something that irritated Leonard. (It was so slight that I didn’t even notice!) The little boy slapped his pencil down, scowled at Meg, and snapped, “Can’t you see I’m trying to get my work done? You just stop all that disruptive behavior.”

“Disruptive behavior?” I said to myself. “Since when does a fourth-grader talk like that?” As I stared at the boy who’d just used such an unexpected expression, the realization dawned: “That’s an adult expression. He heard that somewhere.” Suddenly, the whole picture became clear: the children treated Meg the same way their teacher did!

> At our meeting, Miss Johnson was very open about her feelings toward Meg. Her voice edged with frustration, she told me what her days were like. "All day long, it's 'Meg, get back to work,' 'Meg, get back in your seat,' 'Meg, quit pestering Melissa.' I get so sick of trying to make that kid behave I could just scream." Miss Johnson stopped abruptly, looked earnestly at me, then asked, "Have you ever had a student you just plain didn't like?"
>
> "Yes," I said. "Every few years, there's one that just rubs me the wrong way." Grinning, I added, "But I prefer to call it a 'personality conflict.'"
>
> Miss Johnson was too upset to appreciate my attempt at humor. With a heavy sigh and a look of shame, she concluded, "Every day on the way to school, I hope Meg will be absent."

Children adopt attitudes similar to those of the adults around them. Thus, to improve the relationship between a child and his classmates, the teacher must start by changing her own relationship with the youngster. It is the teacher who takes the lead in developing an atmosphere of acceptance toward an LD/ADD student.

The collage-making technique discussed in chapter 6 is designed to help teachers develop positive attitudes toward students. It is ideally suited for situations where one or two youngsters are "ruining" a class. Any child who sticks out as disliked or disruptive is a prime candidate for a custom-made collage picturing his transformation into a much-appreciated, thoroughly enjoyed star of the class. It is inappropriate to have the offensive child take an active part in such a project; it is the *teacher's* expectations that need changing. After creating the collage in private, the teacher should hang it in the classroom in an inconspicuous place where she can view it frequently without the need for explanations to the children. No hint of the specific child intended should be visible in word or illustration. Students who ask about it can be told "It's a picture of my goals" or "I use it to remind me of what I want for all my students." In extreme cases, a group collage showing the wonderful atmosphere of mutual respect and cooperation we all dream of might be produced by the entire class. A large mural of words and illustrations can make an impressive and attractive display of the actions and attitudes we hope to find in *all* those around us.

Any person who does not recognize the talents as well as the weaknesses that make the LD/ADD child different will find it difficult to be supportive. The classroom teacher involved with a student who has a learning disability and/or an attention deficit disorder is faced with a three-step process: first, she must learn to understand and accept the child; then she must develop strong positive expectations of success for the youngster; and finally, she must lead the class to do the same. The key is in developing a firm belief that this child, too, can grow into a happy, productive adult.

Adjustments in Texts, Materials, and Assignments

CHAPTER 12

FOR THOSE WHO INTEND TO PULL LD/ADD STUDENTS out of their failure patterns, a new approach is essential. Children who have a learning disability and/or an attention deficit disorder don't learn successfully with standard textbooks; teacher's guides rarely suggest instructional strategies that work for them. As their continued apathy and failure clearly demonstrate, these students need major changes in teaching materials and assignments if the instructional approach is to be compatible with their nontraditional style of learning.

When it comes to adjusting materials, homeschoolers have a distinct advantage. They are not bound by anyone else's choices. Parents who teach their own offspring can custom-design every element of their curriculum to fit the needs of just one student. They have the luxury of being able to adopt the textbooks most likely to succeed with an individual child. And if those don't work, they can move on to others. Classroom teachers who struggle to modify inappropriate materials daily can well appreciate what a delight it would be to have the freedom to select books and activities that truly fit an LD/ADD child.

Yet whether instruction is done in the home or the school, budgetary restrictions and time limits force the teacher to make choices. For both parents and professionals, many compromises are necessary. And the first order of business is always the same: teachers must develop techniques that enable them to determine how each child learns so they can select materials and make assignments that are likely to work, and be ready to revise them if they don't. With that end in mind, a general overview of the weaknesses of LD/ADD students is the first step.

Potential Problem Areas

Students who are categorized as learning disabled usually have trouble with language-based skills. Typically, the boys find it difficult to master the word-attack process that turns written symbols into spoken language. Just because they have seen a word before does not mean they will remember it when they see it again. Without careful, systematic remedial instruction, they are unlikely to learn how to figure out unfamiliar words. LD girls, on the other hand, tend to have most of their language-based difficulties in reading comprehension. They usually develop the ability to read a passage with acceptable accuracy but have trouble understanding what it means. And once they do acquire a clear concept of the content, it leaks out of their memory before they have a chance to demonstrate their knowledge on tests. Learning-disabled females often come across as "airheads."

In math, the labels *LD* and *ADD* tend to be applied in ways that cause confusion. Most children with attention deficit disorder have serious trouble with math. They copy inaccurately, tend to transpose numbers, overlook the signs that tell what process to use, can't remember the multiplication table and other basic facts, and forget the sequence of steps required to arrive at a correct answer. Some LD children have trouble working with numbers in addition to having difficulties with written language; some do not. Students whose main area of difficulty is math seldom get classified as learning disabled; they are more likely to be labeled as having an attention deficit disorder. When girls have trouble with arithmetic, it is likely to be shrugged off as insignificant, rather then identified as part of a learning disability or an attention deficit disorder; yet most females with reading comprehension problems also have serious difficulty with math.

Spelling is the most sensitive indicator of a learning disability, particularly among males. Any student who is labeled LD *or* ADD is likely to be a very poor speller. And books that use a weekly spelling list are not effective tools for helping them overcome their limitations in recalling the precise letter sequences required for correctly writing words. Even with long-term one-to-one remediation tailored to the learning style of the individual student, few LD/ADD youngsters ever become more than barely adequate spellers. Those who develop the ability to work around their problem learn to rely on spouses, secretaries, pocket-size spell-checkers, and the programs built into today's word processors. Under Section 504 of the Individuals with Disabilities in Education Act of 1990, schools are required to make accommodations for poor spelling among students categorized as LD and/or ADD. Usually, this means that teachers do not count off for incorrectly written words in content areas and make a number of modifications in spelling class as well.

It is in their problems with producing written language that LD and ADD students look very much alike. Typically, both groups have extreme difficulty getting their ideas down on paper. Their handwriting is atrocious. Their spelling is abysmal. They have trouble organizing their ideas to form a convincing argument, an accurate description, or a detailed explanation. (They rarely have trouble in creative writing and often love to write poetry.) And they hate the whole process.

As students get older, their writing problems look more and more like the result of a bad attitude and poor work habits. In high school and college, LD/ADD students "forget" due dates, fail to get started in time to make the deadline, turn in hastily thrown-together papers full of mechanical errors, produce work that does not follow the directions or meet the minimum requirements of the assignment, request extensions, and take incompletes. It never looks like the assignment is too hard for them. They themselves insist that they are capable of producing a satisfactory paper, but the books they needed were all checked out of the library . . . their car broke down . . . their printer jammed . . . they had it all on disk and lost it . . . their job schedule changed . . . there was a family crisis . . . they've been sick . . . they've had an unusually heavy load of homework . . . all their other courses had papers due at the same time . . . they were in a play . . . it was football season . . . they were out of town. . . . Always, the blame goes to circumstances rather than their inability to make themselves complete a task they find extremely difficult. Regardless of whether the student is a first-grader or a Ph.D. candidate, the inability to produce a satisfactory piece of written work looks like a problem with motivation and organization, not the difficulty with written language that it really is.

By altering texts and materials used with LD/ADD students, teachers make it possible for them to learn despite their weakness in some of the basic skills. It's not that these youngsters can't think or understand. They can usually learn the material being presented. What they can't do is read the regular book and do the routine writing required on assignments, reports, and tests.

Using the Regular Text

It is often possible to adapt a student's work in such a way that he gains enough efficiency to use the standard text with ease and speed. Such alterations enable the LD/ADD pupil to succeed with "regular" work.

MATH WORKBOOKS AND WORKSHEETS

Many students with a learning disability and/or an attention deficit disorder have trouble copying math problems out of a book. Through workbooks, sets of ditto masters, and photocopied worksheets, teachers can eliminate the need for copying while still providing the child the arithmetic practice he needs. If the LD/ADD student is in a regular math group, it's best to use the worksheet approach with the entire group.

OLD COPIES OF TEXTBOOKS

Most LD/ADD students have trouble writing out the answers to questions that routinely appear at the ends of chapters in textbooks. To avoid the need for extensive writing, the student can be provided with an old text which he is allowed to mark up. Thus, instead of writing out the answers to end-of-the-chapter questions, he can record the number of the page on which the answer is found and circle the information where it appears in the text.

Some highly motivated students develop a study technique based on this simple process. In order to condense a chapter's information, they photocopy the questions at the end of the section, make copies of the passages that discuss the questions, and glue them into a notebook that becomes their personal study guide.

AN EXTRA SET OF BOOKS

"I forgot to take my book home" sounds like just another excuse to get out of doing homework. Yet for those LD/ADD children who are poorly organized (and that's most of them), constantly forgetting books is a very real problem. Having a duplicate set of texts at home can save everybody a lot of trouble.

> Steve was in Mrs. Phipps's tenth-grade American literature class. To help the LD/ADD youth work around his difficulty with reading, his teacher carefully adjusted his assignments. The young lady did everything in her power to give Steve a chance to succeed in her class. Yet by mid-October, the boy was headed toward failure. He rarely did his homework, never brought his book to class, and usually slept through most of the period.
>
> In analyzing the situation, the teacher realized that Steve had a pattern. Day after day, he began class by requesting, "Can I go to my locker? I think I left my book there." Whenever Mrs. Phipps let him go, the boy missed the first ten

minutes of class. As often as not, it turned out he'd left his materials at home anyway.

The youth had had the same difficulty for years. All Steve's past teachers believed his problem was lack of motivation. But Mrs. Phipps was idealistic. She discussed her student's situation with the LD specialist, the school psychologist, the youngster's parents, and the boy himself. None of them offered either suggestions or encouragement.

In a conference, Steve's father tried to get Mrs. Phipps to see his son the same way everyone else did. "Steve don't like school, and he ain't gonna study," the man explained with simple honesty. "The boy's just waitin' to hit sixteen so he can drop out." Shrugging his shoulders, he tried to get the teacher to understand that it would be better for everybody if she'd just let the boy finish out his school career as the poor student he was destined to be.

Mrs. Phipps did not argue. But she didn't give up either. She was determined to make Steve's last year in school a profitable one.

With no one to help her in her crusade, she got a stack of material on learning disabilities and attention deficit disorder from the library. A week of reading gave her only one good suggestion. But it was an intriguing idea.

From an article by a leading expert, Mrs. Phipps learned that it helps if an LD youngster is assigned a duplicate set of textbooks for home use. Because of his parents' attitude, it was unlikely that Steve would study at home, so Mrs. Phipps arranged for Steve to keep his own personal second copy of the American literature text in the school's media center. (The original copy stayed in the classroom.) The boy gladly agreed to have his daily study hall moved to where his literature materials were kept. He was delighted to have access to the computers in the library. Doing writing assignments with a word processor was such a new experience for Steve that he actually got a kick out of it.

The youth did not tell any of his friends what he was up to, and his success did not spread beyond American literature. But for two straight semesters, fifteen-year-old LD/ADD Steve got a B in English. They were the only passing grades in his final year of school.

Many LD/ADD students will gladly do their modified

homework if someone will help them keep track of their books and materials. A duplicate set of texts can make it possible for these youngsters to do their assignments. Being prepared for class is often the deciding factor in whether a student passes or fails. Long strings of zeros in the homework grade book can be devastating to an otherwise passing grade.

A READING PARTNER

A student who finds reading a slow, painful process often has trouble getting himself motivated enough to attempt long reading assignments. Having the support of an assistant can improve his attitude as well as the quantity and quality of his work. A reading partnership provides the LD/ADD student a person to read with, while still requiring him to do at least some of the reading for himself. The partner might be a classmate specially chosen for the job, an older student, an adult volunteer, or a teacher's aide. Although the poor reader and his partner take turns reading the assignments aloud, they do *not* have to divide the material equally. It is perfectly acceptable for the partner to do the majority of the reading.

Reading partnerships do not have to be limited to two people. An adult can easily read with two or three children at once, even if they are hyperactive. The teacher should *not* be a student's reading partner.

A READER

Sometimes, it is necessary to supply the LD/ADD student with a person to read *to* him. When the helper acts as a reader, the LD/ADD child's role involves following along in the book and paying close attention. But he is *not* expected to take a turn reading aloud or silently. This method is ideally suited for those occasions when the reading level of an assignment is too difficult for the pupil, yet no adjusted material is available. A reading partner is an appropriate modification when an LD/ADD student is capable of understanding the content but is not capable of decoding the material with speed and accuracy.

Twelve LD/ADD seventh-graders had their language arts instruction with me. We worked on reading, writing, spelling, grammar, punctuation, literature, and composition for two hours every day.

As a special project, this group of middle schoolers adopted the LD/ADD youngsters in our school's third grade. Twice a week, my students gave up thirty minutes of study hall to work one-to-one with their little partners. Sometimes, they helped with a test or a worksheet. Usually, they acted as readers. By having their own special assistant, the LD/ADD third-graders could do their regular classwork as quickly and easily as their classmates.

A RECORDING

A tape recording of the text can provide the LD/ADD pupil with a "reader" while also allowing him to maintain a degree of independence. If thirty students are reading silently and one or two of their classmates are listening to a recording through a headset, then the entire class is completing the same assignment. Using a cassette player within a classroom need not cause *any* disturbance. Headsets and earphones make its operation silent to all but the intended listener.

There is rarely any problem concerning the operation of electronic equipment. LD/ADD youngsters tend to be good with mechanical things. In our gadget-oriented society, even young children are usually familiar with the operation of stereos, VCRs, CD players, and so forth.

Some school systems have collections of tapes on which all their texts are read aloud. Many have an audiovisual department that makes such tapes on request. Special support services for exceptional children often have an extensive library of taped texts available to any teacher in their region or district. In cases where such resources are not available, several national organizations that create materials for the blind will tape textbooks for students with certain types of learning disabilities. To take advantage of these services, tapes must be ordered at least three months before they will be needed.

Now that "inclusion" has closed most resource rooms and

brought exceptional children back into regular classrooms, it is becoming increasingly common to see taped textbooks specified in an Individual Educational Plan (IEP). In such cases, classroom teachers need not take on mammoth taping projects. There will be times when the instructor will want to make a tape or two, but it is not practical to tape an entire text as a routine part of class preparation.

In middle schools, junior highs, and senior highs, LD/ADD students who use recordings of their texts need these special materials readily available during study halls. Keeping the entire collection stored in the classroom or the media center makes this possible. Even a system of careful control will not prevent the loss of tapes if they are taken outside the classroom or the library. Students of all ages with a learning disability and/or an attention deficit disorder are very bad about losing things. Without strict rules, entire tape libraries will disappear among the junk at the bottom of cluttered lockers.

Adapting the Regular Text

Sometimes, a student's assignment in the regular textbook can be altered to fit his personal level of skills. In this type of arrangement, the child is expected to use the regular material; however, the kind or amount of work assigned him is different from that required of the rest of the class. Many learning-disabled students read well enough to deal with regular texts yet have no chance of success unless the amount of material is adapted for their slow reading speed. With schoolwork that involves writing, LD/ADD children almost always need their assignments adapted. They just cannot be relied upon to produce the same quantity of written material as other students of the same age and intelligence.

It is possible to adapt a child's assignments in such a way that the youngster gains the ability to study independently. The simplest such changes involve altering the size of assignments. If the other students do twenty-five addition problems, the LD/ADD student might be told to do the first ten, every other one, every other row, the last three rows, the last one in each row, etc. If the other children read fifteen pages in their library book, the LD/ADD youngster might be told to read five in his. If the class learns twenty spelling words a week, the LD/ADD pupil might be required to master ten. Some assignments can be cut down without sacrificing mastery of the skills being presented at that grade level.

It can be difficult to adapt reading assignments in subject-matter courses such as social studies, science, health, history, and so on. Having a student read only a portion of the material almost always means he gets only a portion of the information. And most of the systems for selecting the parts to be read are either too complicated for the pupil or too time-consuming for the teacher.

There are four basic techniques that *can* work. Somctimes, one or another of them may be useful in making the most of an otherwise impossible situation. Occasionally, one provides a truly ideal solution.

1. Instruct the student to read only the boldface type, italics, and crucially placed passages like introductions and summaries. In precisely organized texts with a clear format, this type of adapted reading system enables the student to get the overall concept, plus definitions and other significant details.

2. Get the pupil to read the questions at the end of the chapter *before* reading the text. He can then scan the material in search of the answers. Thus guided toward key passages, he can find the important parts and concentrate on reading them. When the textbook doesn't have a quiz at the end of a section, students can create their own by reading the boldface type and turning each statement into a question. This technique is particularly effective for students who have serious difficulty with concentration. The search for answers keeps them focused and provides them with a reason for reading. This method is also helpful for students who have problems with reading comprehension.

3. Give assignments in terms of time allowed, rather than number of pages required. On a twenty-minute reading assignment, the LD/ADD pupil must read like everybody else, and when his time limit is up, he quits. Whatever number of pages he read is considered sufficient. This tactic can be especially helpful when the student is required to do skimming, scanning, or selective reading of some specially designated segment of the material.

4. Get someone to mark the key passages in the student's text. By concentrating only on the underlined material, the pupil can skip over less-important passages. With this approach, the youngster reads to get general concepts. This technique sounds terribly time-consuming for the teacher, but it doesn't have to be.

> Ralph's reading problem made twelfth-grade world history extremely difficult for him. He could not read twenty to thirty pages per night. And although he was a good listener, he could not master all the information merely by paying close attention in class.
>
> The teacher, Mr. Deal, had taught the course for a number of years. His personal copy of the text had all the important passages underlined. Mr. Deal and Ralph both realized that the teacher's well-marked text offered a solution to the boy's problem with slow reading. If the student read just the material the teacher had highlighted, it would be possible to cut his reading assignments in half without skipping any important passages.
>
> For a while, they tried having the student borrow the teacher's book. That deprived Mr. Deal of his text at just the times he needed it to prepare for the next day's class. The instructor tried doing the marking but found it to be too time-consuming. It took several weeks of experimentation before they found a way to get the copying done. Two volunteers from the community worked at the school regularly. Usually, they graded papers, made bulletin boards, ran off copies, did filing, and carried out other routine activities. They were delighted to be given a chance to do something

> of such direct benefit to a student. In less than a week, they had Ralph's world history book completely underlined for him. For the rest of his senior year, the boy kept up with his history assignments with ease.

All four of the above techniques allow an LD/ADD pupil to read only a portion of the regular assignment. But they enable him to do his reading independently. Although the student never makes up the parts he skips over, he is expected to learn the details through class discussion and oral instruction.

Using Alternate Materials

Whenever students are given specially selected books appropriate to their level of skill, their material is said to have been adjusted. Under such an arrangement, the youngsters are *not* expected to deal with the regular text at all. Some high schools and universities offer classes which have no one "regular" text. In such courses, students must select several books from a reading list. Teachers who hope to work effectively with LD/ADD youngsters have to learn to make many adjustments in materials.

In reading, spelling, and math, appropriately adjusted books are vital. These three areas are so crucial that the classroom teacher should expect the school's LD specialist to take an active role in the selection process. The expert understands the individual LD/ADD pupil's special limitations and needs. Also, she is usually well informed about the special materials that are available. As in all problem-solving conferences with an LD specialist, the wise teacher should get several suggestions rather than just one. From several equally suitable sets of adjusted materials, the instructor can then pick the one most practical for her classroom and teaching style.

> Pete was a very bright sixth-grader whose spelling was at high second-grade level. He couldn't even *read* the words in the regular spelling book, so his teacher put him in the low group with the fifth-grade book. Pete couldn't read those words either, but it was the book being used by the lowest group in the class.

Week after week, Pete failed his tests. His teacher kept cutting down his list, hoping that if Pete had only a few words, he would succeed. But instead of improving, he experienced more and more difficulty. Finally, the boy quit trying.

In desperation, the teacher put Pete in a spelling group all by himself and gave him a third-grade book. The student hated the whole idea. He was constantly losing or forgetting "that baby book." It embarrassed him to be seen with the adjusted spelling materials his teacher worked so hard to provide. The boy's attitude became defiant and surly.

Finally, the LD specialist was consulted. By that time, the situation was such a mess that radical action was necessary. Pete's sessions in the LD resource room were changed to coincide with the period when his regular class had spelling. The specialist had to take over the responsibility for teaching the youth his spelling.

Pete's teacher was wise enough to know that he needed adjusted material in spelling. But she made a bad situation worse by single-handedly trying to solve a problem beyond the average classroom teacher's expertise. In adjusting materials, teachers should not hesitate to ask the specialist for help.

PARALLEL READING

It's nearly impossible to find an adjusted textbook for an entire year's study of a particular subject. Parallel reading designed to fit each separate unit is the most practical approach. A fifth-grader with a third-grade reading level might be provided with an appropriate library book on Egypt when his class tackles that unit in social studies. However, because of the advanced vocabulary, a tenth-grade biology text could never be replaced by a fifth-grade science book. In such situations, LD/ADD students can learn the general principles from easier books but must learn the fancy terminology orally in class.

CONDENSATIONS

High-school courses in literature and history seem specially designed to make LD/ADD children suffer. Even after successful therapy, most LD students are still very slow readers. *Huckleberry Finn, Oliver Twist*, and *Uncle Tom's Cabin* are difficult for teenagers who are strong readers. For students with a learning disability and/or an attention deficit disorder, they are nearly an impossible chore.

All school systems have certain "classics" built into their program. And nobody gets through without reading them. In such cases, the LD specialist or the librarian can help the teacher find a suitable condensation. Many literary masterpieces are available in a variety of condensations. There are a few sets on the third- or fourth-grade level, many editions from the seventh-grade level on, and even a series or two done in comic-book format. *Reader's Digest* has produced a variety of condensations that are readily available. When an entire class is reading a piece of literature and a child with a reading disability must do the same, a condensation appropriate to his reading level is best.

It must not be pretended that a condensation is of the same aesthetic value as the original. In a toned-down, easier-to-read version, at least some of a masterpiece's plot structure, characterization, and elegant use of language must be sacrificed. But for the LD/ADD youngster who could never struggle through all fourteen hundred pages of *War and Peace*, a good condensation allows him to savor at least some of the elements that make the work a literary classic.

SELECTED READING BACKED BY TAPES

With audio cassettes and videos available through most public libraries, teachers often opt to expose LD/ADD students to literary classics by assigning excerpts from the original while providing the full story through tapes. In using such a system, the instructor expects the pupil to read selections from the book *after* becoming acquainted with the entire plot through attending a production, viewing a video, or hearing the work read aloud on tape. If the youngster's reading skills are not sufficient to tackle even a small portion of the original text, the audio version can be used as an oral reader to voice the words while the student follows along in the book.

Many students with no sign of a learning disability and/or an attention deficit disorder find a modification of this approach useful. By giving readers an overview of the story and introducing all the characters, an audiovisual production can be used to lay the groundwork for a careful reading. Since the students already have the overall picture and know what's going to happen next, they can devote their full attention to the flow of language and the development of characters and scenes.

MATERIALS FOR THE BLIND

From *The Canterbury Tales* to the poetry of e. e. cummings, almost all the great literature of the world is available on tapes, CDs, and CD-ROMs. Anything that is studied by a junior-high or senior-high English class is likely to be available in recorded form through the public library. Some of these productions are designed for anyone interested in hearing plays, poetry, and other literary works read aloud. Many, however, are part of the "Talking Books" series for the blind. Students with a learning disability and/or an attention deficit disorder are often eligible to use the extensive "Books for the Blind" collection. For information, contact your local library, your state library, or the Library of Congress. The student is required to have his doctor sign a certificate stating the nature of the learning problem. That's the only red tape involved. Once he qualifies, he's allowed to use anything in the large catalog provided for him. If a record player is needed, one is supplied free of charge.

If it's *Hamlet* every February for all tenth-graders, the teacher should get an LD/ADD student set up with a source for recordings well before Christmas. It isn't always possible to get the adjusted material *for* the youngster. But it is the teacher's responsibility to help the parents make arrangements to see that the special material is on hand when needed.

Changing Writing Assignments

Almost all LD/ADD students have extreme difficulty presenting their ideas in writing. Most have problems with spelling, punctuation, and handwriting as well. Yet only a few have trouble expressing themselves orally.

Adapting materials and assignments to allow for an LD/ADD pupil's problem with writing should be a major concern for the youngster's teacher. Whenever possible, written work should be cut drastically in size or changed to an oral assignment. With older students, it must be remembered that trouble with writing often makes standard note-taking impossible.

Several adaptations can decrease the amount of writing required to fulfill a given assignment without compromising the value of the activity.

1. Eliminate copying.

Writing down the question as well as the answer is usually busywork, not an essential element of the material being studied. In all grades, assignments are generally written on the board so that students can note the subject, chapter, page, number of problems or questions to be done, specific directions, and date due. It's part of the normal routine. But for LD/ADD children of all ages, it causes problems. They can't copy accurately, they write slowly, and they get frustrated quickly whenever they have a pencil in their hand. Thus, even the way the assignment is made needs adapting!

A "good neighbor" can be a valuable tool in making the necessary changes. First, LD/ADD students always need someone to verify that they have copied numbers and instructions down correctly. Also, when their slow writing makes it impossible for them to complete the task in the time available, they require someone else to do it for them. Usually, one of the main jobs of the "good neighbor" is making duplicates of routine classwork that must be copied. When an LD/ADD student asks his "good neighbor," "Will you make me a copy of that?" the teacher need not even get involved.

As schools shifted to "inclusion," the task of copying assignments joined the responsibilities typically delegated to the LD teacher. It is common for IEPs to specify that the classroom teacher and the LD specialist must provide a student with an accurate set of directions for all independent work. Often, this is carried out by checking and initialing the homework instructions which the student or a study partner has written out. In some cases, the two teachers do the actual recording of the directions for the youngster.

"Copy the question out of the book." "Write your answers in complete sentences." For LD/ADD students, both of these requirements are needless torture. Getting the correct answer onto the paper is enough of a challenge. If the student's answer is satisfactory, it can be assumed that the question was adequately read and understood.

Conducting research for reports is supposed to teach a student how to take notes. But copying long passages from an encyclopedia takes an LD/ADD child an incredible amount of time. By using a copy machine, scissors, and glue, note-taking requires no writing. To do cut-and-paste research, the student finds the information needed, gets the pages photocopied, cuts out important passages, and attaches them to file cards. These become his note cards. A computer with a CD-ROM or an Internet connection makes this process extremely simple and efficient.

Defining vocabulary words found in a dictionary or glossary is primarily a copying activity. Partnership arrangements are usually the most logical solution. The LD/ADD student takes an active part in finding the words, reading the definitions, and selecting the one that best fits the assignment. The partner does *all* the writing.

Teachers often ask that older students "make a final draft." Younger children are told, "Go back to your seat and write this over neatly." Either way, it's a copying assignment. The rough draft is full of corrected errors, erasures, crossed-out words, spelling corrections. It's the original, and it's perfect—but it's a mess. In making his final copy, complete with his very best handwriting, the LD/ADD child usually makes so many copying mistakes that the paper is no longer satisfactory.

Helping an LD/ADD youngster produce an acceptable final

copy of a report is *not* a job for an amateur. It is a major tears-and-tantrums task requiring close supervision by a trained professional. Without the assistance of the LD teacher, the classroom teacher, or an experienced aide, students with a learning disability and/or an attention deficit disorder cannot be expected to complete the job satisfactorily, and the assignment should be adapted. Teaching children to use a computer and then making sure one is provided for producing final drafts of writing projects is a realistic approach that usually leads to success. In the absence of this option, a pupil who completes an accurately revised rough draft can read it aloud to his teacher, to the class, or onto a cassette tape as his way of producing a satisfactory final copy.

2. Accept oral work as a substitute for written work.

Although it is ideal for LD/ADD children to present their work to the teacher in a one-to-one conference, that's not always practical. A tape recorder provided by the school and kept in the classroom is a valuable tool for recording reports and other assignments that can be spoken instead of written. Thus, when other members of the class hand in their papers, LD/ADD students can turn in their cassettes.

3. Accept illustrations as well as written explanations.

If a science question is "How does the human heart work?" the correct answer can be pictured through charts, cartoons, graphs, diagrams, or other visual representations. If a comprehension question for a reading story is "What happened to Bob's wagon?" a set of drawings can show the sequence of events involved in the disappearance of the toy. The teacher doesn't have to think up ways for LD/ADD youngsters to illustrate their answers. If the pupils understand that they are free to use alternate methods of presenting answers, they'll figure out good, logical ways to do it.

4. Assign demonstrations and projects instead of lengthy written reports.

Most LD/ADD students learn best when dealing with concrete objects. In order to tell about different types of Indian dwellings, it is possible to use models, illustrations, or blueprints. For a report on teeth, the teacher might eliminate any need for writing. The student could make a large model or poster clearly showing a tooth and all its parts. Then, in a presentation to the class, he could explain everything he'd learned about his subject. IEPs often require that such options be available on major reports. When given the choice, many students *not* labeled LD and/or ADD also find such a hands-on approach appealing.

5. Accept the briefest possible written form of an answer.

One good sentence or a list of facts often presents as much information as a paragraph. For students with a learning disability and/or an attention deficit disorder, all correct answers should be acceptable.

6. Never count off for spelling errors outside spelling class.

Messy papers with poor handwriting should be cheerfully accepted as long as the answers are legible. When an LD/ADD student's version of a word is totally unrecognizable, the issue is easily resolved by asking, "What's that supposed to say?"

"Writing Partners"

A "writing partner" is someone who writes *with* an LD/ADD child. In such an arrangement, the LD/ADD student does all the planning and thinking. If it's an assignment to be turned in for individual credit, the helper writes *some* of the answers and checks *all* of the spelling.

In some situations, LD/ADD students need a "secretary" to write for them. (In cases of dysgraphia, it's even possible to take the SAT and other such entrance exams with the services of a "scribe.") Usually, the person supplying this service is a teacher, an aide, or a volunteer from outside the class. The task is much too time-consuming for a "good neighbor." The secretary's sole job is to translate the student's spoken words into written form. Pointing out errors and making corrections are *not* part of the task. The child does the thinking; the helper merely provides the hand that records the words.

> Kent had a severe learning disability. Although he was extremely intelligent, at age eighteen he was only in the ninth grade. His unrecognized learning disability in reading, writing, and spelling prevented him from succeeding in any of his subjects. His grades were a dismal series of failures.
>
> Glenda, a senior, was Kent's girlfriend. The couple often spent evenings studying together. Gradually, the two developed a system whereby Glenda became her boyfriend's reader and secretary. She read Kent's assignments to him aloud, then wrote out the answers he dictated.
>
> Tests were very difficult, but most of them required little writing. As long as Kent didn't have to write essay-type answers, he got by in spite of his extremely poor reading and spelling. By January, he was doing better than he'd ever done before.
>
> During the second semester, the youth's English class was taught by a student teacher. This young lady quickly realized that Kent could get good grades on tests when allowed to give his answers orally. With his girlfriend acting as his secretary at home and one teacher making special adaptations, Kent made the honor roll!
>
> Unfortunately, the boy's father found out about the homework arrangement and didn't approve. Glenda graduated and went off to college. And Kent returned to his failure pattern.

Word Processors and Computers

Classroom computers offer a whole new set of alternatives to teachers trying to adapt assignments for LD/ADD students with impaired writing skills. From routine worksheets to quizzes and major tests, all can be given to LD/ADD pupils on a disk. Even college entrance exams are commonly done in this format.

For those lengthy writing tasks that have traditionally produced hysteria in the LD/ADD pupil, frustration in the teacher, and failure for everyone, word processors and computers offer a new chance for success. Children can proofread and make corrections with ease by deleting, inserting, rearranging, spell-checking, and otherwise altering the words on the screen. With editing so radically simplified, producing a perfect final draft is a breeze—just push the button marked "Print."

Producing written work with a word processor or computer has several advantages.

1. Because it is so multisensory, a computer makes a tremendous impact on an LD/ADD student's ability to sustain attention. By involving the child's visual, verbal, kinesthetic, and tactile thought processing, it heightens his level of involvement, thus increasing interest and enhancing concentration.

2. It circumvents the panic an LD/ADD child feels when a pencil and a blank piece of paper are all he has at his disposal. Taking the pencil out of his hand tends to free the LD/ADD youngster to think.

3. It removes the criticism and impatience generated by human helpers.

4. It usually produces feelings of enthusiasm and optimism. Most children think of working at a computer as a pleasant, challenging adventure. Those with a learning disability and/or an attention deficit disorder often have a special talent with computers. Somehow, the machines make perfect sense to them. In addition to freeing them from the frustrations they experience when working with pencil and paper, using a computer usually leads them into the "hyperfocus" mind-set that lets them work joyously for hours.

It is vitally important that LD/ADD students, no matter how young, be given the instruction they need to become highly skilled at the use of computers. Developing such competence equips them with skills that will allow them to overcome many of their limitations.

As much as possible, schools need to encourage students with a writing disability to switch to a computer and eliminate the need for pen or pencil. Producing written work on a word processor is so absorbing and pressure-free that many LD/ADD students produce written work of acceptable quality with no help and few alterations in assignments. In addition to providing a method by which they can succeed with schoolwork, this approach offers them an opportunity to develop skills they will find necessary in adult life.

If there are computers in the classroom, they should be *assigned* to LD/ADD pupils for use on written work that would otherwise be difficult or impossible for them. When all available equipment is in the media center or a computer lab, it is wise to send LD/ADD students there when the day's classwork requires a large amount of writing.

Ideally, youngsters with a writing problem might come to class with their own laptop provided by their family, the school system, their school's resource center, or vocational rehabilitation. (College students often find vocational rehabilitation centers a great source of support in providing special equipment and/or services that are otherwise unavailable.) Pupils who have their own computer should use the IEP to specify exactly how and where it is to be used. In general, it can be considered an alternative to writing by hand on assignments and tests and should be explored as a tool for note-taking as well.

In making adjustments to texts, materials, and assignments, it is important to remember that LD/ADD students can often fulfill the requirements if they are allowed to deviate from traditional study methods. Teachers who allow such accommodations are guided by one basic principle: change the form, not the content.

Adjustments in Teaching Techniques

CHAPTER 13

TEACHERS CAN EMPLOY A NUMBER OF SPECIAL STRATEGIES in the classroom to develop new enthusiasm for learning among previously unsuccessful students. When combined, they create an atmosphere in which LD/ADD youngsters are almost certain to succeed.

The first step in this alternate approach to classroom instruction is actually the beginning of a process. Since it forms the foundation and establishes the tone for all other techniques, its importance cannot be overestimated. The basic tenet of all instructional practices is to make classroom activities interesting. At every possible opportunity—when selecting topics for special projects, when making choices about which skills to stress, when deciding on materials to introduce a new concept, when determining which aspect of a subject to emphasize, when creating examples to use in a demonstration—choose a topic guaranteed to hold students' interest.

Sometimes, that's easy to do.

> Fifteen-year-old Harvey was in a special program for youths with severe emotional problems. He had a long history of school failure, a low IQ, a severe learning disability, an attention deficit disorder, and *no* reading or writing skills whatsoever. When he asked to be taught to read, his teachers decided to ignore his weaknesses and give him a chance.
>
> Harvey's enthusiasm was short-lived. Keeping him on task was impossible except when he had a pencil in his hand. Then he was cooperative and eager to learn.
>
> His instructor soon realized that handwriting, not reading, was what held real interest for Harvey. The youth thought he could use elegant penmanship to impress the ladies. In his mind, the ability to write a romantic little note would give him an advantage over less sophisticated competitors.
>
> Harvey quit coming to his lessons long before he learned to read, but he did stick with them long enough to gain a skill *he* believed was useful. He mastered cursive writing. Somebody had to help him with spelling, but he could write gorgeous love letters. And with beautiful, flowing script, he could sign his own name.
>
> Harvey's interest in learning to write gave him the motivation he needed to benefit from one part of his instruction. Like most teenagers, he wanted to look "cool" among his peers and was willing to put considerable effort into learning something that would impress his friends and help attract the opposite sex.

Students who have never tasted academic success are seldom as motivated as Harvey was. Those trapped in the failure pattern think of all schoolwork as boring and stupid. They aren't going to put any effort into some task they view as just another dumb assignment. Their attitude is part of the problem.

Failing LD/ADD students rarely see any relationship between schoolwork and their personal lives. They don't see how learning something in school gains them anything of value in the real world. They don't believe academic accomplishments are useful. These are attitudes of defeat. Lack of a desire to learn goes along with lack of motivation and lack of success.

When a student has no interest in the subject at hand, the teacher must use strong motivational measures before attempting any serious program of instruction. In the world outside the classroom, the technique is called *salesmanship*.

> A teacher in southern Georgia used this concept to rescue an LD/ADD teenager just as he was about to drop out of high school. She knew the boy would not be swayed by a logical explanation of the advantages of a high-school diploma. Instead, she pointed out what his life would be like if he passed all his classes and got promoted to the eleventh grade.
>
> "You'd be a junior," she said. To make sure he got the full meaning of that lofty status, she added, "We're talking class ring."
>
> The teacher never mentioned that the youth had F's in all his courses. She kept him focused on the rewards available through staying in school. She helped him picture the details. "We're talking prom," she said. Then she helped him imagine how lovely his girlfriend would look. "Can't you just see Carol Anne all dressed up for the prom? With a pretty new dress, a corsage, and your class ring on a gold chain around her neck?"
>
> This young man really wanted all the pleasures his teacher described. He stayed in school, got serious about his studies, and became eligible to rejoin the football team. We're talking letter sweater! This boy found that success in school can be fun.

Sometimes, students have their own reasons for wanting to learn something. Sometimes, the teacher has to provide a picture of the benefits available through mastery of a task. Either way, the amount of progress the student makes is closely related to how much interest he has in learning the skill. Those with a learning disability and/or an attention deficit disorder have to be convinced that an accomplishment is important to their personal life before they can be expected to master it.

To break the pattern of hopelessness, teachers need to be sure all assignments make sense to LD/ADD pupils. Every task must be seen as a step toward a desirable goal. Even the dullest drill will be done cheerfully if it is viewed as part of the process of mastering a skill important to the students.

Setting Goals

When dealing with LD/ADD students, the first goal is to show them they *can* learn. Teach them something. Give them a taste of success. To make that happen, the teacher has to be observant, persistent, compassionate, and clever.

Many children with a learning disability and/or an attention deficit disorder are highly resistant to success. Over and over, they sabotage their own efforts and snatch defeat from the jaws of victory. To the casual observer, and sometimes even to their teachers and parents, it looks like they'll do anything to get out of doing their work. What they're really trying to avoid is pointless activity. LD/ADD youngsters are often assigned tasks that teach them nothing. Their motivation has been killed by busywork that serves no purpose other than keeping them quiet and in their seats. Either their schoolwork is so difficult that failure is inevitable or it's so easy that no learning takes place. Failing students are rarely given a chance for honest success. They are not accustomed to real challenges.

Work doesn't have to be difficult to be challenging. Even a small amount of real effort should give the student a chance for success. But failure must also be possible. Success has no meaning if it's attained too easily. When good grades and high praise are just given away, students are robbed of the satisfaction of real achievement.

Students need to know what constitutes success in any given task. They need to know exactly what they're learning to do. Teachers should define success so clearly that there can be no room for disagreement later. It must be possible to give a definite "Yes" or "No" response to the questions "Are we getting anywhere?" and "Has the goal been reached?" In order to do this, work has to be organized so there is a definite point at which it can be said the material has been mastered.

When setting goals for LD/ADD youngsters, avoid making success dependent on mastering something by a specific date. Their progress is rarely steady and predictable. Missed deadlines have been a major part of their pattern of failure. Pupils should be allowed weeks or even months to learn the material used to create that first taste of success. No time limit or continuous threat of failure should loom over the work. As long as progress is being made, it doesn't matter how long it takes to reach mastery.

This is a radical departure from the normal approach to instruction, in which the pace and sequence of teaching are controlled by the textbook. Texts are written in chapters and units that jump from one topic to another. They don't allow students to stick with one concept until they really get the idea. Math books usually present a week or two of addition, a unit of subtraction, a few lessons on weights and measures, then a page or two of geometry. It might be more than a month before work on addition is resumed. By then, LD/ADD youngsters have forgotten what they learned in the previous section on addition and have to start over. For them, the "little dab at a time" approach is deadly.

When teaching LD/ADD children, the rate at which they learn *must* be taken into consideration. They must be taught at their own speed. This can be accomplished by presenting a concept, then keeping the student supplied with materials until he masters it and is ready to move on. This approach is called "conceptual teaching."

The human brain learns in a conceptual format. It takes in related pieces of information until it catches on to the pattern and recognizes the overall concept. That's when the student says, "Oh, now I get it!" This usually takes place after repetition and practice. Getting the new knowledge into long-term memory requires even more practice.

Traditional textbooks almost never provide enough material for LD/ADD students to master any one topic. Conceptual teaching requires a good assortment of supplementary materials.

> I once taught a regular fourth-grade class in which I had five reading groups. This arrangement allowed each of the thirty-four students to get some conceptual teaching every day, and it sent me scrambling to pull together a huge supply of workbooks and worksheet masters.

In language arts, ten minutes a day were scheduled for a project on dictionary skills. Each of the five groups worked at a different skill level. Four or five children had never learned the alphabet. They completed the easiest book in one series and, when they still hadn't mastered the skill, went on to the same material in the beginner's book of another series. These struggling, unrecognized LD/ADD youngsters often required material from three or four different sources to get enough work on one concept. During the same time period, the good readers breezed through alphabetizing, syllabication, and diacritical marks. They rarely needed more repetition than that provided by one or two workbooks.

It took a few weeks to get this daily dictionary work organized, but once I established a system it was easy keeping children supplied with appropriate materials.

All the students learned as fast as they could. They checked their own papers, charted their progress, and found great satisfaction in the steady gains they were making. Since they weren't all expected to master the same material by the same date, no one failed. There was no deadline. If a student didn't fully develop a skill by the end of the unit in his book, he was simply provided with another book and encouraged to continue practicing. Enthusiasm stayed high. Self-confidence grew. All the students learned enough to feel a strong sense of accomplishment.

The opening ten minutes of language arts became the best part of the school day. It was one of the few times in my career as a classroom teacher when I could honestly say *all* my students were learning satisfactorily. Total success felt great.

Deadlines cause pressure. For LD/ADD students, pressure can create the kind of anxiety that leads to mental shutdown. It's not unusual for these children to become school-phobic. They often confess that the least bit of pressure makes them nauseated or gives them sweaty palms. Weeks of insomnia and diarrhea are common among LD/ADD adults who enroll in adult-education courses at community colleges. Years of failure make them panic every time they enter a classroom.

Teachers who focus on competence instead of deadlines create an atmosphere of calm. Their attitude eases tension and eliminates anxiety. It helps students develop the kind of poise that allows them to tell themselves, "If I don't get it today, I'll get it tomorrow. If I do get it today, I'll still have to do it again tomorrow." Freeing students from deadlines makes learning a natural process similar to physical growth.

Using Alternate Techniques

Since it can safely be assumed that an LD/ADD student *can* learn, it's up to the teacher to determine *how* he learns and to use methods suited to his preferences, interests, and abilities.

Multisensory techniques are almost always effective with an LD/ADD pupil. Teaching to all the sensory channels tremendously increases the chances for success. To employ this instructional style, teachers must keep alert to opportunities to get the student's entire body involved in the learning process. Put his hands to use drawing, building, writing, or manipulating something. Explore body positions other than sitting. Letting the child stand to work at the chalkboard can be helpful; kneeling on the floor to write on newsprint or poster board often enhances concentration and increases recall. Some youngsters think better on their knees. As long as they don't disturb classmates, alternate postures should be encouraged.

Adding a touch of color to written material can create the kind of visual interest that makes information easier to understand and remember. Instead of underlining the subject once and the verb twice, write the nouns in blue and the action words in red. When putting math problems on the board, write the process symbols in a bright color that stands out from the white or yellow of the numbers. Encourage students to take notes in different colors or underline texts with several different highlighters. Every time color is introduced, it makes material more multisensory.

Some students need to talk their way through thought processes. They shouldn't be discouraged from moving their lips while reading or discussing things with themselves quietly when thinking. Verbal cues can help get facts stored in memory. Mnemonic devices almost always include a strong verbal element. Rhymes, jingles, songs, and chants help most learners fix sequences in memory. Many people never learn to do alphabetizing without using the ABC song.

The following instructional practices should be helpful in establishing effective verbal communication:

1. Use words that are short, simple, positive, and in the present tense

2. Employ colorful descriptive language that evokes mental pictures and imaginary scenes

3. Present ideas in sweeping statements that share feelings and opinions

4. Tell of dramatic experiences in an animated, expressive style

5. Communicate through analogies, metaphors, and parables

6. Use jokes, paradoxes, puzzles, and riddles to illustrate important or complex concepts

7. Point out connections and relationships

The following should be useful in teaching new concepts and making assignments:

1. Work an example or do a demonstration to *show* students the appropriate procedures that will lead to success on an assignment

2. Point out relationships between new concepts and material previously introduced

3. Have students work a few examples under close supervision to get the feel of new material

4. Show how the assignment fits into the big picture

5. Provide students with the correct answers and let them figure out how to arrive at them

The following concentration enhancers can help students build positive attitudes and minimize distractibility in the classroom and in private:

1. Notice, point out, and respond to humor in the environment

2. Hum, whistle, sing, recite rhymes or poems, listen to music, or beat out a rhythm

3. Maintain a playful, carefree attitude

4. Get involved in methodical, mundane, mechanical activities

5. Move about or maintain constant repetitive motion

To lead students to success, assign tasks that require them to do the following:

1. Imagine, visualize, or pretend

2. Sketch, draw, or print illustrations; work with colors, shapes, and patterns

3. Explain a process or demonstrate a procedure nonverbally

4. Create an original design or picture

5. Touch, feel, or manipulate real objects

6. Grasp messages conveyed through body language and tone of voice

7. Hypothesize possible solutions to a problem

8. Read between the lines for subtleties and unspoken messages; find meaning in symbolism

9. Provide answers that are rough guesses or estimates

10. Seek the new, the different, the unusual, the non-traditional through risk-taking and improvisation

11. Act quickly and immediately; be spontaneous

12. Use analogical thinking and intuition

13. Experiment with the untried; design by trial and error; learn by doing

14. Gain information through charts, maps, graphs, and illustrations

These techniques seem ridiculously simple. It's hard to believe they can lead to profound changes in classroom atmosphere, students' attitudes, personal study habits, and academic success attained by LD/ADD pupils. To prove that they really do work, try the following experiment. Take a routine vocabulary list of twenty words and divide it in half, making sure the two parts are of equal difficulty. Present the first half to the students with the "standard approach" outlined below and the second half with the "alternate approach" that follows.

STANDARD APPROACH

Day 1 Have students copy the words off the board and arrange them in alphabetical order. Help the class use syllabication rules and phonetic principles to decode the words orally.

Day 2 Have students look each word up in the dictionary, break it into syllables, correctly place all accents and diacritical marks, note what part of speech it is, and write its definition. Have them complete the assignment as homework if necessary.

Day 3 Check and discuss the previous day's work. Have students write an original sentence using each word. Have them complete the assignment as homework if necessary.

Day 4 Check and discuss the previous day's work. Review and practice using matching, multiple-choice, fill-in-the-blank, and true-false items. Check the work and send it home with the students for study and review.

Day 5 Give a test on the week's list using any format appropriate to the age level of the students.

After one week, test again with a pop quiz. After thirty days, retest with an unannounced quiz. Record the scores for comparison with those from the other part of the experiment.

ALTERNATE APPROACH

Day 1 Write the words on the chalkboard before class starts. Read them one by one to the class. Have the students repeat each word with correct pronunciation. Randomly assign three words to each student. (For instance, if this is a biology class and all the words are about fish, put the ten words on bobbers or colored pieces of paper cut out in the shapes of fish and have students draw them out of a fishbowl.) Each word will be repeated several times, depending on the number of students. Have each student look up his three words in the dictionary, break them into syllables, correctly place accents and diacritical marks, note what part of speech they are, and write the definition. Have them complete the assignment as homework if necessary.

Day 2 Give the students a list of all ten words complete with syllabication, accents and diacritical marks, part of speech, and definition for each word. Leave a blank place for students to fill in synonyms later. Read the list of words to the students. Have them repeat the correct pronunciation of each. Using the same words assigned the previous day, have each student do the following four things.

1. Select three pieces of colored construction paper, one that is appropriate for each word.

2. Print one of the words in large letters across the bottom of each sheet, using crayons or chalk in a color that contrasts with the paper.

3. Find a picture in a magazine to illustrate each word, then glue it on the colored paper. Even the most subtle abstractions can be illustrated if the word's meaning is clearly understood. For example, the word *prevaricate* means to tell a lie. The concept might be conveyed in an endless number of ways. A picture of a human face could have a long nose added to look like Pinocchio. A table fork and a tongue could be combined to portray the Indian expression "Speaks with forked tongue." A picture of a politician caught in a lie could also communicate the idea. The word *unctuous* could be explained by an ad for cooking oil. *Salacious* could be expressed by an advertisement for an X-rated movie. Students will have to stretch their imaginations to make these connections, and the results will often be funny.

4. Display one illustration by each student in a prominent place on a wall or bulletin board. The assignment may be completed as homework if necessary.

Day 3 Read the list aloud *with* the students. Discuss definitions of the words and help the class decide on good synonyms; list them on the board. Have the class write the synonyms in the blank space on the definition sheet given out the previous day. (Have extra sheets available for those who have lost theirs.) Have the youngsters write sentences using each of their three words and the appropriate synonyms on the backs of the illustrations created previously. The sentences should explain the words' relationship to the picture on the front of the paper. "Pinocchio's nose grew every time he prevaricated (lied)." "All oils are unctuous (fatty)." "Salacious (lustful) movies are usually X-rated." Have the students share their illustrations and sentences with the class. As long as no offensive language is used, humor should be encouraged. Hang the illustrations in a prominent place for display and later use. The assignment may be completed as homework if necessary.

Day 4 Read the list aloud *with* the students. Have the class repeat each word correctly and say its synonym as recorded on the definition sheet the previous day. Help the children think of rhyming words for each of the ten vocabulary words; list them on the board. (For instance, *prevaricate* might have *coagulate* and *miscalculate*; *unctuous* might have *scrumptious*, *amongst us*, and *rambunctious*; and *salacious* might have *spacious*, *pugnacious*, and *good gracious*.) Have the students create rhymes, jingles, or limericks with each of their three words, plus any of the others they find appealing. Don't expect quality poetry. The sillier these are, the better.

> My blood will coagulate
> if I prevaricate.
>
> People get rambunctious
> when they feel something unctuous
> being poured in their hair.
>
> Good gracious,
> that movie was salacious!

Choose a student to record one or two of the best rhymes for each of the ten words. Photocopy the verses and hand them out at the end of class for use as a review sheet.

Day 5 Get the children to gather up their illustrations from walls, bulletin boards, and other display areas; place them out of sight. Give a test on the week's list using any format appropriate to the age level of the students.

After one week, test again with a pop quiz. After thirty days, retest with an unannounced quiz. Record the scores for comparison with those from the other part of the experiment. Compare the results of the "standard approach" to those of the "alternate approach" by asking the following:

1. Which approach was more time-consuming in terms of preparation?

2. Within the classroom, which took more time?

3. Which took more energy?

4. Which was more pleasant?

5. Which got the students more motivated and cooperative?

6. Which produced the better test results at the end of the week?

7. Which yielded the better test scores after a week without review?

8. Which produced the better results in long-term memory, as demonstrated by the quiz after thirty days?

9. Which students showed marked improvement with the "alternate approach"?

10. Which students achieved higher scores with the "standard approach"?

Good for One Can Be Good for All

Research studies have repeatedly shown that the human brain learns best when experiencing concrete reality. This principle applies to *all* youngsters and *all* subjects. But it is doubly true for those with a learning disability and/or an attention deficit disorder. The following hierarchy shows how this concept applies to classroom practices:

1. Rather than having him read about it, tell him about it

2. Rather than telling him about it, show it to him

3. Rather then showing it to him, let him touch it, handle it, observe it, feel it, build it, work it, or do it

In classes where instruction is based on experiments and demonstrations, LD/ADD children are likely to excel. They are usually most successful in classes that use a hands-on approach to learning. Such methods allow them to combine their high level of curiosity with their unusual powers of observation and their talent for dealing with three-dimensional objects. They can reason out what's going on, draw their own logical conclusions, and remember the concept presented. That's good learning.

In classes where instruction is based on reading the book and answering questions, LD/ADD children are likely to be bored, unmotivated, and inattentive. Such teaching techniques force them to rely on areas where their skills are weak. Due to their slow, labored reading, they forget the beginning of the paragraph before they get to the end. Misreading and skipping over hard words give them only a hint of the concept being presented. Rather than wade through masses of words explaining some abstract theory, they investigate the freckles on the backs of their hands. That's also good learning. But they're learning about freckles, not the topic being presented.

Teaching techniques that are appropriate for LD/ADD students are appropriate for others as well. Anything done to help an LD/ADD pupil become more attentive and better organized tends to have the same effect on the entire class. Special instructional methods adopted to help one such youngster frequently result in better learning for all the students and increased efficiency for the teacher.

> After his second unsuccessful year in the seventh grade, Fred was diagnosed as having a mild learning disability combined with a severe attention deficit disorder with hyperactivity. Since there wasn't a single LD specialist in the boy's small hometown, the clinic where he was tested agreed to send an expert to consult with his school. Fred's eighth-grade teachers were given the kind of guidance they needed in order to work effectively with this LD/ADD youth.
>
> As the semester progressed, Fred's teachers got discouraged. With each monthly visit, the consultant found that another teacher or two had given up.
>
> "All he wants to do in class is socialize," Fred's science teacher complained. "If he'd pay attention, I could help him. But all he does is talk and fool around." Obviously, science class wasn't interesting enough to lure the boy's attention away from his friends.

"I can't get him to do his homework or bring his materials to class," the youth's English teacher said. "It's gotten to the point that he just sits there and looks out the window—and I let him." Despite all the changes she had made, this teacher hadn't figured out a way to work around the child's problem with disorganization.

Fred's reading teacher didn't like his attitude. She gave up when he failed to produce a book report after repeated warnings and postponements.

The youngster's math teacher remained optimistic until the middle of the semester. For her, the final blow came when a routine notebook grading revealed that Fred was at least a month behind.

One by one, all of Fred's teachers threw their hands up in defeat.

All but Mr. Ward, the history teacher. At every monthly meeting, he discussed the problems he was having with Fred and asked the LD specialist for new suggestions. With patience, Mr. Ward listened to the advice he was given, then went back to his classroom to put it into practice.

The history teacher used tremendous ingenuity in working to solve his LD/ADD student's classroom problems. With insight, flexibility, and creativity, Mr. Ward made radical changes in his teaching techniques. All the alterations paid off handsomely for Fred, for his classmates, and for Mr. Ward.

1. Instead of lecturing from notes he'd written on file cards, Mr. Ward changed to outlining his lectures on a plain sheet of paper. Every morning, he ran off about a dozen copies of the day's material. One copy automatically went to Fred. Others went to students who had missed class. Pupils who lost their notes got replacements from the teacher's master file. Many youngsters requested sets as a study guide for tests. By the end of the semester, Mr. Ward was making his lecture notes available in all his classes.

2. In lecturing, Mr. Ward often gave names, dates, and other details not recorded in his outline. Since Fred was a very poor speller and made many reversals when writing dates, the teacher devised a two-part system. When introducing important names and dates, Mr. Ward wrote them on the blackboard and on a file card he kept at his podium. The entire class was expected to record the information in a special section of their notebook. As a backup measure for the LD/ADD boy and any others unable to copy accurately, a pupil with good handwriting used carbon paper to make a duplicate of the list. At the end of each period, this "class secretary" gave a copy of all the material on the board to Fred, who stapled the facts to his daily notes before leaving the room. As other students recognized the value of such a service, the class secretary's notes increased in popularity.

As the second part of his system, Mr. Ward dated and filed the card he'd used to record the list of details. Students who were absent or who lost their notes found the teacher's file of the daily lists useful.

This well-organized history teacher soon noticed that Fred's class was doing better work than the other groups he taught. Oral reading and discussions went more smoothly. Fred's classmates had little trouble remembering difficult names. Their test grades were consistently higher than those of his other history classes. The daily information list was such an effective study aid that the instructor also introduced this system in his other sections.

3. During movies and filmstrips, Mr. Ward routinely jotted down the main ideas so they could be discussed, reviewed, and included in tests. Normally, he expected his students to make their own record of the important facts. But Fred couldn't take notes. To help his LD/ADD pupil, Mr. Ward had to devise an alternate system.

First, during the presentation, the teacher made his own notes as a master. By running off copies, he always had a good set of notes available for Fred. Then, since he had the material available anyway, the teacher went one step farther and used it as a lesson in note-taking for the entire class.

Immediately after a film concluded, Mr. Ward would announce, "This movie had one major subject, three main points, and twenty-three important details. Check your notes and see what *you* have."

After the students counted up their record of the topics presented, the teacher led a point-by-point discussion.

"What was the major subject?" he asked.

Students volunteered answers until there was general agreement.

Mr. Ward continued, "What was the first main idea?"

After that was answered, he challenged, "There were eight important details about that one main idea. What were they?"

Students called out the points they had listed in their notes. Groaning over their defeats, proudly smiling with their triumphs, they always made the discussion lively. Even Fred participated actively.

At the end of class, each student was given a copy of the teacher's notes to compare with his own. No grades or scores were ever given.

What started as an adjustment to help one LD/ADD student survive became a technique that helped an entire class.

4. To get away from writing daily assignments on the blackboard, Mr. Ward handed out a weekly homework sheet every Monday. In addition to relieving Fred of the difficult copying task, this allowed him to get a head start on reading assignments that he couldn't complete in one night.

Major reports, tests, and projects were assigned well in advance. Week by week, the sheet reminded students to prepare for tests and projects.

Mr. Ward found this technique to be such a timesaver that he put all of his classes on a weekly assignment program.

5. Fred had a major problem with attention. His mind constantly drifted off into daydreams during class. To keep the youngster's attention focused on the work at hand, Mr. Ward saw to it that the boy took an active part in all discussions. If Fred's hand went up, he was always called on. If Fred's hand didn't go up, he was often called on anyway. For some LD/ADD youngsters, this would be torture. But since Fred loved to talk and knew a lot about history, it was an effective and reasonable technique.

6. Once a week, Fred and his history teacher had a fifteen-minute conference. The time was mainly used as a way to keep Fred organized. He and his teacher looked over the assignment sheet and checked off the work he'd done. Then Fred reported on his progress with special projects or preparations for a large test. Mr. Ward approved, advised, prodded, made suggestions, wrote a note to his pupil's parents, requested special material from the library—whatever was needed. He helped Fred organize the notes and lists that had accumulated over the last week. Anything that was missing was replaced from the file.

Mr. Ward did not start weekly conferences with all his eighth-graders. But he did find that if he left his files open, many students came by to organize their own materials.

How was it that Mr. Ward succeeded where other teachers failed? He was willing to change more than materials and assignments. He went to the core of his program and altered his teaching techniques. Most teachers are very reluctant to change their instructional methods.

Teaching techniques must not be confused with *teaching styles.* There are many sound instructional techniques. They are easily adopted, adjusted, and discarded. Finding a new way to teach the same old thing can excite and challenge a class. Varying instructional methods helps fight boredom in both students and teachers. Creative instructors tend to have an open-minded, experimental attitude toward teaching techniques.

That is not the case with teaching styles. Personal teaching styles differ widely but are always a reflection of the entire individual, an expression of a personality. When a teacher tries to imitate the words, behavior, and attitudes of some other person, the result is likely to make the instructor and the students intensely uncomfortable.

Julia was a highly intelligent college senior doing her learning-disabilities internship under my supervision. She was a pleasant and agreeable person who definitely had an honest, up-front, straight-from-the-shoulder approach to life.

The first time I observed Julia teaching a one-to-one lesson, she used a variety of acceptable LD techniques. But her teaching style didn't fit her personality at all. In presenting material to her fourteen-year-old pupil, she treated him as though he were a baby. Smiling and talking in a little, high-pitched voice, Julia praised his good work by cooing, "Oh, you did such a wonderful job on that, Walter. I'm so proud of you. And it was hard, too, wasn't it?"

The young woman's behavior puzzled her student. He glanced at me and rolled his eyes.

Not noticing her pupil's discomfort, Julia went on. "As a reward for doing such good work today, I'm going to let you play this special game. Doesn't that look like fun?"

I couldn't stand it. I left the room. The poor teenager had to stay and put up with it.

Later, when we discussed her lesson, I bluntly asked the intern, "Why were you doing all that gushing?"

Julia understood immediately. "I thought I was *supposed* to do that," she replied.

"You treated a teenage boy like a seven-year-old."

The intern looked tremendously relieved. "You mean I don't have to do that?"

"Certainly not. Whatever gave you the idea you did?"

"All the teachers I've observed treated their pupils that way. So I thought I had to do the same."

It turned out that Julia had visited three LD classrooms to do some observing. Two had been first-grade classes where the "oh, this is going to be so much fun" attitude was appropriate. In the clinic, the girl had observed one of our finest therapists. Mrs. Collins was an old pro in her late sixties. With a wonderful, warm smile and a deep Southern drawl, she addressed everybody as "Honey," "Dahlin'," "Sweetheart," or "Sugah." The director of the clinic, the psychologists, the secretaries, other therapists—Mrs. Collins gushed over everybody. It was just her way. In Mrs. Collins, the constant, effusive sweetness was real. Students of all ages loved it and responded well. In Julia, it came across as phony, and her student hated it.

Instructors who adjust their teaching techniques must guard against the tendency to revise their teaching style in the process. A new instructional method feels awkward for a while. But an altered teaching style that does not fit the educator's temperament feels uncomfortable always. When a teacher feels that she's putting on an act, she is probably using an unsuitable teaching style that does not allow her to express herself honestly.

Change the Presentation, Not the Content

When instructors make adjustments in their teaching techniques to help LD/ADD students succeed in a regular classroom, there is one general principle that can always provide a guideline: make alterations in the way material is presented, *not* in the material itself. Adjusted instructional methods are supposed to make it possible for LD/ADD students to learn without having to rely on their weak skills in reading, writing, copying, math, and/or spelling.

1. Keep directions clear and simple.

A teacher might say, "John, today is the day we solve your problem with numbering on your spelling test. Instead of numbering your paper before the test, I want you to try a new method. I really think it will help if you write down the numbers as we go along. That way, you'll get the right number for each word. You won't get mixed up because all you'll have to do is write down what I say. I think this will be a lot easier for you. Don't you think it will help?"

It would be better to say, "John, don't number your paper now. As I give the test, write the numbers when you hear me say them. Today, write the numbers with the words during the test."

In the latter example, the teacher gives *one* message three different ways: first as a command, then with detailed instructions, then as a summary. That's not a good conversational technique with spouses and friends. But in the classroom, speaking to LD/ADD children, giving the message in three different forms can be very effective. It's important to notice that the child isn't given an explanation of *why*. When he finishes the test, has all his numbers correct, and looks up at the teacher with the "Wow!" of success, he'll understand why he was told to do it.

Explaining the assignment in words is only the first step in a three-part process. Working a sample for the student is the second. The teacher *shows* the youngster what to do. At the end of the example, the pupil is usually nodding and saying, "I've got it."

The third step, which requires the student to do a sample for himself, really imprints the idea on his memory. LD/ADD children often forget what they hear and see. But once they've done something for themselves and gotten the feel of it, they usually remember.

The tendency that students with a learning disability and/or an attention deficit disorder have to forget what they're supposed to do can usually be overcome by clear, simple directions and a three-step approach: *tell* them, *show* them, have them *do* it.

2. Avoid giving multiple assignments.

When presented with more than one type of study activity at a time, students with a learning disability and/or an attention deficit disorder are likely to become confused. Directions for one segment get mistakenly applied to another.

If an LD/ADD child is required to do three separate worksheets, he needs to have them explained to him one by one as he does them. Even when all the work is routine, problems arise in shifting from one type of thinking to another.

3. Avoid techniques based on sequencing.

Many good teaching techniques are based on the human mind's ability to remember a long series of things in a particular order. For most people, sequencing is a memory aid. However, these techniques can frustrate LD/ADD children.

> Mary Louise was in the ninth grade but had never mastered long division. Year after year, her math teachers tried to help her learn the process by saying, "It's just five easy steps that you do over and over: divide, multiply, subtract, compare, bring down. All you have to do is get those five steps into your head, and you've got it."
>
> And every year, Mary Louise stayed bewildered as she failed to get those simple steps embedded in her memory. She also had trouble remembering the four seasons and the twelve months of the year in order. But none of her teachers noticed her glaring weakness with sequencing.
>
> Finally, at the age of fourteen, Mary Louise ran across a math tutor who taught her a trick for keeping the long-divi-

> sion steps in order without relying on her sequencing skills. At the top of her paper, right under her name and the date, the girl learned to put "DMSCB." That stood for "Does McDonald's sell cheeseburgers?" It gave her the cues she needed to keep the division steps straight as she successfully worked the problems.

It's bad enough when a teaching technique is based on sequencing. Many times, an entire lesson is based on this skill. For LD/ADD students, such a task gives them no real chance for success. They are simply not able to keep a complicated series in the correct order.

4. Avoid techniques based on directional patterns.

Once children get beyond the age of playing Simon says, it is assumed they understand *up, down, left, right, under, over, beside,* and *around.* Using directional patterns helps most children master new tasks.

For instructors who want to teach long division without relying on sequencing, there is another common memory trick. It is based on the use of directional patterns. "It's just a matter of working in a circle with a series of big loops," children are told. "Start with the number on the far *left* and divide it into the number on the *right.* Put the answer up *above*, starting on the *left.* Multiply the number *above* the line by the one to the far *left* and put the answer at the bottom *left.* Subtract the numbers at the *bottom* and compare the answer with the divisor at the far *left.* If it's smaller, look *above* . . ."

Such an explanation helps most children master the complex maneuvers involved in long division. But for a child who can't tell left from right, a technique based on such directions makes a difficult task impossible.

Sometimes, the only way to teach a skill involves directional patterns. In such cases, teachers can show the pattern with arrows instead of describing it with words.

Teaching young children manuscript and cursive writing is usually based on directional instructions. The most common technique teaches youngsters to talk their way through the process of forming a letter. "To make a cursive capital *J*, start on the line. Go *up* and around to the *left, over* the top to the *right, down* below the line, around to the *left*, back *up* to the *right*, and cross at the line." After demonstrating once or twice, the teacher tells the child, "Say it with me as we do it together." In unison, they form the letter while saying, "*Up* to the *left, over* to the *right, down*, around to the *left, up*, and *over*." It's an effective method for most children. But for those with a learning disability and/or an attention deficit disorder, it's usually not very helpful. They get lost in all the words.

LD specialists teach writing by telling children where to start, showing them how to do it, then getting them to feel it. Sometimes, they help students trace the patterns on sandpaper, in a pan of grits, in shaving cream on the floor, or on bumpy letters designed for the purpose. Usually, they have youngsters trace the movement over and over. They rarely use words to explain the direction of the movements.

In teaching students to deal with maps, charts, graphs, football plays, gymnastics moves, dance steps, techniques of dissecting a frog or setting up a chemistry experiment, and a host of other activities, the standard method of instruction is based on verbally describing directional patterns. These techniques can be adapted by shifting away from *telling* and placing the emphasis on *demonstrating* and *illustrating*. LD/ADD students can learn the process through imitation.

5. Avoid instructional methods that require a great deal of independent work.

To the inexperienced, LD/ADD students placed in regular classrooms look like ideal candidates for the kind of individualized instruction in which all their work is specially designed for them. The theory is that they should be taught one-to-one, then allowed to work independently on assignments created to meet their particular needs. It sounds wonderful. And since individualized instruction is so much work for the teacher, the inexperienced tend to think it must be good for the child.

In the case of youngsters with learning disabilities and/or attention deficit disorder, that is not true. Because of their problems with organization and attention, LD/ADD students almost always have trouble working independently. They do not do well with work that, although designed specifically for them, requires them to work unsupervised. Their minds wander. Often, they never succeed in getting down to business at all.

On their own, LD/ADD students are usually not very productive. They need structure and firm guidance. They thrive under close supervision but falter under a heavy load of independent work.

6. Spare the child the embarrassment of demonstrating his weaknesses in front of his classmates.

In classes other than reading, it is not necessary for all the students to read aloud. If an LD/ADD pupil volunteers to take a turn at oral reading, a short, easy passage is appropriate for him.

The annual spelling bee is usually unavoidable. Mercifully, LD/ADD pupils are almost always eliminated in the first few rounds.

Writing on the blackboard is another awkward situation that is best avoided unless the youngster volunteers.

Publicly displaying their weaknesses makes LD/ADD children terribly ashamed. It also opens the door for unkind remarks from unsympathetic classmates. It puts all the students in a position where social problems are likely to develop.

Most LD/ADD students sit in class praying they won't be called on to read aloud or put something on the board. Wise instructors see to it that their prayers are answered.

Teachers who take the time to explore and apply the techniques presented in this chapter will notice a significant difference in their entire class almost immediately. The improvement in the performance of *all* students is sometimes startling.

A North Carolina biology teacher named Donna Oliver was

the 1987 National Teacher of the Year. In a newspaper article, she was quoted as saying, "My top priority is to prepare and plan my lesson for today so that it is an exciting lesson for my students and me. That's first. The other things have to work around that." Teaching that captures interest does more than transmit information. Exciting teaching gets children involved. It builds enthusiasm, generates optimism, and develops motivation. To teach in ways that transform lives, we have to touch hearts as well as minds.

Adjustments in Homework

CHAPTER 14

FUNDAMENTAL TO ALL EDUCATIONAL PHILOSOPHY is the belief that formal instruction equips the individual to think independently. Schools are intended to do more than teach skills and transmit information. They are also responsible for preparing students to use knowledge on their own. The process of education is not complete until the individual can apply learning in real-life situations.

The practice of assigning schoolwork to be done at home is a logical product of this philosophy. Through homework, pupils develop skill in working independently.

Within actual classrooms, these lofty ideals tend to get lost. Many teachers no longer assign homework regularly. They have found the traditional system to be more trouble than it's worth.

Among homeschoolers, homework is extremely unpopular. Most of them are so anti-homework that they consider the entire concept ridiculous. In choosing to teach their offspring at home, they usually opt for educational practices that are not open to consideration for those in a classroom environment. Homeschoolers who place a high value on self-reliance and self-confidence usually include a great deal of independent work in their program without ever using the word *homework*.

LD/ADD students can quickly kill a teacher's faith in any kind of homework program.

Is Homework Success REALLY Important?

Homework is the single most visible evidence of LD/ADD students' lack of academic success. Every night, their parents go through a battle that keeps their home in constant turmoil. At the beginning of every school day, a zero goes into the grade book to announce their failure to their classmates. First thing every morning, the teacher's frustration is renewed before the lessons even begin. Lack of success with homework daily reestablishes LD/ADD students as dummies, misfits, and losers.

Parents and teachers rarely figure out what to do. The situation is allowed to persist even as it erodes the child's self-esteem and destroys the patience and optimism of the frustrated adults around him.

This pattern is totally unnecessary.

Homework is the one area in which a significant change almost always can be achieved in a single semester. All it takes is one determined teacher and one cooperative family member, and a youngster's homework habits can be totally altered.

Teachers who want to put serious energy into reversing an LD/ADD student's homework failure need to start by analyzing their own attitudes about home assignments. They can't be expected to make a success of a program they don't even believe in.

Teachers often hate to adjust the homework given to LD/ADD pupils. They think it's unfair if one student isn't required to do as much work as the others. Teachers have always assigned work in terms of the size of the finished product. Every member of a class is told to read the same number of pages, answer the same set of questions, and perform the same set of operations or activities in accordance with directions that apply to everyone. The variable is how long it takes each student to accomplish the task. And that is considered fair.

When seen from this traditional perspective, home assignments are related to the needs of the instructor, the curriculum, and the school—not the needs of the child. There is an assumption that a certain amount of work must be completed in order for the entire class to finish the book by the end of the school year. With this approach, the standard is set according to the size of the finished product rather than the amount of time involved in producing it. Thus, good students are rewarded for working quickly. In less than half an hour, efficient workers can read a social studies assignment, write the answers to the end-of-the-chapter questions, have a snack, and go off to play with friends. Meanwhile, LD/ADD youngsters are punished for working slowly. In two hours, they can figure out about half the words in a social studies assignment, write garbled, misspelled answers to a few questions, have a tantrum, and go off to sulk in their room. Rather than go through all that agony, most youngsters with a learning disability and/or an attention deficit disorder simply avoid the situation. They "forget" to bring their books home or lie to their parents in claiming that they don't have any homework.

Students with a learning disability and/or an attention deficit disorder usually don't do any homework at all. Everybody else works. They do absolutely nothing besides play, feel guilty, and cause trouble. Yet even more than other pupils, LD/ADD youngsters need the benefits daily independent study can provide. They need opportunities to be productive despite their tendency toward disorganization and forgetfulness. They need that sense of accomplishment that comes from doing a satisfactory job on even the tiniest assignment. They need the feeling of self-confidence that comes from working successfully on their own.

LD/ADD students know that a system that gives everyone an equal amount of work treats them unfairly. Teachers have to come to the same realization. Until educators shift away from the traditional method and make a radical change in the way homework is selected and assigned, they're not in a position to make appropriate adjustments in the homework of LD/ADD students.

The First Parent-Teacher Conference

Homework is schoolwork assigned by the teacher to be done at home under the supervision of the parents. It directly involves both the home and the school. If an LD/ADD student is to be successful with homework, there must be coordination and cooperation between the parents and the teacher. Mutual understanding must be developed from the very beginning.

During the first two weeks of school, the classroom teacher needs to have a formal conference with the parents of each LD/ADD student in her class. The school's LD specialist should be included as well. Through such a meeting, the teacher takes the lead in establishing good communication between school and home. And she accomplishes three major objectives. First, she gains helpful information about the youngster and his previous school experience. Second, she has an opportunity to explain the way she runs her class. Third, she and the parents can thoroughly discuss homework. Although it is too soon for the teacher to give details on just how the student's homework will be altered, she should give the parents an idea of the general approach that will be used. The mother and father need to understand exactly how often their child will have home assignments. The teacher needs to understand just how much supervision and help the parents are willing and able to provide.

> From the time their sons entered school, the Dixsons were positive that both their boys had dyslexia. Books and magazine articles confirmed their suspicions, but they couldn't get educators to do anything to help. Since the father's work moved the family all over the country, the two boys were tested in various clinics and schools.
>
> When George was twelve and Bill was nine, they were finally diagnosed correctly and provided appropriate therapy. Despite his severe learning disability, George had successfully passed grades one through five. He was in the midst of squeak-

ing through grade six. As a third-grader, Bill was still a non-reader. Though he was always on the brink of failure, the child had passed the first and second grades.

What success the boys had achieved was totally due to the efforts of their parents. For six solid years, the Dixsons had devoted all their evenings to schoolwork. They hadn't merely helped their sons with homework. They had systematically retaught everything that had been done in school. Reading to their sons, recording their answers to questions, explaining, drilling, discussing, practicing, studying for tests—for all practical purposes, they were homeschooling George and Bill. For all four of the Dixsons, "family life" meant schoolwork shared.

It took two years of LD therapy to get Bill and George to the point where they could do their own homework. Then it took another two years under the supervision of a psychiatrist to get the family to break away from its long-established pattern of spending its entire time together huddled over schoolbooks.

Even though it had been absolutely essential for them to become involved in their sons' studies, Mr. and Mrs. Dixson had found helping with homework to be habit-forming.

It is common to find that parents of LD/ADD children have either given up or never gotten involved with homework in the first place. There are also families who care very much and provide encouragement and supervision yet are not capable of supplying the assistance the child needs. Many LD/ADD children have LD/ADD parents. Before the teacher designs a system to alter the child's nightly assignments, it is important to find out what kind of assistance can be expected in the home.

Twelve-year-old Brad was the fourth of the Johnsons' six children. He and his three older brothers all had a learning disability along with an attention deficit disorder. His two sisters were having no trouble with school, but they were only in the first and second grades.

Brad's parents had never been officially diagnosed, but it appeared that they, too, were LD/ADD. Mrs. Johnson had to read recipes six or eight times to figure them out. She had dropped out of high school because of her trouble with reading comprehension. Mr. Johnson had dropped out of college because of his difficulty with writing and spelling. The man often confessed, "When I'm on a business trip, I have to call my secretary to get her to spell words for me."

There were eight wonderful, warm, loving people in the Johnson home. Every one of them was eager to offer Brad any kind of assistance he needed. But there wasn't a single one capable of helping him with his sixth-grade homework.

No matter how much help is available for the child at home, teachers should adapt assignments so that LD/ADD students are able to do the majority of their homework on their own. In the first conference, parents should be encouraged to avoid *any* direct involvement in their youngsters' nightly assignments. They should be guided to understand that their role is to provide an appropriate time and place to study, to show interest, and to offer encouragement or sympathy when needed. Other than that, they should stay out of homework as much as possible.

For students who have previously found homework to be an insurmountable hurdle, developing independent study skills needs to be addressed as a major goal and included in the IEP. Such remedial action requires a step-by-step plan designed to lead students to develop the organizational strategies, time-management procedures, and study skills necessary to reverse the failure pattern.

Bryan was a high-school senior. He had a 1480 on his SAT and an acceptance to a good college taped to the mirror above his dresser. But in the middle of his last semester, he was in danger of failing three courses and not getting his diploma! He had gotten so far behind with papers, projects, and routine homework assignments that his good test scores were being ruined by long strings of zeros.

The midterm report warning Bryan's parents of his impending disaster made the cause of the boy's problem very clear.

Honors English classwork C
Homework F
Exam A

Grade F
Book reports and term paper never turned in.

Physics classwork C
Homework F
Exam A-
Grade C

AP Spanish V classwork C
Homework F
Exam C+
Grade D

Economics classwork B
Homework F
Exam A
Grade A-

AP Calculus classwork F
Homework F
Exam C-
Grade F

Honors World History classwork D
Homework F
Exam B+
Grade F
Major project never turned in.

In courses where reports, projects, and term papers were included as part of the homework, Bryan's poor performance on independent assignments outweighed his good grades on exams. By getting behind in his reading and ignoring homework assignments, he was seldom prepared to take an active part in classroom activities, and his classwork grades suffered accordingly.

This bright young man used a quick mind, highly developed listening ability, a strong memory, outstanding test-taking skills, and excellent reasoning power to master his course material and make good grades on tests. But his high IQ couldn't help him overcome his disorganization, his lack of motivation, and his absent-mindedness. Since Bryan was certified as LD and ADD, his IEP allowed for his poor spelling and his difficulty with writing. But no attempt was made to accommodate his problem with disorganization through either time-management instruction or modification of the work required. He was being penalized for weaknesses over which he had no control. And his family knew it.

As it turned out, the youth squeezed by and graduated with his class. If Bryan had not managed to bail himself out of the mess, his parents could have come back to the school with a lawyer and made a convincing case that by not making accommodations for their son's difficulty with organization the school had been out of compliance with Section 504.

In most academic environments, the inability to fulfill homework requirements is a much greater handicap than poor spelling and writing. In terms of life skills, the ability to work successfully without supervision is crucial.

For youngsters who have a history of getting bogged down on homework assignments, it is best to treat the problem as a separate issue unrelated to success or failure in any one subject. Just as LD/ADD students are not penalized for poor spelling outside spelling class, those with weaknesses in organizational techniques and study strategies should not be penalized for poor homework performance. Until the student is led to develop the skills and habits necessary for successful completion of home assignments, homework should be removed from the list of factors that determine his grade in regular classes.

Enabling the Student to Work Independently

In order to change homework to fit the limitations of an LD/ADD pupil, the teacher has to shift from thinking of home assignments as a way to cover material quickly and instead use them as a way to develop reliability and self-sufficiency. By making assignments in accordance with the following guidelines, teachers can use homework to help LD/ADD students develop independence, establish good study habits, and build self-confidence.

1. Carefully consider the attention span of the particular LD/ ADD student.

Under the best of conditions, how long can he work at one stretch? In the controlled environment of the classroom, can he work for ten minutes on math? How many minutes of spelling can he do before his mind drifts off? For young children, the answer is probably two to five minutes at best. For older ones, ten minutes is usually about the maximum.

Find out how long the youngster can concentrate and start with that. The student may be given three or four different assignments in one night, but no single one should require more time than is contained in one of his short bursts of attention.

Keep in mind that for the child with a learning disability and/or an attention deficit disorder, doing homework includes getting organized. Five minutes of actual work takes ten minutes of finding papers, sharpening pencils, getting to the right page, figuring out directions, and so on. Changing from one subject to another means the student needs another ten minutes to get reorganized.

2. Be sure the student understands the directions and has two samples to copy—one that was done for him, one that he did himself.

The LD/ADD pupil may remember how to add numbers today but not tomorrow. The fact that the youngster did a certain kind of work in class every day this week does *not* mean he'll remember how to do it at home tonight. A good set of directions and two samples can refresh his unreliable memory when he forgets.

3. Be sure the student has the exact assignment written down correctly.

Children with a learning disability and/or an attention deficit disorder cannot be trusted to remember their homework assignments. The most effective way to work around this is to insist that they carry a small spiral notebook with them at all times. Every home assignment must be recorded in this notebook. And someone must check to be sure that it is written down accurately—an ideal job for a "good neighbor."

Disorganized students rarely catch on to the use of a memory-jogging system immediately. In fact, most of them are highly resistant to the idea. Many of the most scatterbrained LD/ADD youngsters insist that they have a perfectly good memory and are insulted that adults should even suggest an improvement is necessary. When they do agree to add an assignment book to the clutter at the bottom of their backpack, it gets lost right along with all the other school materials that slip out of their possession so easily. "It was right in the back of my notebook," they protest when they can't produce it at homework time. It takes close monitoring for at least six to eight weeks before an LD/ADD student can even begin to use an assignment book effectively. Those who are willing to go through the process of establishing such an important habit deserve the eternal gratitude of the child's family, his future spouse, and a lifetime of employers and coworkers.

4. Assign only work that involves concepts the student has already mastered in class.

If the skill is just in the process of being learned and the pupil is still having trouble with it, it should not be practiced outside the close supervision available in the classroom. If subtraction problems with borrowing always confuse him, he shouldn't be expected to tackle them alone. As much as possible, assign tasks at which the student is nearly certain to succeed.

5. Give the child an escape route.

Even when a teacher takes every precaution to select the perfect assignment, there are times when a student cannot successfully complete it as designed. It is especially hard to judge how long it will take a given child to do a particular task. A bail-out clause makes it possible to deal with such situations without damaging the chances for future success.

All of us have an occasional off day. The frustration of such times must not be allowed to build to the exploding point. It's important that students learn to recognize situations where it's best to back off. An upset student can go stretch his legs, get a drink, or get a breath of fresh air before going back to work. There is no shame in this. Recognizing the limits of one's patience is part of wisdom and maturity.

Many LD/ADD students are perfectionists. For them, the desire to complete a homework assignment must not be allowed to cause tension or anxiety. Such stress contaminates other areas. If the determination to succeed becomes so all-consuming that the youngster takes no interest in anything else, it's time to ease up.

For children who can use a clock, a time limit is ideal. In the front of his assignment notebook, the pupil should have a list of the maximum time allowed on each subject. If the study schedule includes fifteen minutes daily for spelling, the limit for that subject should be about twenty minutes. After putting serious effort into the assignment for the full time allowed, the child should draw a line, write down the time spent, and quit. For youngsters who have not learned to tell time, a parent or other "homework helper" should take responsibility for calling "Time!" and getting the student to set the task aside.

When used properly, a bail-out clause can actually improve student performance. Pain studies have shown the benefits of such an escape agreement. When patients are allowed to have medication anytime they request it, they tend to require drugs less frequently and in smaller dosages than other patients. Doctors believe that the tolerance for pain is increased by knowing it can be stopped on demand. The same principle applies to students learning to complete homework independently. Their ability to endure frustration increases when they have control over the situation causing it.

When an escape route is made available, there will be times when students choose to use it. Their right to do so must be respected.

6. Adjust the assignments in size, not quality.

If, in five minutes' time, a student is capable of doing ten easy math problems *or* five hard ones, choose quality over quantity. Assign work that is challenging. Do not give homework that is so easy that it's an insult to the pupil's intelligence. Emphasize building speed. Even the most mundane drill becomes challenging when increasing the rate of work is a goal.

7. Eliminate copying entirely and keep writing to an absolute minimum.

In an unsupervised study situation, the LD/ADD student's frustration with writing can grow so intense that he gives up in disgust. If it's necessary to assign a writing task, it's better to have it done at school, where someone is available to help when he gets stuck, to sympathize when discouragement sets in, and to pick up the pieces when he blows up. Homework should increase learning, not frustration.

8. Always do something to recognize that the assignment was successfully completed.

Homework does not always have to be collected or corrected. But at the time it is due, the teacher must at least scan it, comment on its overall quality, and give the student credit in the grade book. Neglecting to credit home assignments gives the impression that they're not important. When the completion of home assignments isn't recognized, students often decide that doing independent work is optional. If their efforts aren't regularly acknowledged, LD/ADD children are quick to turn off to homework.

Education courses teach that every piece of student work has to be corrected, scored, and recorded in the grade book. The traditional belief is that if a pupil's paper isn't going to be looked over carefully, it shouldn't be assigned.

Using that old rule, there are lots of times when conscientious teachers hesitate to make an assignment. The students might need the work, but it shouldn't be assigned because the instructor can't handle any more papers to grade! It's especially difficult to teach expressive writing, where just one batch of essays produces a mountain of homework for the teacher. For years, teachers have felt trapped between what is best for the students and what is humanly possible for the instructor.

> One fall, I tried a revolutionary approach based on the ideas of Daniel N. Fader and Elton B. McNeil in *Hooked on Books: Program and Proof.* To develop my LD/ADD seventh-graders' skill in expressive writing, I assigned a one-page essay *every* night. But not all the papers they produced were corrected. In fact, most of them were never even read. As in music lessons, where the pupil spends an hour or so daily perfecting his technique, most of my students' nightly essays were considered "practice." At the beginning of class, I looked over and checked off every single paper as completed and of acceptable appearance, then discarded the entire batch. Once a week, I kept the essays for careful evaluation, proofreading, correction, and grading.
>
> My students had some surprising reactions to this experiment. Only one part of the assignment gave them trouble: the teenagers found it terribly difficult to think up suitable topics on such a regular basis. Most of them had to rely on the ideas that I provided daily. It made perfectly good sense to them that one should practice writing in much the same way one practices the piano. They rarely complained that their work was not graded. As long as they got credit for the assignment, they were content. Also unexpected was their reaction when I chose papers to keep. My teenage pupils always responded enthusiastically when I announced, "The random-selection machine says today's papers—these gems I now hold in my hand—will be graded."
>
> From the day our project began, the students never slacked off. Each night, every pupil put maximum effort into producing an essay of good quality. Night after night, they created papers they were proud of! And the quality of the students' writing improved so dramatically that they got great satisfaction out of the progress they were making.

By always taking the time to recognize a successfully completed assignment, teachers give students a daily opportunity to taste success. Just by glancing at the grade book, pupils can see that they have attained the skills needed to conquer their old enemy—homework. That moment of triumph feels wonderful. Students with a learning disability and/or an attention deficit disorder need to experience the "Wow!" of success repeatedly. It's not enough to wait for the surge of emotion that comes when a major goal is reached. To break the old habits of failure, success must be frequent and must be noticed.

Most LD/ADD students have so little experience with success that they fail to recognize their academic achievements when they see them. They shrug their shoulders and assume that their progress is just a fluke. Daily records help them see that they are moving toward their goal and give them cause for celebration at each step of the process. With each tiny check, they move closer to the point where they see themselves as people who have the power to succeed.

9. Assign nothing that the children cannot complete successfully on their own.

A youngster might be using a social studies book successfully at school even if it is just barely within his reading level; in the classroom, a "good neighbor" can help when he gets stuck on a word. Adjusted assignments that are realistic in the classroom are often too difficult for independent study.

10. Develop a routine.

LD/ADD youngsters thrive in structured situations. Doing the same old thing day after day does *not* bore them. In fact, it makes them feel secure and helps them get organized and stay focused.

> In my self-contained LD class of fifth- and sixth-graders, our day always started with a highly structured session of LD therapy. We did half an hour of tracing, copying, and handwriting; twenty minutes of phonetic practice; forty minutes of word-attack exercises and reading; and half an hour of dictation, proofreading, and correcting.

Though I tried hard to keep the work challenging and fun, by midwinter I thought it was getting deadly dull. I saw myself as some kind of lunatic who hung from the rafters spouting phonics.

One gloomy Friday morning in late February, I indicated my boredom to the twelve boys in my class. "Well, guys," I groaned, "do you think you can stand it one more time?"

Bobby, one of the more outspoken students, tartly replied, "What do you mean by 'stand it'? This is the best part of the day!"

The others immediately chimed in their agreement.

"Yeah, we like this stuff."

"I'd rather do this than math."

"Ain't nothing about this that's so bad."

Even the more sophisticated twelve-year-olds indicated that they found nothing objectionable about our morning routine. The students approached our daily sessions in much the same way an athlete approaches warmup exercises—as a necessary part of preparing for peak performance.

Until that moment, I'd never thought about it. But my boys were right. Those two highly structured hours were the most productive part of our day. All the students kept a close eye on the increasing scores that gave evidence of their growing skills. It *did* feel good to have two hours every day when we knew we were being successful.

In setting up a homework program for LD/ADD students, teachers should recognize that the more steady and predictable the routine, the better. Ten minutes of math every night. (Every night means Monday, Tuesday, Wednesday, and Thursday—not weekends.) Ten minutes of spelling every night. Fifteen minutes of reading every night. Ten minutes of science, social studies, or health every night. This helps the student establish a system, develop a rhythm.

In junior and senior high, teachers need to work together to coordinate the homework assigned LD/ADD pupils. If a youth has five subjects, each teacher should agree to give a certain amount of homework regularly. If each holds assignments down to a maximum of fifteen minutes per night, that is an hour and fifteen minutes of work, plus organizing time. For older students, that's a reasonable amount of time for homework. Younger children should spend slightly less time on independent work at home.

An important part of building success involves helping LD/ADD students discover a study system that works for them. Unsuccessful pupils rarely understand that repetition and routine are essential elements in learning. They have no idea what regular practice can accomplish. They've never tried it.

Through carefully assigned homework, teachers can provide LD/ADD youngsters with an efficient and realistic study schedule. The ideal pattern calls for a small amount of review and practice daily. Through closely monitored homework, teachers can lead students through the process of developing new study habits and create clear proof that, when using appropriate study methods, real learning takes place. Youngsters with a learning disability and/or an attention deficit disorder don't believe those who tell them they can learn. A taste of honest academic achievement demonstrates their own ability to them.

Working with the Family

No matter how much help is available for a student at home, the teacher should adjust assignments so that an LD/ADD child is able to do the majority of his homework on his own. This can be accomplished if the classroom teacher and the LD specialist begin the school year with an investigative attitude toward the LD/ADD pupil and his homework capabilities. By adjusting, revising, experimenting, and readjusting, the pupil and his teachers must find out exactly what he can and will do independently.

During the first four to six weeks of school, parents should be encouraged to avoid direct involvement in their LD/ADD offspring's homework. Their role is to provide him an appropriate time and place to study, to show interest, and to offer encouragement or sympathy when needed. Other than that, they should stay out of homework as much as possible. It may not be wise to maintain this hands-off policy throughout the entire school year, but in the opening weeks, it is highly recommended.

After the suggestions presented earlier in this chapter have been implemented, the project proceeds into a second phase. At this important point, another parent conference is necessary.

Because their role is vitally important, parents need to be included in *two* conferences. The first one is conducted at the opening of the year as part of the process discussed earlier. The second one needs to be scheduled five or six weeks later. It is in this second meeting that the teacher and the LD specialist should explain the details of the youngster's school program and homework assignments. By then, the teachers have had time to get to know the student and choose methods, materials, and assignments appropriate for him. They have also had the opportunity to give careful consideration to the various homework adjustments likely to be useful with the child. It is at this point that the teachers should enlist the parents' cooperation and establish a clear understanding of the role they are to play in dealing with their child's homework.

The "Homework Helper"

After the LD/ADD student has demonstrated how much he can do independently, it may be decided that his needs and his home situation are suitable for a "homework helper" system. The person selected to act as an LD/ADD youngster's homework helper must have a cooperative, understanding attitude toward the child, must be available at regular study hours, and must be willing to take on the job. One or both parents, a brother or sister, a relative living nearby, a neighbor or family friend, a volunteer from a church or community center—there are many candidates available. The person chosen must clearly understand two basic rules: the helper will not work with the child for more than an hour and a half daily (less for younger children), and the youngster must do at least half his homework on his own.

Anytime the pupil is given an assignment to be done with his helper, the teacher should explain exactly what role the helper is to play. "Get your mother to read these five pages of social studies to you." "You and Barbara take turns finding the vocabulary words in the dictionary." Either the helper should feel free to use his or her judgment on the type of assistance needed or the teacher should provide a reliable method of getting this information to the helper.

A simple code system can indicate the degree of help needed. When the student writes down his assignment, it can get one star if a "reader" is needed or two stars if a "secretary" is needed. Work to be done independently gets no star. No matter what method is devised, the LD/ADD student's homework helper should have the teacher's home phone number for emergencies.

1. A "reader" or reading partner

A good reader can cover many pages in a short time. The average fourth-grader probably needs twenty minutes to get through the same material an adult can read aloud in about half that time. Thus, in adapting an assignment by having it read *to* the child, it is *not* necessary to adjust the size of the assignment. As much as possible, LD/ADD students should be encouraged to do at least some of their own reading. However, the use of a reader is recommended for large assignments in history, science, and literature (especially poetry—poor readers butcher the rhythm, rhyme, meter, and flow of verse).

2. A "secretary" or writing partner

> While still in high school, I had a part-time job working with a very bright ninth-grade boy who was a total nonreader. I was not his teacher or his tutor. I was his secretary.
>
> In all his classes, Rob completed the regular assignments by having me do *all* the reading and writing. To do reports or answer questions at the ends of chapters, he dictated to me just as a business executive would to a stenographer. Since I didn't know shorthand, I was often hard-pressed to keep up with the flow of ideas that poured from his quick mind. My job was to record exactly what Rob said. The school graded all his work for content only.

As discussed earlier, helping an LD/ADD student write a major report is not a job for an amateur. Unless special arrangements are made between home and school, the homework helper should not be expected to provide assistance with assignments that require more than one page of writing. Twenty English questions requiring answers of two to three sentences each—yes. A short story—no. Five discussion questions of one to two paragraphs apiece—yes. An essay on democracy—no. Notes on material read for a term paper—yes. The term paper itself—no.

3. A copyist

Copying math problems from the book to the paper is often a routine part of the homework helper's job. For some students, an assistant might need to do *all* copying on all types of assignments. In other situations, the child might be able to use a partnership approach or merely a proofreader.

4. A proofreader and editor

Youngsters with a learning disability and/or an attention deficit disorder need to be encouraged to do as much of their own writing as can reasonably be expected. Assistance with proofreading and corrections is often the only help that is needed.

Example A

A fifth-grader who has difficulty with copying and spelling but has little trouble with reading, handwriting, and math is assigned the following homework: read five pages of social studies and answer three questions at the end of the chapter; answer ten true-false questions on a reading worksheet; do twenty math problems; write one sentence using each of five spelling words.

The child can complete his social studies and reading by himself. He can also do a rough draft of the five sentences for spelling.

When his helper joins him, she can proofread and correct the sentences, act as his partner or secretary with the social studies questions, and conclude her part of the day's work by copying the math problems out of the book.

The student can then use the last part of his study time to work his arithmetic problems on his own.

Example B

A tenth-grader with little trouble in reading and handwriting but serious difficulties in copying, spelling, and punctuation has the following homework assignment: read a short story and write two- to three-sentence answers to six discussion questions; read four pages of biology, draw a leaf, label each part, and write one paragraph to explain how each major part works; do a math worksheet; look up five words in the glossary of the history book and copy the definitions onto file cards.

This student can begin by doing all the reading on his own. He can probably write the answers for English and get the history definitions copied onto file cards. He can definitely do the math worksheet and draw and label the leaf.

When the helper enters the picture, she can start by proofreading and correcting the spelling and punctuation on everything the student has written or copied. For the biology paragraphs, she can act as "secretary."

Anytime an LD/ADD student is capable of doing his own writing and copying, encouragement and proofreading should be liberally provided.

5. A "typist"

This is really a copying task and does not necessarily call for the use of a typewriter or word processor. But it is a specialized kind of service that is often needed.

After getting their written work proofread and corrected, LD pupils are frequently told, "Copy this over so the teacher can read it." That job is impossible for most LD youngsters of all ages.

Regardless of the size of the assignment, the student's homework helper usually has to provide this copying service. Although the final draft might not be produced right before the youngster's eyes, the service counts as time used by the homework helper.

> William, an eleventh-grader, had a very efficient homework system. His mother helped him with history, English, spelling, writing, and "typing." His father assisted in science and math. Although the two parents worked with their son separately, they never gave more than a combined total of an hour and a half of help per night.
>
> A term paper was assigned for English class in the spring. William's class started working on the project right after Christmas. The youth's teacher led him through every step of the process. Only three parts had to be done outside school: reading, taking notes, and writing the final draft.
>
> As soon as the research began, William and his parents started cutting down his nightly help by five minutes. By the end of two months, the boy had accumulated three hours of reserve time for his mother to use for the typing process; if it ran over, he would have to work off the rest afterward. William and his mother had a firm agreement. He was to have the perfect but messy first draft in her hands at least three days before the term paper was due. And she was to have his finished copy—either typewritten or longhand—ready on the appointed day.
>
> Their system worked beautifully.

For students who do their rough drafts on a word processor, the "typist" can provide proofreading and editing by making corrections on the disk and then printing out the final copy.

6. A drill director

LD/ADD students almost always need someone to call their spelling words out for them. They also require help in learning factual information like definitions, important names, and special dates. Some of this type of practice is likely to be included in almost every homework session.

Through the use of the following technique, the homework

helper can be of great assistance as the LD/ADD student struggles to get facts firmly planted in his memory. The two should develop a drill pattern based on a three-step process in which the child *reads* the fact aloud, *repeats* the fact aloud from memory, and *writes* the fact (copying if necessary). For mastering spelling words, the same basic approach applies. The student *says* the word aloud, *spells* it aloud (reading if necessary), then *writes* it (copying if necessary).

When practicing any kind of material to be memorized, always have the student write the fact or word. Children usually hate this step, but it is absolutely necessary. When preparing for a test, calling out the answers is not sufficient; paper and pencil are required. LD/ADD youngsters are often able to spell a word accurately with their mouth but not with a pencil. They need to get the "feel" of a word or fact before they can hope to remember it. For practice purposes, writing in the air or with one finger on the top of a desk is a helpful variation.

To be sure a word or fact goes into long-term memory, connecting the new concept to some previously mastered rule or information can be beneficial. When trying to remember a word that is difficult to spell, using some kind of mnemonic device is extremely helpful.

7. An interpreter

Despite the teacher's having carefully explained the directions and seen to it that students have two examples, there will still be occasions when LD/ADD youngsters need someone to help them figure out what they're supposed to do. Although the assistant may not need to get involved with carrying out the work on the assignment, it's often necessary to help students get started.

8. A timekeeper

Since the teacher assigns homework to LD/ADD students according to the specific amount of time to be allotted for each subject, pupils usually need someone to help them keep an eye on the clock and tell them when their time is up.

Regardless of the pupil's age, the home and the school must agree on the maximum amount of time that can be devoted to each subject in one night. There should also be a time limit governing the length of an entire home-study session. These limits should be written down and strictly enforced.

Unfortunately, many LD/ADD youngsters are perfectionists and drive themselves mercilessly. For them, success is not enough. They don't want a C+ or even a B. They want an A every time. They expect things of themselves that are not realistic. Unless someone stops them, they'll just keep torturing themselves. It is the homework helper's responsibility to say, "You've done enough." Situations requiring such action sometimes qualify as emergencies, and the teacher should be called for advice. When the LD/ADD student cannot complete assignments night after night, something is wrong with the system.

During the homework session, the assistant needs to supervise the student's pace. The LD/ADD child's faulty concept of time does not allow him to balance his work so he gets everything done. Without someone to move him from one subject to another, he spends close to an hour on a reading assignment that should take fifteen minutes, then doesn't have enough time left to even start on his math and spelling.

A stopwatch can be handy for this type of monitoring. Students who are dawdling along at five minutes per math problem often pick up the pace if a timer is introduced to make them aware of the need to move at a faster clip. For most LD/ADD students, increasing the speed intensifies the concentration. When their attention is drifting, ticking off the passing minutes with a metronome or other timer prods the child to be mindful of the need to work efficiently.

9. An organizer

LD/ADD students have such a poor concept of time that they usually need someone to organize their daily study schedule. Every day, the helper should look over the list of work to be done and draw up a "battle plan." The helper should say, "We've gone over the directions. Do all the reading and write your five sentences for spelling. Call me when you're done. And if it takes more than twenty-five minutes, I'll come and tell you to stop."

Keeping track of books and materials is also an area in which children with a learning disability and/or an attention deficit disorder need patient, close supervision. They can be real space cadets when it comes to remembering where they put things. If they are left to their own devices, their books and papers get scattered all over the house.

Forgetting to take completed assignments back to school is a common—and major—problem among LD/ADD students. The homework assistant should help the youngster develop a foolproof system whereby he always remembers to grab his papers and books as he heads out the door in the morning. It is the child's responsibility to get completed homework into his teacher's hands. It is not the helper's duty to chase the school bus down the street every morning yelling, "Have you got your homework?"

When homework is done successfully, students get satisfaction from both the finished product and the process that created it. When assignments are designed to assure pupils' success, studying becomes a challenge with attainable, worthwhile rewards. In the hands of a wise teacher, nightly assignments can build students' interest, confidence, and motivation.

Adjustments in Testing

Chapter 15

Testing provides an opportunity to apply new skills. Athletes run laps, lift weights, and do calisthenics as part of their training, but that's not the same as running a race or playing a game. As much as possible, students need opportunities to apply their skills to real-life situations. Tests help learners turn practice into real performance.

LD/ADD students must be taught to learn independently. Routine testing gives them the facts they need to take charge of their learning. Test scores allow students to measure their progress and see where they stand in relation to their goal. By giving a clear picture of the skill development taking place, testing allows students to monitor their advancement. A decrease in the rate of mastery can signal the need to adjust the study methods or revise the schedule. A sudden increase in progress can lead to discovering some change in the environment or routine that has enhanced learning.

When LD/ADD students begin developing new habits that allow them to learn successfully, they need to *see* their success. They need to demonstrate their new skills in ways that *prove* to them that academic achievement is taking place. In a goal-oriented program where objectives are clearly stated and understood, attaining a passing grade on a final test brings the closure necessary to celebrate the completion of the task. It is the feeling of victory gained through success on the current test that equips struggling students to move on to the next one with new confidence. Eager learners are built, not made. Every triumph generates the enthusiasm that drives students to seek greater accomplishments. Every time a pupil passes a test, there is an opportunity to build a chain reaction of success.

Getting Out of the Failure Trap

For decades, students with a learning disability and/or an attention deficit disorder have flunked tests covering material they truly have mastered. Even when they fail because they don't try, their lack of effort is usually a direct result of a system that allows them no chance for success. Either the questions were written in a way too difficult for them to read, or the test format caused them confusion, or they didn't have enough time to finish, or they couldn't record their answers in the form required, or the setting was so distracting that they couldn't concentrate. When LD/ADD students do study, they often fail tests anyway.

For the pupil who can't read the words or understand the directions or record answers accurately, an F means lack of success in dealing with the test itself. It says nothing about the student's knowledge of the subject matter.

> After two years of LD/ADD therapy, Janet entered the tenth grade in a private college-preparatory high school. Full of resolve, she was confident her new organizational skills and study habits were going to help her overcome the difficulties that had plagued her in the past. But by the middle of the first semester, the girl was in danger of failing biology.
>
> Janet's mother went to the school for a conference. The

biology teacher, Miss Johnson, explained that Janet had gotten an A+ for producing an outstanding bug collection. She had a perfect record with homework. Although she sometimes had difficulty with her lab notes, she had passing scores on all her work. But she had failed all four major tests. Altogether, her grades averaged out to a low D.

Fortunately, the mother understood the types of problems that resulted from her daughter's learning disability and attention deficit disorder. In a previous conference, she had gotten all of Janet's teachers to agree to provide a private room for testing and to remove the time limits from all tests. In hopes of discovering the problems causing her daughter's low test scores, Mrs. Richards spread the test papers on the table, then requested that the teacher help her analyze Janet's mistakes. "She always has done poorly on tests," the mother commented. "But maybe there's something that makes these particularly difficult."

The teacher immediately replied, "The only thing that always costs her a lot of points is spelling." Miss Johnson picked up one of the papers to demonstrate her point. "The first section is fill-in-the-blank. Out of twenty questions, Janet missed twelve. Seven were misspelled; five were totally wrong."

The student's mother tried to be diplomatic and hide her surprise, but still her eyebrows shot up. "If the answer is misspelled, you count it wrong?"

"Yes, of course." To the teacher, the system seemed perfectly logical. She returned her attention to the test paper. "On the multiple choice, she usually does pretty well. Here, she has twenty out of twenty-five. That's definitely okay."

Mrs. Richards nodded.

"On the true-false, she got fourteen out of twenty. That's not bad."

The mother agreed, then added, "Janet doesn't read with precise accuracy. She usually finds true-false questions difficult."

Miss Johnson went on. "On these last two sections, she did very poorly." The teacher pointed to a page covered with red circles and *X's* to mark the numerous errors. "On the three essay questions, it was possible to score fifteen points. Janet got five and a half. And on the labeling section, out of twenty points possible, she got six!"

"Janet is such a poor writer that I'm surprised she does that well on the essays," the girl's mother said.

"Oh, she doesn't do that badly," Miss Johnson countered. "I can always tell that she knows what she's talking about." She indicated the first essay question as an example. "On this one, Janet got four points. Her answer was very good. But since she made more than three errors in spelling, punctuation, capitalization, and so forth, she lost half her credit."

The teacher turned to the last page of the test, which featured a large picture of a frog. Long arrows pointed to twenty different parts of the animal. Miss Johnson scanned the words Janet had written in the blanks at the ends of the arrows. "It was her poor spelling that made her get so many wrong on this part, too. If she had spelled all the names correctly, she'd have gotten thirteen points for her labeling. As it is, she got six."

"I think Janet would have passed this test if she hadn't lost so many points because of her bad spelling," Mrs. Richards concluded.

The teacher admitted, "It's possible."

"Could you count it up and see?"

To satisfy the mother's curiosity, the biology teacher scored the test without counting off for spelling. "If she hadn't made all those mistakes, she'd have gotten a seventy-three. That's quite a difference."

Mrs. Richards sighed, then asked, "Why do you count off for spelling in a biology class?"

"It's department policy" was the simple reply.

Mrs. Richards made a sweeping gesture toward her daughter's test. "This F does not say anything about Janet's success in learning biology. All it says is that she can't spell!" She paused, then stated the crux of the issue. "Janet has a learning disability. It's not fair to fail her in biology because of her poor spelling."

Miss Johnson tried to be sympathetic. She talked about high standards, college-preparatory programs, school policy, and the grading procedures used in the science department. Finally, she suggested a possible solution. "Janet really does need to improve her spelling. If she could cut down on all these careless spelling errors, her test scores would increase significantly." She paused, then presented what she believed to be the only alternative: "Or she'll have to study harder so she can make up the points by doing better on the rest of the test."

The mother's voice was no longer sweet and calm. "Janet has been working to improve her spelling since second grade. Those are not careless errors—they are evidence of a learning disability." Crisply, she pointed out the simple arithmetic of the teacher's suggested solution. "If Janet loses twenty points per test for spelling, a perfect paper with every single answer correct would only get her an eighty! If she missed just ten questions, instead of a high B for a ninety, she'd barely pass with a seventy!"

By this point, both women were very frustrated. Miss Johnson was irritated that this mother wanted her to lower her standards. She didn't believe in teaching some watered-down course and passing it off as biology. Mrs. Richards was disgusted with a system that cheated her daughter out of what success she achieved. She was tired of fighting the same old battle. She was tired of well-meaning teachers who simply didn't understand what the system did to LD/ADD children.

After a minute, Mrs. Richards quietly asked, "Would it be possible for you to give Janet two grades on her biology tests—one for her answers and one for her spelling?"

The teacher shook her head. "I'm sorry, but I couldn't do that."

The mother persisted. "Would it be possible for the head of your department to give you permission to do that?"

Despite the cool tone of her voice, the teacher maintained a cooperative attitude. "She would probably have to consult with the dean. But yes, she would have the authority to make that decision."

Gradually, Miss Johnson and Mrs. Richards resigned themselves to the fact that they did not have the power to resolve the problem. The teacher provided Janet's mother with photocopies of the girl's four failed tests, along with the name and phone number of the department head.

The mother and the teacher managed to part on friendly terms. It was obvious that Janet's parents were *not* going to stand idly by and let their LD/ADD daughter fail biology because she couldn't learn to spell the names of the parts of a frog.

In negotiations with the head of the science department, the academic dean, and the headmaster, it was agreed that Janet would be allowed to bring a portable spell-checker with her to all classes and exams so she could verify the spelling of words she wasn't sure of. But no attempt was made to adjust the low grades she'd made prior to the special modification to accommodate her weakness with spelling.

To be fair, tests must be designed to let pupils show what they have learned in the subject being evaluated. Teachers must guard against test situations that merely provide added proof of the LD/ADD child's deficiencies in the basic skills.

A few simple guidelines can help teachers make test adjustments that are both practical and fair.

1. If LD/ADD students have not been exposed to all the information presented to the rest of the class, it is not fair to test them on points that were never presented to them in assignments or discussions.

An adjusted test is easily created by omitting or striking out inappropriate items on the copy of the test given to LD/ADD students, then adjusting the scoring accordingly. All questions that are deleted should be clearly marked *before* the examination begins. Crossing them out is more effective than merely circling their numbers. Since LD/ADD children get mixed up on numbering, this is not a task to be assigned to the pupils themselves.

2. Because LD/ADD students read slowly and have so much difficulty with concentration, they are rarely able to finish a test in the normal time allowed. It is often most practical simply to shorten their test by crossing out some of the questions. This method saves the children from the social pressure that makes them want to hurry and finish so that they can appear just like everybody else. It also spares them the embarrassment caused by adjustments that single them out.

Some teachers allow the students to decide which parts shall be omitted. If the examination is made up of several sections, they get the pupils to select entire sections to be skipped. For instance, on her biology test, Janet would have been wise to skip the essay questions or the labeling. Most LD/ADD students have specific formats that cause them confusion. Those with poor spelling and writing skills do best with short-answer questions, matching, true-false, and multiple choice. Some can write a great essay but get mixed up on multiple-choice questions. In universities and graduate schools, it is common for LD/ADD students to be given alternate forms of exams so they can avoid the formats that prevent them from demonstrating their knowledge. These special accommodations have to be worked out well in advance, usually with the help of the school's Section 504 coordinator.

There are several ways to shorten a test without adjusting it to accommodate students' weaknesses. Pupils can be told to do a certain portion of the questions in each part. They can select a certain number of pages to be omitted. Or they can merely start at the beginning of the test and work straight through until they run out of time. When teachers use these approaches, the questions that were not attempted are not counted. For example, if an LD/ADD youngster answers the first sixty-eight questions on a one-hundred-item exam, his grade is based on how many he gets correct out of the sixty-eight he tried. His test is cut down in size by thirty-two questions.

The most common method of adjusting a test to fit the slow pace of students with a learning disability and/or an attention deficit disorder involves giving them extra time. Unfortunately, this method is often ineffective. Teachers frequently say, "I let him have as much time as he needs." Usually, that means that if the child asks for more time, he may have it. Also, it normally means the student has permission to stay in his place and keep working. No matter what goes on in the classroom—noise, children moving about the room or changing classes, the teacher starting a different lesson—he's allowed to keep working on his test. But unless the teacher can see to it that an LD/ADD pupil is provided adequate time *in an appropriate environment*, she should use some other method of adjusting a test to fit his pace.

3. Because many students with a learning disability and/or an attention deficit disorder are poor readers, the pressure of a test can make even the easiest material too difficult. Special provisions need to be made for a youngster who has trouble reading *any* of the words on a test. If the child needs to ask, "What's that word?" someone should be available to help.

The "good neighbor policy" can be effective during tests as long as the LD/ADD child does not require much help. Teacher's aides and volunteers are especially appropriate people for providing LD/ADD students with help during tests. It is also common for the LD specialist to assist with exams. When a pupil has been officially identified as learning disabled, the special education department and the LD teacher can usually be relied on to help the teacher make adjustments required by the IEP. When students need help reading test questions, it is *not* practical for the classroom teacher to assume the role. She cannot adequately supervise the rest of the class while she is out of the room reading test questions to one of her pupils. Helping the child within the classroom doesn't work well either. All the talking disturbs the other children and makes the LD/ADD student embarrassed. Singling a child out publicly usually leads to resentment from the other students and social problems for the youngster involved.

A cassette player makes the ideal reader for an LD/ADD student during tests. Even the GED and college boards allow for the use of tape-recorded versions of the test for certain types of LD/ADD students. Such a modification allows the pupil to work independently while being provided the support necessary to overcome a weakness in reading.

After two years of LD therapy, Joel had overcome almost all of his reading problems and was doing fine in a regular sixth-grade class. The boy had gotten to the point where he needed special adjustments only when taking tests. Like many LD/ADD students, the youth panicked when faced with an examination and forgot all the skills he'd learned. Under pressure, Joel could not read material that was easy for him at any other time.

This sixth-grader did not need someone to sit at his elbow and struggle through every part of a test with him. He was ready to work independently. But he did need confidence. It was necessary to give Joel just enough help to get him past his panic so he could use his own adequate skills.

All of Joel's tests were read onto a cassette tape. The boy had to take his exams in the classroom in the standard way. If his parents had taken a strong stand and gotten the modification placed in the boy's IEP, arrangements could have been made for him to take his tape-recorded tests in a quiet, private place. That would have been an ideal way to provide him the assistance he needed *without* making him look different from his classmates.

Having each question read aloud by a cassette player wasn't much help. But for Joel, it was enough. Once he was certain he knew what a question said, he had no trouble figuring out the answer. Without the tape recorder, Joel's test grades were in the fifties and sixties. With it, he made Bs and Cs.

4. Because LD/ADD students have trouble writing, certain types of tests should be radically adapted or avoided altogether. Essay questions almost always put LD/ADD youngsters at the worst possible disadvantage, requiring them to rely on their weak skills in handwriting, spelling, organization, and expressive writing. As much as possible, students with serious writing difficulties should be allowed to avoid essay-type test questions entirely. If a test segment that requires a great deal of writing cannot be omitted, then a method of adaptation is essential. This can be accomplished through two basic approaches.

A. Keep the essay format but change the form from written to oral. The student still has to present an answer in well-structured sentences and paragraphs, but he dictates his essay to the teacher, an aide, a volunteer, or a tape recorder.

B. Have the student write out his answer but don't require it to be in the form of carefully structured interlocking paragraphs. In a list or rough outline, the pupil presents the substance of what would be contained in an essay.

Most LD/ADD students also have trouble writing out definitions, answers that must be in complete sentences, and quotations from long memorized passages. Wherever possible, these should be eliminated or adjusted to fit the student's weakness in writing.

What kinds of test questions are best suited to most LD/ADD pupils? Any type that keeps the need for writing to a minimum. True-false, multiple choice, fill-in-the-blank, matching—these rarely require more than one word per answer.

5. Because many LD/ADD students have trouble with math, teachers must be prepared to adjust tests in other subjects that involve working with numbers. Many youngsters with a learning disability and/or an attention deficit disorder have difficulty with science courses. And charts, graphs, and statistics sometimes make it difficult for them to succeed in social studies.

Margaret was a high-school senior. She had never had any trouble with reading, writing, or spelling. Math was her weakness. By counting on her fingers, she had reasonable skill with addition and subtraction. Multiplication was difficult for her because she had never been able to memorize the multiplication table. And she could not do division at all.

In her physics class, Margaret did acceptable work with everything except the problems that had to be solved mathematically. She could memorize the formulas. She could even set up equations. But she could not manipulate the numbers and come up with the correct answers.

She flunked her first two physics tests. She got every question that required mathematical computation wrong.

After a conference with Margaret, the physics teacher adjusted her tests. The student no longer had to concern herself with working out the math and coming up with correct answers. For Margaret, using the proper formula and setting up the problem correctly was considered proof that she had mastered the material. The LD/ADD student's teacher understood that a wrong answer meant Margaret was not good at working math problems. It did *not* mean she didn't understand physics.

For the LD/ADD student with a disability in math, arithmetic errors should not count off on work outside math class. For the LD/ADD student with a language disability, spelling errors should not count off on work outside spelling class.

6. Because LD/ADD youngsters have difficulty with concentration, they need a test environment that is isolated and quiet. They often find it impossible to tune out distractions for more than a few minutes at a time. Just knowing others are in the room can prevent them from focusing their attention on their work. From first-graders to Ph.D. candidates, students with a learning disability and/or an attention deficit disorder usually need a small, private place where they can take tests. Under Section 504 of the 1990 Individuals with Disabilities in Education Act, this accommodation is considered reasonable for students of all ages under most circumstances. Sometimes, providing a suitable location places a strain on teachers and administrators, but the legal requirement is clear.

The library is *not* the ideal spot. What's needed is a place where the student can be alone. And the smaller it is, the better.

One resourceful teacher converted her elementary school's book storage room into a quiet place for LD and ADD students to use when taking tests. Floor to ceiling, all four walls had shelves of textbooks. Carpeted, air-conditioned, and windowless, the tiny room was totally private and soundproof. It was an ideal spot when used individually by those who did examinations orally with cassette recorders.

Many teachers felt uncomfortable inside that small, windowless little cubicle. But none of the children showed any reluctance to use it. They seemed to find it safe and cozy.

A huge old high-school building had a strange three-room suite of chemistry laboratories. In the most inaccessible and least-used of these rooms, there were two "gas chambers" that looked like the isolation booth on a TV quiz show. Created for use in experiments requiring special ventilation, they were also soundproof. When the school's LD specialist asked the faculty to set up some private areas where distractible students could take tests, the science department chose these two chambers. The English department adopted a tiny workroom off the library as its isolation area. The math teachers used the office assigned to the head of their department. All over that antiquated building, little nooks and crannies were set up as test booths for students with a learning disability and/or an attention deficit disorder.

But the "gas chambers" in the science department were the ones the students liked best. Even when taking tests in other subjects, they tried to reserve a space in what they jokingly referred to as "the Inner Sanctum."

Children who are labeled LD and/or ADD do not always outgrow their distractibility. At all ages, they need special adjustments to help them perform well despite their problems with concentration.

7. Because they have trouble understanding and following directions, LD/ADD students need to have test instructions explained to them one section at a time. This calls for use of the three-step process: tell the student, show him, have him do one for himself.

The teacher gets the pupil started on the first part, but then questions may arise over who will help with directions for the other sections. If the child is taking his test outside the classroom, he must have someone to go to for help at the end of each segment of the test. More than likely, the teacher will assume this responsibility while supervising the others taking the exam. The student could also get help from the LD teacher, an aide, a volunteer, the librarian, or even the school secretary.

When an LD/ADD pupil takes a test in the classroom, his "good neighbor" can explain directions as needed. When the "good neighbor policy" is allowed during tests, both children must understand clearly the types of problems they are permitted to discuss. Generally, the helper is permitted to assist with three kinds of questions: "What are we supposed to do?"; "What's that word?"; and "How do you spell ——— ?" If the student has other difficulties, he must consult the teacher.

8. Because youngsters with a learning disability and/or an attention deficit disorder become easily lost on a printed page, certain types of tests confuse them and put them at an unfair disadvantage.

To save money in administering standardized tests, schools often provide children with answer sheets so that the test booklets can be used year after year. Answer sheets full of circles or squares are easy to check. Often, they're even machine-scored. But though they are efficient for the teacher, they can cause LD/ADD pupils great difficulty. Some children cannot keep their place among the little spaces numbered to match the questions. Skipping lines by mistake, putting answers in the wrong column, marking two answers on the same line—there are many ways in which LD/ADD students make a mess out of an ordinary answer sheet. Allowing LD/ADD children to record their answers directly in the test booklet saves everybody a lot of time and annoyance.

Occasionally, teachers concoct an examination that has a truly unusual and complicated format. Matching tests with as many as forty or fifty items are sometimes used. Once in a while, a student is required to flip back and forth between different pages or sections. Questions presented in confusing forms make it impossible for LD/ADD students to demonstrate their knowledge of a subject.

> An ingenious test was created by a teacher who was tired of doing the same old stuff with her seventh-grade English classes. She knew its complex structure would give Wayne difficulty. As the boy's LD teacher, I acted as his helper when he took the test.
>
> On the first page of the test was a short story. The directions at the top merely said, "Read the story below." Wayne did that silently with no difficulty.
>
> The second page was a solid mass of fill-in-the-blank comprehension questions on the story. My student got tired of flipping back and forth to find answers and copy words. With patience and determination, he managed to do it on his own.
>
> The real fun began on the third page. Directions covered the top, blank lines filled the bottom, and the middle was divided into three columns. First, the students were told to go back over the story on the first page and underline all the verbs. After that, each of the verbs was to be copied into one of the columns. The descriptive active verbs went into column A. Those that were just regular active went into column B. And the last column was for those that were passive or showed a state of being. It nearly drove Wayne crazy. He'd find a verb on the front page and decide what type it was. Then he'd reread the directions on the third page to see which column was for that category. But by the time he was ready to choose the column, he'd forgotten the word. Then, in the process of going back to find it, he'd forget where to put the answer.
>
> In desperation, he asked me to help. My job was to remember the word while he struggled to figure out what to

> do with it. Wayne read, "The old man sputtered." Without glancing up, he instructed me, "Okay, you remember *sputtered.*"
>
> I jotted the word down.
>
> Mumbling under his breath, my student made the decision that the word was active. "But is it descriptive?" he asked himself. "Descriptive active or regular active?" To refresh his memory on the difference between the two, he reread the examples. "If it says, 'He bounded across the porch,' that's descriptive. If it says, 'He walked across the porch,' that's just plain active." He paused, looked at me, and asked, "What was the word?"
>
> "*Sputtered.*"
>
> "*Sputtered.*" Then he returned to thinking out loud. "'The old man sputtered' or 'The old man said.' It's gotta be descriptive." Looking at me again, he asked, "*Sputter?*"
>
> "*Sputtered.*"
>
> "How do you spell it?"
>
> For the other students in the class, this clever test was a pleasant break from the routine. They completed it successfully in one fifty-minute class period. For Wayne, it was fiendishly difficult. It hit all his weaknesses. Even with a trained professional helping him, it took the LD/ADD student more than two hours to complete the test.

Some test formats require a child to use skills he does not have. If some other method of examination cannot be arranged, the teacher must consider it her duty to provide the LD/ADD pupil with a professional helper. Guiding an LD and/or ADD student through a test that he finds complicated and confusing is *not* a job for an amateur.

Adjustments in Grading

CHAPTER 16

Sally had always had trouble with math. In grades one through five, she was in the bottom group of the lowest track. She could read, write, and spell. She was sweet and cooperative. But no matter how hard her teachers tried, they couldn't seem to help her learn arithmetic.

Sally's family moved to a different state. The girl's new school used a math program that was totally individualized. The students were assigned work at their own level. All work was graded pass/fail. Report-card grades simply indicated how quickly the pupils were progressing through their individualized arithmetic lessons.

Since Sally was a hard worker, she faithfully completed all the material assigned her. Her work was nowhere near sixth-grade level, but at the end of the year, the math grade on her report card was an A.

That summer, the family moved again. Sally's application was submitted for entrance into a private school. The prospective student and her parents went in for an admissions conference with the school's headmaster. When asked about their daughter's academic record, the parents produced her sixth-grade report card. A solid year of high grades attested to the fact that Sally was an excellent student. Except for math, that was a true picture of the girl's performance in school.

The parents carefully explained their daughter's good grade in sixth-grade arithmetic. "All it means is that she finished the book." They made it clear that Sally was *not* good at math. The headmaster nodded, assuring them the child would be placed in an appropriate class.

When her new private school began, Sally was assigned to the top seventh-grade math class. It was prealgebra. She lasted about three days! Recognizing the error in their judgment, the school moved her down to a regular class. She did better. But after a few weeks, she began falling behind. During the sixth week of school, Sally was switched again. This time, she was put into the low math group, where she should have been placed in the beginning.

Because of that one deceptive A, the new kid in town had to deal with the embarrassment of looking stupid in front of three different groups of schoolmates. And after only a month and a half of school, she was already behind the other students in the lowest math class.

The teacher who gave Sally that A in math did not do the girl a favor!

A single letter grade cannot give a fair indication of a learning-disabled child's progress in school. A student can be making phenomenal progress while working far below grade level. A grade of A would indicate his great attitude, excellent work, and strong improvement, but it would also imply superb work at or above grade level. Such a mark would not be fair to the youngster, his classmates, or his next teacher.

Failing a child when he is doing the best he can is equally unfair. An LD child who is far below grade level shouldn't be given D's and F's when he's working hard and making good progress. Any success he achieves deserves a reasonable reward.

Arthur had an adjusted spelling list. His classmates did twenty words a week out of a sixth-grade book. Most of them spent about fifteen minutes a night on their spelling. Arthur had eight words a week from a third-grade book. He struggled to master two a night. To pass his weekly test, Arthur spent at least forty-five minutes on spelling every night.

The system was working. Arthur passed all his Friday tests with a score of at least 80 percent. The youngster was delighted by his accomplishment. For the first time in his life, he was highly motivated.

At the end of the first marking period, Arthur's report card had a D- for spelling. The boy was crushed. When his mother came in for a conference, the teacher sweetly explained, "He can't do sixth-grade spelling at all. I really should have given him an F. But I just couldn't flunk a child who is trying so hard."

The mother took the matter up with the principal, supervisors, and several high-level administrators. The school system felt that the teacher was generous to give Arthur any kind of a passing grade.

There was nothing anyone could do. No matter how hard Arthur worked, the best grade he could possibly get was a D-.

Or he could quit trying.

The boy gave up. But in the traditional pattern of failure, he did not merely give up in spelling. It started there but gradually spread to include a special hatred for his teacher, serious behavior problems, total lack of interest and effort, failure in all his subjects, and finally a two-week expulsion from school for stabbing another student with a fork.

Arthur was not a bad boy. But for him, sixth grade was a very bad year.

Standard grading and reporting procedures simply do *not* fit the needs of teachers trying to give an honest evaluation of an LD/ADD student's progress. Three adapted methods are available. None of them is ideal.

1. The double grade

It is often possible to give two marks for different aspects of the same work. Rather than combining effort and progress with level of achievement, the two can be kept separate. A fifth-grade

LD/ADD youngster who is working hard and having good success with his adjusted assignments at third-grade level might get a B for effort and progress. The level of difficulty should then be indicated separately from his grade. In the appropriate box on his report card, he might get a B/3.

LD/ADD children are not very fond of this method. It reminds them that they're not quite like everybody else. But at least it *is* fair. And it's honest.

An alternate method allows teachers to separate form from content. For the LD/ADD pupil who writes his own papers, marks like B-/D+, A/D-, or C+/F might accurately describe knowledge of the subject (the first grade) and quality of presentation (the second grade). The double grade is also appropriate when an assignment has been drastically adapted. On a tape-recorded term paper, a logical mark might be C-/0 or B+/LD. The *0* or *LD* indicates that only the content can be fairly evaluated.

Another use of the double grade enables teachers to honestly state the level of achievement without judging effort or progress. A seventh-grader with third-grade reading skills might be marked 3/LD. Such a grade makes no comment on the student's progress yet explains the reason for his low achievement level.

2. The "nongrade"

Sometimes, it is impossible to evaluate an LD/ADD student's performance in a particular subject area. Fifth-grade report cards often have a blank where teachers are to grade the quality of the cursive writing students use in their regular classwork. LD/ADD pupils at that age are often just beginning to learn cursive and aren't yet competent enough to use it at all in class. Rather than giving an F (which wouldn't be true) or a 0 (which wouldn't be fair), the teacher can either leave the space blank or enter a "nongrade" like *LD* or *ADD*.

Some schools do not allow teachers to use double grades. Without such a system, it is impossible to give students with a learning disability and/or an attention deficit disorder honest marks in subjects such as reading, spelling, math, high-school

English, and any others that have been heavily adjusted. In such situations, a "nongrade" like *LD* or *ADD* instead of a letter or number is reasonable. The parents will understand, the child will understand, and next year's teacher will understand.

3. The written report

A fair explanation of an LD/ADD youngster's progress in a subject can usually be presented in one concise paragraph. Such an approach allows the teacher to be both fair and honest. Unfortunately, it takes a great deal of time to produce good written reports.

For those teachers willing to write out an explanation of a student's progress, a typewritten statement can be stapled to the regular report card. Each page should have a basic heading stating the student's name, his grade placement, the subject being evaluated, the current date, and the teacher's name. One paragraph should be written to cover each of the basic subjects. Each paragraph should evaluate attitude, effort, material covered, homework record, test scores, concepts mastered, adjustments made, and special difficulties. The grade level at which the student is working may be included when known and applicable.

Sample A

Carl has been working very hard in his sixth-grade spelling class. Using a weekly list of five words from the third-grade book, he has passed all but one test with a grade of 80 percent or better. He has failed to bring in his homework only twice. Carl finds it especially hard to locate the words in the glossary and break them into syllables. He has mastered saying the alphabet in order and is having good success in learning to alphabetize. Overall, I'm pleased with Carl's progress in spelling.

Sample B

Helen has been neglecting her work in our seventh-grade math class for the past eight weeks. Out of thirty-two homework assignments, she failed to bring in eleven. She is often inattentive and uncooperative in class. Despite daily help one-to-one, Helen is still unable to do long division. Through the use of a new game, she has made some progress in mastering multiplication. She can now multiply three-digit numbers by two-digit numbers. On tests, she passes the sections on addition and subtraction. Helen has improved in working with decimals and fractions. Although she is not in a regular math book, she is now working successfully on about a high fourth-grade level.

Whether or not teachers use the written report at the end of each marking period, it should be considered a *must* at the end of each semester.

Adjusted Scoring Systems

To simplify scoring and grading, teachers try to devise tests and assignments that work out to an even one hundred points. Many assume that adjusted assignments throw the whole system off. That's not necessarily true. By using a variation of the normal system, teachers can get adapted work to yield normal percentage scores.

For example, a teacher may choose to omit an essay question worth fifteen points from an LD/ADD student's test. Thus, a total of eighty-five points is available. This figure is the new adjusted total of points possible and becomes the bottom number of a fraction. Adding up the points for correct answers gives the top number. If the student gets sixty-three answers right, his adjusted score is computed by putting the sixty-three over the eighty-five ($^{63}/_{85}$). Dividing the top number by the bottom one ($63 \div 85$) gives the percent the student got right. The resulting 74 percent can then be entered in the grade book and converted to a letter grade.

No matter what the method used to alter the assignment, the

basic principle of adjusted scoring remains the same. How many were possible? How many did this child get right? Make a fraction with correct answers on top and number possible on the bottom. Divide the fraction. The result is a percentage score.

Most children do a twenty-word spelling list every week. Since a perfect score is 100 percent, the twenty words count five points (5 x 20 = 100). If a child's list is cut to ten words, they count ten points each (10 x 10 = 100). If the student has only five words to learn, they are worth twenty points each. One misspelled word on the test gives a grade of eighty. Missing two words means a failing sixty. The fewer words on the list, the more points each one counts.

> A custom-designed spelling program was used with a class of LD/ADD eighth-graders. Each week, the class had a list of twenty words. Numbers one through five were always easy. The next five were more difficult but still part of the basic sight-word vocabulary. Numbers ten to fifteen were more challenging. And the last five were on or above eighth-grade level. From this weekly set of twenty words, every student was assigned his own personal list.
>
> Three boys with severe problems in spelling were assigned only the first five words. Those who were not so severely disabled were given the first ten or twelve. Those who had already mastered the basic words were assigned numbers one through fifteen. Two very bright students with no problems in the language area had the whole list every week. For them, numbers sixteen through twenty provided a challenge and the first fifteen acted as review.
>
> The class had thirteen students each working on his own version of the spelling list. Yet it was not at all difficult to administer and grade the weekly test. When the children numbered their papers, each wrote down only the numbers for the words he had studied. Everybody had the first five. Some had been assigned the first seven or the first twelve. A few had truly personal lists composed of a combination from the different categories of difficulty. At the top of his test paper, each pupil also put a number from one to twenty to indicate how many words had been assigned him for that week.
>
> The teacher gave percentage scores for the tests. After a

few weeks, she began using the following conversion table. (Note that some of these figures are rounded off.)

5 words = 20 points each
6 words = 16 points each
7 words = 14 points each
8 words = 12 points each
9 words = 11 points each
10 words = 10 points each
11 words = 9 points each
12 words = 8 points each
13 words = 7½ points each
14 words = 7 points each
15 words = 6½ points each
16 words = 6 points each
17 words = 5¾ points each
18 words = 5½ points each
19 words = 5¼ points each
20 words = 5 points each

For example, in a list of seven words, the teacher counted fourteen points off for each mistake. A child who made two errors got twenty-eight points off and a score of seventy-two.

Adjusted assignments make a revised grading system essential. Those discussed above are easy, fair, and objective.

Grades Can Be Good

Like everyone else, students with a learning disability and/or an attention deficit disorder need standards—something to measure themselves against as they strive toward real success. They need something that tells them how good "good enough" is. When the goal is attainable, aiming for 100 percent is a challenge.

Many educators think LD and/or ADD pupils should not be given grades. They believe that by abandoning grades they can make the youngsters *feel as if* they're succeeding. Eliminating grades does relieve children of reminders of failure. But it also deprives them of the rewards of success.

Youngsters with a learning disability and/or an attention deficit disorder have very little experience with success. They usually fail to recognize their own academic achievement when they see it. Routine scores and grades help them notice that they are moving toward their goal—and give them cause for celebration at each step of the process. As they begin to understand that successful learning feels good, they begin seeking it on their own.

LD/ADD students must be taught how to gain knowledge independently so they can be lifelong learners. Tests and grades give them the facts they need to take charge of their learning. Number and letter scores allow them to measure their progress to see where they stand in relation to the goal. Grades are like yardsticks that allow us to watch a plant grow. They enable us to see development actually taking place.

Realistically, grades do not harm children. What hurts them is failure. Tricks that hide failure do not create success.

By adjusting the work of LD/ADD students, teachers make it possible for them to succeed. Then grades put a twinkle in the children's eyes as they tell of *real* success.

PART 4

The Final Analysis

Chapter 17

For more than sixty years, scientists struggled to come up with a logical explanation of what causes learning disabilities. Medical doctors, psychologists, and other highly specialized researchers studied brains, chemicals in the blood, genetic variables, body chemistry, teaching methods, nervous systems, and any other factors that might conceivably be connected to the problem. Many came up with theories. None of them offered conclusive—or even very convincing—proof to back up their ideas.

A whole new field of research opened up in the late 1950s. After ten years of careful investigation, a group in California released the results of its "split-brain studies" in 1968. The findings revolutionized our concept of the human brain.

The original discoveries were based on studies done with a small group of epileptics who had the connecting link between the two halves of their brain severed in an attempt to control their seizures. Doctors had always known that the human brain is shaped like the meat of a walnut, with one thick piece of connecting tissue joining the two halves. But the relationship between the two hemispheres had never been adequately explained. The left side was pretty well understood. The workings of the right half remained a mystery. With the cooperation of the split-brain patients, scientists were able to experiment on living humans to determine exactly how the two brain hemispheres function.

Through ingenious and fascinating tests, it was discovered that while the two sides of the brain are almost mirror images of each other, they work in entirely different ways. They take in different types of information, and they do their processing by radically different methods.

The left brain is designed to deal with abstract information. It is highly organized and analytical. Its processing is called *reasoning*. The left hemisphere is the seat of the "computer" which rules the realm of logic.

The right brain is designed to deal with concrete reality. It is highly intuitive and creative. Its processing is called *feeling*. The right hemisphere is the seat of the "spirit" which rules in the realm of inspiration.

The following summarizes the characteristics of the two hemispheres of the human brain.

Left Brain	**Right Brain**
1. VERBAL PROCESSING: thinks with words and numbers	1. VISUAL, KINESTHETIC, EMOTIONAL PROCESSING: thinks with pictures and feelings
2. ABSTRACT THINKING: deals with ideas and controls thought processing	2. CONCRETE THINKING: deals with tangible reality and controls doing
3. TIME: maintains awareness of an inner clock to design schedules and establish priorities	3. SPACE: notices, plans, organizes, and manipulates imaginary three-dimensional space

Left Brain, continued

4. SEQUENCES: takes in, organizes, processes, and stores information in chains of symbols linked in a specific order (alphabetical, chronological, left to right, top to bottom)

5. NARROW FOCUS OF ATTENTION: concentrates attention by tuning out non-essentials

6. ANALYSIS: breaks concepts into component parts which are compared, labeled, classified, and evaluated

7. LOGIC: uses a well-organized decision-making process that prioritizes, plans, and evaluates by predicting outcomes with mathematical precision

8. REASON: reaches conclusions through a step-by-step decision-making process based on logic and analysis

9. SENSE OF ORGANIZATION: creates systems and rules that use analysis, sequencing, and reason to impose order on objects and ideas

10. PREPARATION FOR MEMORY: processes information with sequencing systems that provide easy access and fast retrieval of facts

Right Brain, continued

4. RELATIONSHIPS: takes in, organizes, and stores information by connecting ideas according to similarities and patterns

5. WIDE FOCUS OF ATTENTION: expands attention to notice everything

6. SYNTHESIS: builds and develops original concepts by experimenting with new connections and relationships

7. EMOTION: plans, responds, and expresses with feelings, sensations, and actions

8. INTUITION: gains sudden insights all at once as a whole

9. SENSE OF THE ABSURD: finds humor in situations and makes fun of human foibles

10. PREPARATION FOR CREATIVITY: recognizes possibilities previously unexplored and brings them into form

Sometimes, the two hemispheres work together as a team. To play tennis, the right brain controls the body movements while the left brain plans the strategy. In writing a short story, the right hemisphere supplies imaginative ideas while its counterpart takes charge of spelling, grammar, and punctuation. In such endeavors, both sides of the brain are involved in different aspects of the same project.

For other tasks, the two hemispheres take turns. Balancing a checkbook is best done with cool, calm reason. Creativity or emotion would complicate an otherwise simple manipulation of factual information. Dancing is best done in the free-flowing manner of right-brain processing. A rational, analytical frame of mind would kill the beauty and spontaneity of the movements.

Ideally, an individual shifts back and forth between the two modes of thinking as needed. But this is not always the case. When the natural division of labor does not take place, the two hemispheres work in opposition to each other. One side can insist on doing a task for which the other is better suited. The left side of the brain has a strong tendency to dominate. For that reason, it's sometimes difficult to restrain it to minimal involvement in an activity. It wants to take over, or it wants no part of things.

In "developed" countries, society admires the man of reason. Formal education fosters skill in intellectual pursuits. Through training and the process of acculturation, children are deliberately shifted to near total reliance on the left brain. Thus, it is common for intelligent, highly educated adults to say, "I'm not very creative," "I'm not very good with my hands," or "I can't even draw a straight line." Such individuals—and there are many of them—have almost no access to the tremendous capabilities of their right brain. Their creative mind cannot produce insights and inspirations because their reasoning mind refuses to relinquish control. For adults thus trapped in their left brain, it is a long, hard struggle to reestablish contact with the right. Meditation, jogging, gardening, yoga, weaving, sewing, drawing, painting, playing a musical instrument, dancing, drugs, biofeedback, backpacking, self-improvement courses—Western man is working to get back in touch with the right side of his brain and restore balance to his life.

People with an "artistic temperament" consistently favor the right-brain mode of thinking. Many writers devote their energy to ideas and insights. They rely on editors to take care of the tedious details of grammar and punctuation. Musicians love to perform and create. They pay managers to organize schedules and take responsibility for business details. These artistic types *can* do left-brain thinking, but they make the shift only when it's absolutely necessary.

As soon as results of the split-brain studies were released, experts realized that individuals with a learning disability and/or an attention deficit disorder tend to have weaknesses in left-hemisphere processing and strengths in the kind of thinking done by the right side of the brain. On first hearing an explanation of split-brain theory, LD/ADD adults almost always recognize the connection. One former student asked me, "Do you think my left brain has died?" Another claimed, "I feel like I'm trapped in my right brain."

Once Roger Sperry and his colleagues at Cal Tech introduced the world to the unexpected differences between the two halves of the human brain, the door to a whole new avenue of exploration flew open. Thinking, learning, remembering, and concentrating could be examined from an entirely new perspective. For the first time, there were logical explanations for many of the puzzling aspects of academic failure and success. Those who were interested in learning disabilities immediately initiated studies to investigate the connection between brain structure and specific types of difficulties with learning and paying attention.

Discoveries accumulated rapidly. By watching brain activity during thought processing, a Canadian researcher found that many LD/ADD individuals are built as though they have two right brains. Several groups of educators discovered that LD/ADD youngsters learn best when the methods of instruction teach to the right side of the brain. Books on how to do this popped up all over the country. British doctors began experimenting with a drug that stimulates the left side of the brain. When this chemical is administered to dyslexics, the resulting increase in left-brain activity improves their skill in reading.

From the work of scientists all over the world, a new theory developed: youngsters who have a learning disability and/or an attention deficit disorder are different because the left side of their brain does not operate effectively. They are right-brain learners. They have special skills and talents not available to most of us. When placed in schools designed for the left-brain majority, they not only cannot succeed, but their unique gifts are systematically destroyed. When placed in an appropriate setting, they learn and thrive.

The terms *learning disability* and *attention deficit disorder* focus on left-brain deficits without pointing out right-brain attributes. When seen from the perspective of brain-hemisphere function, it becomes obvious that labels that refer to *disabilities* and *disorders* are not appropriate. These youngsters are not defective. They are *right-brain learners.*

In the learning-styles research of Drs. Rita and Kenneth Dunn, students who do their best thinking in the style associated with the right brain are termed "global" learners; those who are more adept at doing their thinking in the left-brain style are "analytic" learners. Global thinkers have the characteristics commonly found among those with a learning disability and/or an attention deficit disorder. The typical classroom of the 1990s does not help them learn successfully.

They Are Reality-Oriented

Global learners are firmly rooted in concrete reality. The real world—the one that can be touched, tasted, smelled, heard, watched—is the world that makes sense to them. It's what draws their interest, leads to understanding, produces responses, and lodges in their memory. Reality-oriented children live by their senses. It's in concrete reality that they are comfortable and competent.

Reading and writing involve deep levels of abstraction. The

printed symbols represent letters that stand for sounds and go together to produce a graphic picture of a spoken word, which is in turn a group of sounds blended into one unit and used to express symbolically an idea or a name of an object or action that did exist, will exist, might exist, should exist, could have existed, or does now exist in concrete reality. Language is abstract. Global thinkers are not oriented toward the abstract. Their minds thrive on the tangible, the physical, the real.

How does this show up in the classroom? At every opportunity, a global learner shifts from the abstract to the real. Instead of filling in the blanks on a reading worksheet, he draws pictures on it, punches holes in it, or folds it into an airplane. When dealing with abstractions, he has trouble concentrating. He's easily distracted or just can't "get into it." Once he shifts his attention to the concrete reality of a fly buzzing against the window, he has no further problem with distractions. He is absorbed completely. When his mind and body are both involved, he has an incredible intensity of concentration. The reality-oriented youngster succeeds in concentrating, performing, and learning when the task allows him to immerse himself in it physically as well as mentally.

The global thinker is built like an old-fashioned string of Christmas tree lights—one missing bulb and the entire string refuses to light. Either the individual is totally involved in an activity—eyes, ears, head, hands, heart, muscles, feelings—or he's not involved at all. His senses must work in unison with his mind. It's as though he thinks with his whole body. This enables the youngster to learn beautifully. It also prevents him from learning in the ways preferred by schools.

Tying the abstract to physical reality gives global learners a chance to take in the sensory information they need to activate attention, understanding, and memory. The highly abstract *can* be taught to them, provided it's done by methods that are rooted in reality. One of the oldest and most highly respected methods of LD therapy is the Orton-Gillingham approach. Its effectiveness is largely based on the fact that it is multisensory. Almost all of the pupils' senses are employed in the teaching of reading, writing, spelling, and math. It is reality-oriented and therefore well suited to the global thinkers it's designed to reach.

With few exceptions, modern educational systems are based on developing the verbal and abstract. The natural tendencies and talents of global learners are unexplored, denied, and abused.

They Are Spatially Gifted

Years ago, a well-known researcher studied a large group of dyslexics. This scientist believed that all those with a disability in reading, writing, and spelling must have one particular "symptom" in common. After careful investigation, she did find one characteristic shared by all her subjects. But much to everyone's surprise, it was not a deficit. It was an attribute. Every one of them had a talent for dealing with objects in space. They were all spatially gifted. The three-dimensional world made more sense to them than it does to most people. Their minds were ideally suited to perceiving, understanding, manipulating, visualizing, and remembering concrete objects that exist in space. They had the special talents needed to be builders, inventors, actors, designers, mechanics, sculptors, architects.

Split-brain research has clearly demonstrated that spatial ability is a function of the right hemisphere of the brain. Since LD/ADD children are right-brain thinkers, it is not surprising that they should have a talent for dealing with three-dimensional objects.

The spatially gifted can comprehend a whole and the relationships of all its parts regardless of its orientation. In concrete reality, size, shape, and location are relative. For example, a carburetor is at the end of the gas line and distributes fuel to the pistons. If seen from directly above, it is round. From the side, it looks rectangular. From above and to the side, it appears oval. From beneath, it's hidden by the engine block. But no matter how its shape and location appear to vary, the actual carburetor remains the same.

To deal effectively with objects in space, orientation must be taken into consideration. That's a major aspect of spatial ability. But when this same processing technique is applied to the abstract world of letters and numbers, the effect is disastrous.

If their orientation is not considered to be fixed, how are a *u* and an *n* different? To someone who does not consider orientation in space to be significant, how are a *p*, a *g*, a *d*, and a *b* different? They're all the same! They are the exact same configuration viewed from different sides and angles. You can't fool the spatially gifted global thinker. He knows a stick and a ball when he sees one. Turn it any way you want, it's still a line and a circle.

Teachers point out that a *d* faces one way, a *b* the other. The global learner thinks of that as a phenomenon that occurs sometimes, not as a permanent condition. Sometimes, a carburetor looks long and thin; sometimes, it looks round. To the spatially gifted child, orientation is always conditional, just as it is in concrete reality.

They Have No Inner Clock

Split-brain studies have proven that functions concerning time and space are divided between the two hemispheres in a way that is nearly mutually exclusive. The right brain does the spatial processing and deals with spatial tasks. The left brain is responsible for keeping track of time, doing sequencing, and dealing with temporal matters. Global learners thus have a pronounced weakness in their concept of time. They live as though time doesn't exist. They don't think in terms of time, don't measure their lives or events by standards related to time. Of all the students with a learning disability and/or an attention deficit disorder I have encountered, I have never met one who dealt with time in a totally "normal" way.

One LD/ADD adult I know is a good example of the global learner's strange contrast of abilities. At the age of twenty-four, he was a talented and highly successful landscape architect. His spatial gifts made him ideally suited for his profession. But his lack of an inner clock made it difficult for him to supervise crews of workmen. Unless the men kept an eye on the clock themselves, their young boss forgot about breaks and meals. In this situation, as in many others, the unusual characteristics of a global thinker acted as both a blessing and a curse.

Albert Einstein, the physicist and mathematician who pioneered the theory of relativity and proved that time and space are two aspects of the same thing, didn't learn to tell time until he was in his teens. He used to say that since he explored the subject at a more mature age than most people, he went into it much more thoroughly. Despite his intellectual understanding of mathematical and theoretical concepts of time, Einstein exhibited personal habits that were very much those of the absent-minded professor. Most LD/ADD adults have a lifelong problem with clocks, calendars, schedules, punctuality, and work pace.

In a newspaper interview, a well-known artist referred to his struggles with time management by commenting, "I was born late." When asked about his concept of time, he said he didn't picture days flowing by. He never imagined himself marching through weeks or past markers that measured out the years. Instead, this hypoactive adult saw time as though it were contained in a giant bucket. When he needed some, he just reached in and dipped some out. To him, the supply of time was endless. He never felt the need to hurry.

The hyperactive have the opposite view of how time passes. They always feel there is more work to do—or fun to be had—than there is time available. They don't dare slow down to wait their turn, work neatly, check over their answers, be polite. To them, time flies by. They are always in a hurry, racing against the clock.

The perception of time seems to be closely related to the chemistry of the brain. Those who "self-medicate" to control ADD find that sugar, caffeine, nicotine, alcohol, and a long list of other substances alter the inner clock. Some of the most popular street drugs—and many legal drugs sold over the counter or by prescription—have a profound effect on the user's concept of time. Marijuana makes five minutes feel like half an hour. Cocaine makes time pass quickly and creates enhanced awareness of details.

Hard-core drugs like crack and heroine tend to remove the awareness of time altogether. Amphetamines make the user feel like his whole body has speeded up. No wonder stimulant medication improves handwriting and increases concentration. By removing the inner pressure that makes the hyperactive feel that they must rush through their work, these drugs give students the patience to take their time, to work carefully and deliberately, and to pay close attention to details. There's no need to hurry; work is already going fast.

Sequencing is a technique that orders objects or events in time. Global thinkers have no sense of time; consequently, they have no sense of sequence either. They order reality in terms of relationships and space. In assembling a model airplane, spatially talented children rarely follow the printed directions. The sequence they use is not based on the step-by-step instructions of the manufacturer. They put the seat, controls, instruments, and pilot into the cockpit before they glue on the canopy. They determine this order in accordance with the logic of working with objects in space: the interior parts must be completed first because you can't get to the inside after it's buried under the outside.

That's an effective way of functioning when it comes to concrete reality. It's called "good common sense." Usually, global thinkers have a lot of that.

This kind of nonsequential spatial reasoning does not work in the realm of the abstract. To impose order on the abstract, sequencing in time is necessary. Instructions that must be followed step by step are tremendously useful to most youngsters. But to the global learner, they are of no importance whatsoever. They're something he doesn't notice on his own; they don't make much sense to him even when they're pointed out; and they don't stick in his memory at all.

These three factors—a strong reality orientation, a facility for dealing with space, and the lack of an inner clock—make it all but inevitable that the global thinker will have great difficulty learning to read, write, and spell. It seems a horrible irony that his greatest strengths combine to cause his greatest weaknesses.

They Are Unusually Observant

Global thinkers are tremendously observant of what's going on around them. No sight, sound, or sensation is too small to escape their notice—*if* it interests them. Constantly monitoring their environment, their mind is everywhere at once. This expanded focus of attention is a great asset when walking across a busy intersection or riding a bike through the park. In the real world, where both danger and beauty can spring up anywhere, keen powers of observation promote safety and provide an avenue for added pleasure.

One highly respected expert has suggested that many of history's great warriors were LD and/or ADD. He believes that the global thinker's trait of being super-observant enabled Alexander the Great, George Patton, and many others to lead men successfully in battle.

Yet in today's typical textbook-and-worksheet classroom, global learners are constantly criticized for not paying attention. Their expanded focus is considered undesirable. Teachers say these children are "distractible." They think youngsters who notice everything have a short attention span. Schools that make reading, listening, and answering questions the primary methods of instruction require students to develop and sustain a narrow focus of attention. They want pupils to zero in on their work and tune out everything else. Global thinkers can't comply, and in their failure to do so they are accused of being uncooperative, disrespectful, and unmotivated.

Being highly observant is a tremendous advantage in the real world. In the vast majority of today's schools, it's a handicap.

They Prefer Intuition over Logic

Schools train children to use logic. Great emphasis is placed on developing skill in the use of structured thought-processing patterns. Sound reasoning is the only acceptable method of arriving at a conclusion. Teachers make sure a pupil's correct answer is not just a lucky guess. Get the facts, remember the facts, add up the facts—that's the rigid system used in formal education.

This highly organized reasoning process does not appeal to global learners. Their preferred thinking style is based on sudden leaps of insight. Just as they are unusually observant in concrete reality, they are highly attuned to intuition. Their active minds thrive on the hunches and brainstorms of inspiration.

Thomas Edison was operating on this principle when he invented the incandescent light. The idea came to him as a fully developed realization produced by intuition. Others told him it was a crazy notion. Yet after nearly two thousand unsuccessful attempts, he produced a bulb that would actually light. First came the inspiration; then came experimentation and a process of elimination; last came logic, which was applied to explain *why* the device worked. In thinking by intuition, logic comes last. Its function is to explain why something happens in reality. The truth of what is discovered through intuition and experimentation is proved through reasoning.

For aborigines and Indians who live close to the land, for artists and writers and inventors, for students in project-based educational programs, this is an effective way of thinking. But this type of thinking is *not* effective in "read the book and fill in the worksheet" schools. In the traditional classroom, the intuitive approach is called "wild guessing." Teachers dislike it intensely. Global learners rely on it heavily.

In an elementary-school reading circle, global learners give a classic portrayal of the attempt to apply intuition to a situation that requires logic. A systematic method of word attack is not their style at all. Rather than trying to figure out a word, they call out what they expect to be there. Based on the pictures, the reading of the other students, and the cues and corrections provided by the teacher, they piece together their own version of the story. Thus, the oral reading of global thinkers is full of substitutions. Pronouns, articles, and prepositions are especially vulnerable to transformation in their improvisational approach to reading. Yet almost always, the word inserted makes good sense within the context of the sentence or story. In trying to read "Come down from there right now," students who read by intuition might try any of the following: "*Get* down from there right now," "Come down *off* there right now," or "Come down from there *this minute*."

As global learners get older, their reading usually improves with or without special instruction. By the time they get to fifth or sixth grade, they've learned to look at the first letter of a word and then guess. Some get to the point that they look at the first and last letters—before they make their guess. This technique produces errors like *carefully* read as *comfortably* and *Tuesday* read as *Thursday*. For those few who learn to pay attention to whole syllables before applying intuition, mistakes are made on more difficult words: *consternation* becomes *conservation* or *conversation*, *formally* is read as *formerly*, and *Austria* is pronounced *Australia*.

At every level, the tendency toward improvisation remains strong. And always, it's the little words that are the most likely candidates for substitutions. Typically, global learners improve their skill at controlled guessing. But ultimately, the intuition that serves them so well in reading people, nature, and reality hinders them when reading books.

They Are Creative

The left side of the brain, with its controlled, predictable processing methods, is perfectly designed for analyzing. The left hemisphere has a natural tendency to break wholes into component parts. It automatically identifies and labels pieces as an aspect of verbal thinking. It is also the mind's center for judging, comparing, and evaluating. Once information has been gathered and judgments made, the left brain places the pieces into categories. Through some method of numerical, alphabetical, or chronological sequencing, these groups are then arranged and organized. If used immediately, the facts are added up in systematic fashion so that a decision is easily reached. If filed away for later reference, the exquisitely organized material is neatly stored in memory.

Analysis is a process unique to the logical left brain. It is also the direct opposite of the special thinking unique to the right hemisphere.

The right side of the brain, with its sudden insights and surprising revelations, is ideally suited to the task of synthesizing. The right hemisphere has a natural tendency to put things together and build. In its type of processing, details and pieces are important only in terms of their relationship to the whole. As an aspect of nonverbal reasoning, it automatically manipulates visualized images of real or imagined objects. It tends to rely on mental pictures as it searches for similarities. Synthesizing is aimed at an end result that has nothing to do with logical solutions and is in no way bound by tradition.

The right brain's findings are not of the type that can be categorized and organized. That's just as well, because the synthesizing mind has no method of organizing anything systematically. It operates outside time and sequence. It is guided by curiosity. Synthesizing is a mental adventure that can be pursued with no sense of hurry. As long as options can be found, they are explored.

Skill in analyzing tends to go along with a good memory. The two occur together because they're closely related. People who live by logic usually have a good memory for factual information. But since they are analytical thinkers, they are not particularly creative. Facility in intuition and an aptitude for synthesizing produce just the opposite result. They usually occur in conjunction with a high degree of creativity and a poor memory. Albert Einstein could never remember his own phone number. When he wanted to call home, he had to refer to a card on which he had written the information. Global thinking is great for some things. But memory of sequences isn't one of them.

Everyone is familiar with the vague kind of recollection produced by dreams. The setting, theme, and emotional reaction may be recalled. "I had this dream that I was in a gambling casino and I won all this money. Boy, was I happy." But the details slip away. Eventually, the whole thing fades. Global thinkers seem to remember in much the same fashion. They often say things like "Miss Jones tried to teach me that last year, but I don't remember" or "I did a bunch of problems with carrying last week, but now I've forgotten." Memory seems to rely heavily on the organization, logic, and analysis used by the left brain.

The process of analysis prepares material so it can be stored for easy accessibility in the future. Apparently, the brain cannot file away new information unless the big concepts are broken down into manageable pieces that are labeled, categorized, and organized. Logic both draws on and feeds into memory.

The mind's ability to synthesize makes it possible for humans to create. The right brain's special processing methods enable the individual to develop the *new*. By using intuition, focusing on the whole, and processing by means of synthesis, the global thinker repeatedly comes up with innovative ideas. Not bound by the way things have always been, he yearns for the different, the improved, the bigger, the better, the stronger, the prettier, the more wonderful. Never convinced that there is only one way to get something done, he looks for methods that are faster, easier, cheaper.

It has been scientifically established that global learners are more creative than their analytically inclined classmates. They have a special flair for developing the original. In problem-solving situations that come up in daily living, they have a knack for devising ingenious solutions. Teachers see this quality and rarely appreciate it. They prefer predictable, reliable students. In the classroom, it's considered essential that pupils work in the prescribed, logical, fixed way. Innovations are not desirable.

The global thinker has a fabulous mind as long as he applies it to the type of mental processing for which it is suited. He was not designed for the left-brain world of the abstract, where thought processing is based on reading, writing, spelling, and remembering facts. His realm of excellence is the world of the concrete, where he can explore, learn from experience, synthesize, and create.

They Are Highly Sensitive

Global thinkers are observant, intuitive, and creative. They have an artistic temperament. They are unusually perceptive and extremely sensitive. They are strongly affected by what they feel. They tend to base their actions on emotion rather than reason.

LD/ADD children are very, very sensitive. Over the years, they lose their tolerance for teasing. No matter how carefully hidden or sugarcoated, any form of rejection hurts them deeply. Behind all the bluff and boisterousness they project, they are usually tender-hearted, caring people. Their sensitive nature tends to make them compassionate toward the world's underdogs. Their sensitivity applies to themselves and everything and everyone around them.

Many global thinkers have an uncanny ability to read people. Their unusual powers of observation allow them to pick up on body language, tone of voice, and other unspoken signals. Their high degree of intuition often leads to amazing depths of insight. These youngsters are especially attuned to "vibes." They seem to sense the feelings of others. (Note that even though they are global learners, children with a severe attention deficit disorder often have a glaring weakness in these people-reading skills.)

This sensitivity enables global thinkers to see through to the depths of situations. They can't read the words on the page, but they can read between the lines and in the margins to understand messages conveyed without language. They usually get what's implied, suggested, hinted, buried, or even camouflaged. They are often brilliant in understanding metaphors and symbols. (With youngsters who have an extreme attention deficit disorder, the opposite is sometimes the case. They tend to take all language literally.)

The global learner has a strong sense of the absurd. He is likely to be labeled the "class clown." His spontaneous wit allows him to produce quips and one-liners based on the moment. The jokes are clever, subtle, and quick. They almost always reveal a deep perception of human nature, specific individuals, or the particular situation. Some adults notice and appreciate this style of humor. Many do not. When a student drops a hilarious remark to explain away his forty-seventh consecutive morning of tardiness, his teacher is not likely to be amused. The global learner's sense of humor is rarely understood by his peers. To them, his unusual jokes merely prove that he's weird.

Their sensitive nature makes these creative youngsters vulnerable to pressures toward conformity. Global learners are not damaged by being different. They are damaged by people and a system that cannot accommodate their differences.

A New Perspective

By viewing those with a learning disability and/or an attention deficit disorder from a new perspective, unexplored possibilities emerge. Once it is recognized that global learners are not defective, modifications and accommodations are no longer enough. We need to provide them with an educational system that honors their basic nature.

As of 1997, that means alternative schools or homeschooling. A few public schools are now in the process of developing very creative experimental programs. Some of them show promise for increasing the quality of learning for *all* students.

Through the pioneering learning-styles research of Drs. Rita and Kenneth Dunn, educators are coming to see LD and/or ADD students as part of a spectrum that includes left-brain analytical learners at one extreme and right-brain global thinkers at the other. In their workshops and publications, the Dunns offer guidance for creating academic environments that can meet the needs of all types of learners. LD/ADD youngsters are usually much happier and more successful in schools that investigate pupils' learning styles in order to acknowledge their differences and provide an appropriately customized setting.

The work of Dr. Howard Gardner has led educators in totally new directions. As applied by David Lazear, Gardner's theory of the seven aspects of intelligence—verbal/linguistic, mathematical/logical, visual/spatial, kinesthetic, musical, interpersonal, and intrapersonal—is the basis for a whole new set of teaching methods useful in any setting with any curriculum. For example, when global learners are taught by hands-on (visual/spatial and kinesthetic) methods, they have no trouble concentrating; activities that involve their whole body tend to shift them into the kind of focus where it's possible for them to stay immersed in an undertaking for hours. And when musical thinkers use rhythm and melody to help them remember information they would normally find difficult and boring, there is a noticeable improvement in both their attitude and their level of achievement. When each student's preferred mode of thinking is taken into consideration in the preparation and presentation of classroom instruction, LD/ ADD children have little difficulty with boredom, restlessness, and leaky memories.

Gardner's ideas can also be applied productively to collaborative learning.

> A staff-development workshop was not going well. The classroom teachers and LD teachers were doing hands-on projects while their superintendents sat back and socialized and their aides stood around shuffling their feet waiting to be told what to do. Only the few who got actively involved were learning anything. No amount of cajoling and encouragement made any difference. For at least half the seminar participants, the sessions were a complete waste of time—until the groups were re-formed in accordance with Dr. Gardner's seven classifications.
>
> On the third day of the summer institute, right in the middle of yet another ill-fated project, the training specialist called everything to a halt. The seven aspects of intelligence were presented, explained, and discussed. Participants were given materials to analyze personal strengths and weaknesses and then told to put symbols on their nametags to indicate areas of special talent and interest. The original work groups, comprised of teams of colleagues from one district or another, were disbanded. New groups were assembled. Each had to have one representative for each of the seven aspects of intelligence.
>
> When work on the projects resumed, the room was abuzz with enthusiastic activity. Teacher's aides gained new confidence and stature. Superintendents clearly understood their area of responsibility to the team and participated eagerly. Regular teachers assumed roles that fit their temperaments and talents. Everybody was happy—and very productive. Scis-

sors flashed and colored paper flew as the groups created simple props and costumes that could capture the attention of even the most resistant students. There were no more reluctant learners being dragged through a chore. Instead, there was humming, singing, whistling, and laughter as every participant got actively involved. When it came time to demonstrate the lesson plans they had developed, every single group produced an outstanding example of the lesson style assigned.

Reorganizing the groups so that every member was asked to contribute from an area of personal strength and interest transformed the whole class.

Entire schools are organizing classrooms in accordance with Gardner's principles. At all levels, kindergarten to college, programs that are designed to fit the talents of each individual pupil can produce a transformation of attitude and accomplishment that is truly amazing.

Another application of Gardner's ideas can be seen in the museum-based approach to academic instruction. Programs of this type take students outside the school building and immerse them in hands-on study. When children's museums are used as the basic educational environment, youngsters get to explore, investigate, and experiment under the supervision of a trained naturalist or curator. Since this approach offers whole-body learning while also appealing to students' high level of interest in the world around them, LD/ADD global thinkers thrive. As children grow older and their interests become more refined, an apprenticeship system can offer a whole range of sites for developing a mature level of skills through direct experience and hands-on methods.

A few alternative schools are offering a museum-based curriculum. And many homeschoolers are adopting it as well. Families who live in major metropolitan areas have a vast array of museums to choose from. Whether the focus is science, industry, natural history, local history, aviation, art, or ethnic groups and cultures, even rural areas have access to historical societies, nature/science centers, art galleries, and zoos eager to participate in educational projects. As more and more parents find the courage to take unhappy LD/ADD children out of traditional schools and provide a custom-designed program of home-based education appropriate for global learners, museum curators will be among those who lead these whole-body thinkers to the delights of successful learning.

Another alternative is available through schools committed to experiential education. In this type of reality-based curriculum, the entire world becomes the classroom. Through Outward Bound–type programs, educators teach children the skills necessary for developing direct contact with the natural environment. Backpacking, hiking, rafting, skiing, rappelling, caving, scuba diving, biking—the activities tend to be very physical. Such adventure-based programs are ideal for global thinkers who love the outdoors and like to be constantly on the move. Whether by traveling cross-country in a chartered bus or exploring a city via subway, experiential education often includes extensive travel. Historical sites, industrial sites, parks, recreation areas, theaters, museums, and centers of local and regional government are but a few of the real-life venues available for educational activities.

> A "school on wheels" makes an annual three-week visit to a hospice for the terminally ill in a small Southern city. During the teenage students' stay, their daily schedule includes two hours of classwork (grammar, algebra, literature, geography, history, formal discussion), a four-hour shift caring for guests or working on maintenance projects around the grounds, day trips to local museums and historical sites, and private time for work on crafts and personal projects. One boy is developing an extensive butterfly collection. Two girls carry a portable darkroom with them and devote many productive hours to photography. One of the camera buffs is collaborating with three budding young writers in producing photographs to illustrate a slim volume of original poetry.
>
> When the traveling academy leaves the hospice, the next stop is a sheep farm in Virginia.

This type of on-the-road education is very popular among homeschoolers. It's well suited to missionaries and traveling families who spend part of the year working craft shows, conferences, rodeos, races, crops, or carnivals. Most people think of mobile academic programs as a hardship forced upon children by difficult circumstances. In reality, quite the opposite is true. For most students, experience-based education is ideal. For global learners, basing educational activities on real-life experiences can be considered essential.

> Albert Einstein is the hero of the learning disabled. They find it very encouraging that his lack of success in school did not prevent him from maturing into a mathematical genius whose discoveries altered our understanding of the universe. Most of his little LD/ADD admirers assume that nothing special was done to bring about his transformation from abysmal failure to world-famous scientist and humanitarian. Most of his fans believe that Einstein just outgrew his learning problems.
>
> Nothing could be farther from the truth. When young Albert was in his early teens, his family moved to Switzerland. It was there that the youth was placed in a school founded by Johann Heinrich Pestalozzi, an educational reformer of the early 1800s who is still recognized as the father of "show and tell." At this alternative school, Einstein was taught by a hands-on approach called "sense realism." With all his academic activities solidly based in real-life experiences, he learned how to control and direct the powerful intellectual gifts that eventually led to a lifetime of prominence and success.

The list of researchers grows by the minute. Even popular magazines are offering new approaches to educating the masses in a way that's fair and successful for all types of students. If the goal of public education really is to make every citizen literate enough to participate in the democratic process, we have to rethink the basic organization of schools entirely.

The idea of "getting back to the basics" has much appeal. But the classroom of the 1940s featured much more than a simplistic emphasis on reading, 'riting, and 'rithmetic. There was prayer and fierce patriotism. In both the home and the school, a general attitude of "spare the rod and spoil the child" undergirded strict requirements of neatness, obedience, and punctuality. By example as well as precept, families, churches, and communities worked together to instill in children a sense of duty, a respect for discipline, and a total commitment to the American work ethic.

Even if a wave of some magic wand allowed the perfect teacher from the past to step into a classroom and establish a true "back to the basics" atmosphere, a positive transformation would not occur as some advocates believe.

Today's children are different. They bring a different brain to school than was seen fifty years ago, or twenty years ago, or even just five years ago. Since the brain's process of constructing itself is strongly influenced by a child's experiences, minds that absorb television and master Nintendo are bound to be different from those that developed through hearing stories and playing checkers. And not all such influences are under direct parental control. From irradiated milk to ozone depletion, today's generation is absorbing traces of fertilizers, pesticides, antibiotics, food additives, and radiation that didn't even exist in previous decades. And this doesn't begin to consider the increase in street drugs as well as prescription medications pumped into children. For many of these chemicals—legal as well as illicit—the long-term effects are pretty much unknown.

Since today's child comes to school with a brain that is different from his predecessors', every aspect of his learning varies from past patterns. What educators need to do is understand the techniques that promote successful learning in modern children and design facilities, programs, and instruction accordingly. In consideration of the rapidly increasing number of LD and ADD children, it has been suggested that they will eventually become the majority. Many schoolteachers and scores of school districts report that nearly 50 percent of students are on stimulant medication. Experts all over the country whisper behind closed doors, "What's going on? They're coming out of the woodwork." Instead of trying to figure out what's causing the change and assuming that children will someday return to "normal," it's time to deal with the reality of today's children. We need to use our energy to create programs that teach them effectively as they are, rather than hoping they will go back to being the way they were when our methods used to fit!

Appendix: Useful Addresses

CHADD (Children and Adults with Attention Deficit Disorder)
1859 North Pine Island Road
Suite 185
Plantation, Fla. 33317
(305) 587-3700

LDA of America (Learning Disabilities Association of America, formerly ACLD, the Association for Children with Learning Disabilities)
4156 Library Road
Pittsburgh, Pa. 15234
(412) 341-1515 or (412) 341-8077

Learning Styles Network (Drs. Kenneth and Rita Dunn)
St. John's University
8000 Utopia Parkway
Jamaica, N.Y. 11439
(718) 990-6335

* NILD (National Institute for Learning Disabilities)
107 Seekel Street
Norfolk, Va. 23505
(804) 423-8646

NICHCYD (National Information Center for Children and Youth with Disabilities)
P.O. Box 1492
Washington, D.C. 20013-1492
(800) 695-0285

Orton Dyslexia Society
Chester Building, Suite 382
8600 La Salle Road
Baltimore, Md. 21286-2044
(410) 296-0232

Internet Addresses for ADHD Issues

alt.support.attn-deficit
www.chadd.org

* with a focus on Christian schools

Select Bibliography

Learning Disabilities

Hampshire, Susan. *Susan's Story*. New York: St. Martin's Press, 1982.

* Herzog, Joyce. *Learning without Labels*. Lebanon, Tenn.: Greenleaf Press, 1994.

MacCracken, Mary. *Turnabout Children*. Boston: Little, Brown and Company, 1986.

Osman, Betty B. *Learning Disabilities: A Family Affair*. New York: Random House, 1979.

Learning Disbilities Combined with Attention Deficit Disorder

Journal of Child Neurology 10, supplemental issue on learning disabilities (January 1995).

* written from a Christian perspective

Levine, Mel. *Keeping a Head in School.* Cambridge, Mass.: Educators Publishing Service, 1990.

McCarney, Stephen B., and Angela Marie Bauer. *The Parents' Guide to Attention Deficit Disorders.* 2nd ed. Columbia, Mo.: Hawthorne Educational Services, 1995.

Stevens, Suzanne H. *The LD Child and the ADHD Child: Ways Parents and Professionals Can Help.* Winston-Salem, N.C.: John F. Blair, Publisher, 1996.

Attention Deficit Disorder

Armstrong, Thomas. *The Myth of the A.D.D. Child.* New York: Dutton, 1995.

Barkley, Russell A. *Attention-Deficit Hyperactivity Disorder: A Handbook for Diagnosis and Treatment.* New York: Guilford Press, 1990.

———. *Taking Charge of ADHD.* New York: Guilford Press, 1995.

Hallowell, Edward M., and John J. Ratey. *Driven to Distraction.* New York: Pantheon Books, 1994.

The Brain, Intelligence, Learning, and Child Development

Armstrong, Thomas. *In Their Own Way.* Los Angeles: Jeremy P. Tarcher, 1987.

———. *Seven Kinds of Smart.* New York: Penguin Books, 1993.

Healy, Jane M. *Endangered Minds.* New York: Simon and Schuster, 1990.

———. *Your Child's Growing Mind.* New York: Doubleday, 1987.

Text References

Fader, Daniel N., and Elton B. McNeil. *Hooked on Books: Program and Proof.* New York: G. P. Putnam's Sons, 1968.

Gardner, Howard. *Frames of Mind.* New York: Basic Books, 1983.

———. *The Unschooled Mind.* New York: Basic Books, 1991.

Lazear, David. *Seven Ways of Knowing.* Palatine, Ill.: Skylight, 1991.

Instructional Materials

Lazear, David. *Seven Ways of Teaching.* Palatine, Ill.: Skylight, 1991.

Margulies, Nancy. *Mapping Inner Space.* Tucson, Ariz.: Zephyr Press, 1991.

Meirovitz, Marco, and Stuart Dods. *Verbal Thinking.* Unionville, N.Y.: Trillium Press, 1990.

Richards, Regina. *L.E.A.R.N.* Tucson, Ariz.: Zephyr Press, 1993.

Rose, Colin. *Accelerated Learning.* New York: Dell, 1985.

Index